AF278863

FIVE SOULS

By

ASIF MENGHRANI

REFLECTIONS OF THE POLISHED HEART

Copyright © 2025 by Asif Menghrani.
All rights reserved.

No parts of this publication may be reproduced, stored in a retrieval system, or transmitted, in any form or by any means, electronic, mechanical, photocopying, recording, or otherwise, without the prior permission of the author.

ISBN: 978-1-969576-00-3

First Edition

A&A Publishing and Marketing

Visit the website for more information at http://www.5souls.com:

INVITATION
FROM THE AUTHOR

Five Souls is rooted in a universal journey of redemption, healing, and transformation that transcends religion, culture, and nationality.

The soul of this book speaks to all of us who wrestle with light and shadow, grief and grace, and the eternal human search for meaning. It is not a political manifesto. It is an allegory that invites readers to reflect deeply on the human condition — our wounds, our potential, and our interwoven fates. In today's increasingly polarised world, I believe that stories can still act as bridges.

My wish is that readers will take away the message that healing is possible. That redemption is real. And that even in our darkest moments, we carry the potential to reflect divine light. This is a book about the sacred within the broken, and the hope that rises when we choose love.

ACKNOWLEDGEMENTS

The journey of writing this book pushed me out of my comfort zone on so many levels. Left to my own devices, it would have remained nothing more than a scramble of nascent thoughts and ideas sitting in a mental drawer. Destiny decided otherwise and placed people in my orbit to nurture these notions into a literary work. I am sincerely grateful to the many individuals and influences who supported, guided, and inspired me throughout my travels.

My deepest appreciation goes to my exceptional professional team:

- **Don,** for his invaluable mentorship and for serving as an insightful sounding board.

- **Megan,** my developmental editor, whose wise guidance and keen insights helped shape the narrative.

- **Debbie,** whose meticulous eye as a line and copy editor ensured precision and flow.

- **Kristina,** for her remarkable talent in designing a cover that so perfectly encapsulates the essence and spirit of the book.

- **Melissa and Alexander,** for their expertise and dedication in navigating the complexities of bringing this book to launch.

To my cherished friends, who patiently offered their earnest feedback on early drafts, titles, and cover designs. Your unwavering openness, diligent critiques, and generous spirit through countless revisions were truly indispensable.

I would especially like to thank **Kate**, whose own life transitions held a mirror to the journeys I knew I had to take but never began. You taught me that pain cannot heal the scars of war, and that forgiveness elevates us. For your unwavering support, quiet sacrifices, and your ability to see beauty beyond life's battlefields, I will always cherish you.

To the **University of Basel library**, where I spent countless hours immersed in the quiet wisdom of its walls of books, I owe a debt of gratitude for the stillness, the inspiration, and the silent encouragement of all the authors before me who were driven to share their gifts with the world.

My heartfelt thanks go to the countless authors of inspirational books around the world. Your profound works not only provided invaluable reference material for my research but also gently guided me to delve deeper into the reflections of my own heart.

And finally, to my protagonists — **Sergei, Budoo, Anaïse, The Boy, and Noor.** Thank you for leading me on such an extraordinary and transformative ride. It was an honour to write your stories.

DEDICATION

To my daughter and son, Helena and Alexander-Akeem.

Dear Helena, the day you were born, the door to my old life suddenly closed behind me, then dissolved into the wall. Before me, an expansive white canvas opened up, inviting me to create a new image of life. Overwhelmed, I jumped in, not realising how fatherhood would shape me. Thank you for holding my hand on this journey and for the quiet assurance that all would be well. In you I see the spiritual strength of your grandmothers, intuitively understanding what no book can teach.

Dear Akeem, being a part of your life has given me the opportunity to become the father that my own father never had the chance to be. I wish you had met him, gotten to hold him, and learned at his feet as I did. Only after you came into the world did I begin to understand his inner strength, his patience and his wisdom. For this gift of generational healing, dear Akeem, I am endlessly grateful to you. Keep creating amazing stories with your boundless imagination.

In an ideal world, I would love to see how you will both shape the world and embrace even grander versions of all I might have achieved myself. But we all have an appointed time, and no plea will allow me to stay on this earth longer than that. Let the stories in this book remind you of all the conversations we shared at the dinner table, and the journeys we have yet to take.

I hope you will always know how much I love you both. You allowed me to live the most beautiful version of a life that I never knew would be available to me.

TABLE OF CONTENTS

"They say within every soul, two wolves eternally contend. I believe the fate of humanity does not hinge on which one prevails, but on how soul communities learn to walk with both, forging wisdom from shadow and light."

Inspired by Cherokee warrior wisdom
(Light & Dark Wolf)

Prologue

In the veiled interstices between worlds, where the seen and unseen realms converge, two eternal sentinels stand as divine witnesses to humanity's end journey.

The Tree of Life, its roots penetrating the depths of existence, branches reaching toward divine creation and potential, is counterbalanced by the rhythmic, thudding pendulum of the Spiritual Doomsday Clock. Its solitary hand hovers a mere ninety seconds from midnight, an outcome of mankind's hubris. The Earth has been bent to their will, its resources stripped, the very cradle entrusted to their stewardship defiled, just as the Jinn before them once did.

The Nūrāniyān, radiant guardians of the Clock and guides to student souls, gather in solemn assembly. Their faces are etched with resignation as they grapple once again, as they did during the reign of the Jinn, with the timing of the encroaching apocalypse.

Sintra, a guide of profound wisdom, observes the Clock's hand tremble as autumn winds sweep through humanity's seasons, stripping away certainties like leaves from branches. Yet where the Nūrāniyān only see an irreversible cataclysm, she sees transformation, a passage to what can be born from the fire. Sintra steps forward with a desperate gambit — to send forth chosen souls and reclaim valuable seconds from earth's predestined fate. She volunteers her own students, resolute that within their hearts lies the potential blueprint to restore belief in humanity. The Nūrāniyān agree, but the souls' lives must not be tainted by knowing of the trial. Any attempt to influence their choices will accelerate the singular hand of destiny towards midnight. With the veil of deception cast, their journey must be a labyrinth of discovery born of free will.

All the while, the clock ticks relentlessly towards its final destination. The fate of the Divine Tree, and with it, all humanity, now rests in the hands of five souls.

Meeting in the Place of Souls

A rolling meadow stretched to the horizon, the soft lines unbroken save by a craggy tree. Its branches reached high into the heavens; its gnarled roots spread far across the field.

Clusters of wildflowers sat nestled in the vibrant green grass, the multicoloured patchwork dancing in a soft breeze that nudged white fluffy clouds across the azure sky. Bees buzzed among the flowers, and the distant murmur of a babbling brook reached five orbs floating in the tree's cool shade as they gazed into a translucent milky pool filling a shallow bowl carved into the rock. Tiny figures were moving in the pool; it was like peering through a telescope at a distant city where the history of humanity unfolded.

"Why are they so destructive?" Anaïse murmured, her essence radiating calm rationality, searching for patterns to understand humanity's choices.

"They always have," the Boy replied, a ripple of inspiration flitting across his form. "Even in their deepest mistakes, don't you see the seeds of something more? Adam and Eve? Cain and Abel? Ring any bells?"

"It's quite a spectacle, isn't it?" A tall woman shimmering with soft light glided slowly towards them. A white robe flowed behind her, and a warm smile played on her lips. She paused. "Seen from above, human behaviour looks random, violent, capricious. But even in those most self-destructive moments, the greatest opportunities for growth ignite."

"Sintra!" Anaïse brightened instantly. "We figured you'd appear soon."

Sintra stood beside them as they gazed into the pool.

Several crystalline orbs drifted past, each the size of a small bush, souls drifting aimlessly between assignments, the light forming soft, iridescent rainbows of memories on their shiny surfaces.

"I could watch this pool forever," said Anaïse.

The Boy nodded. "Highly educational."

"But if you really want to learn something, sooner or later, you have to join in," Sintra said with a smile.

Sergei huffed. "I knew you'd remind us of that."

Budoo's aura blazed as she stared at the tiny figures. "Their foolishness amuses me."

"Amuses you?" Sintra challenged Budoo, her voice gently firm. "Do you truly see no echo of yourself in their trials and tribulations?"

Budoo slowly lifted her eyes, her unreadable form momentarily hardening, her jaw squared, a hint of self-reproach quickly veiled.

"I try not to," the Boy interjected wistfully. "But even their foolishness — it sparks something, doesn't it?"

"Every action has a reason, however flawed," Anaïse added, an analytical gaze fixed on the pool.

"And those reasons are often so transparent!" the Boy chuckled.

"We all do things we might regret," Sintra said, her gaze encompassing them all. "That's how we truly learn."

"And how," muttered Sergei.

Sintra beckoned to the group as she moved away from the pool into a portal with a winding corridor. The gossamer walls glowed with soft light that ebbed and flowed in a never-ending array of pastel shades.

"You've all chosen your time and location?" she asked as the group fell in behind her.

"I have," said Anaïse. Sintra watched Sergei, his silence in sharp contrast to the excitement of the others. "Does your chosen path trouble you?" she inquired gently.

Small wonder he was apprehensive. Sergei's proposed life would echo the most destructive human attributes the souls had observed.

His orb flickered. "You want me to succumb to my base self and destroy thousands of lives, hoping it saves one soul?"

"She's not just any soul, Sergei."

His salvation would be reciprocally bound to another, both clinging to fragments of each other's humanity. Sintra wished she could show Sergei the incredible counterbalance of love and acceptance he would encounter if he submitted to his journey.

"It's a burden I can't carry. I'm sorry," Sergei murmured.

His refusal was met with concerned silence from the group, the change in energy reflected by his dimmed presence.

"Is there no other way?" Sergei asked.

How could Sintra convey her unshakable belief that his love would save this soul? "Yes. Her destiny would be defined by another who will never feel the need to love her as you will," she replied, hoping this appeal to Sergei's protective nature would help him decide.

The other souls' forms were morphing into the temporary vessels they would inhabit. With each transformation, Sintra knew Sergei's proposed journey weighed more heavily.

"Remember," she said, "Your free will remains paramount. This sacrifice, this act of love, is a heavy burden. Perhaps another path to fulfil your calling exists?"

Stretched stillness gave way to cautious acceptance as Sergei's soul began to take on its physical form. "Without your wisdom, experience, and guidance, we'd be in danger of choosing the path of ease rather than the one most beneficial for us," he replied.

"Sergei's right," added the Boy. "I've gone with your recommendation too."

"I have also agreed with your proposal," said Budoo, her voice laced with a mix of apprehension and anticipation. "The dark path awaits me."

***

As they moved down the corridor, more orbs drifted past, some seemingly aimlessly, others more purposeful amid clusters of five or six moving in the same direction.

Sintra looked at Noor. "Are you certain in your choice?"

Noor nodded slowly, his face serene. "In my heart of hearts, I know it is the right thing to do."

Sintra sighed. "You've chosen a hard road."

"I am ready," replied Noor. "If my companions have made difficult choices, what would I be if I took an easy path?"

"Teacher's pet!" said the Boy with a laugh. His face turned serious. "But good luck. Serious kudos for your choice, Noor."

Anaïse nodded. "By our choices, we are made," she said.

Sintra smiled in agreement.

"And we're each taking on a challenge in our own way," Noor said. He smiled softly. "I think we'll all need a little luck."

"I don't think I'll find much on my journey," grumbled Sergei.

"And yet, as we have each learned," Budoo said, "no matter how dark things might seem, as long as we stay the course, there is always Light."

Sintra smiled softly. "I'm proud of you all — what you have learned here with each other."

They had reached the end of the corridor. An infinite prairie lay ahead, the tall golden wheat swaying on the fragrant breeze. Beyond was a boundless ocean, glinting and sparkling in the sunshine.

Sintra slowly looked at each of them. "It is time."

Sergei let out a pent-up breath.

The Boy clapped his hands as though trying to psych himself up. "Let's do this!"

"I've got butterflies," Anaïse said.

Noor gently took her hand, and the others followed suit, each linking with their neighbour.

"And that's why I love this group," said Anaïse, looking at her companions.

Sintra smiled. "Draw from each other's strength," she reminded them.

With a last glance at each other, they stepped into the waving wheat. Sintra watched their small figures moving serenely through the field, then one by one they merged with the light and were gone. As they disappeared, their voices came floating back.

"See you on the other side," said the Boy.

"Good luck, everyone," growled Sergei.

"May a shower of blessings accompany your journey," said Noor.

"I'm going to miss you guys," added Anaïse. And lastly, Budoo's deep, brooding voice. "Until we meet again …"

Sintra watched until all traces of them were gone. "Good luck indeed," she whispered. Then she turned and dissolved back to the veiled interstices.

The Drunkard
(the unrepentant Soul)

12

"The cage stands open, yet the bird still sleeps,

Dreaming in shadows, while true joy weeps.

It calls for freedom, yet keeps its eyes shut,

Tangled deep in its own self-spun rut."

**Shams-ud-Din Mohammad Hafiz-e Shirazi
(interpreted by Daniel Ladinsky)**

CHAPTER 1

Soviet military training ground, Lviv Oblast, Ukraine

1987

"Lieutenant Colonel Salenko! Come quickly!"

Sergei forced himself up from his desk and straightened his jacket. "What's the hurry, Sergeant?"

"It's Karpin, in the barracks …"

Sergei strode across the polished wooden boards to the door and marched across the square, the sergeant trailing in his wake.

A bitter wind stung his cheeks and tugged at his thinning hair, bringing the first snow of winter. Two privates waiting outside the barracks threw open the door as Sergei approached. He stepped inside to a hubbub of hushed voices which died away on his entrance.

Between the concrete floor and tin roof, forty beds lined the walls. The space was feebly heated by an old wood-burning stove in one corner.

A crowd had gathered around one of the beds, halfway down on the right. The men silently parted for Sergei.

"What's going on?" he demanded.

The group stepped back silently, eyes cast downwards.

Sergei followed their gaze. "Oh, shit!"

Karpin was sitting propped against the wall, his rifle in his hands, the barrel in his mouth, the streaks of blood and brains up the wall already coagulating.

Sergei stared for a long moment. "Clean it up!" he snapped. "I want everybody outside in five minutes, in full combat gear."

"Sir?" The sergeant looked puzzled. "It's ten at night."

"We're going on a little run, Sergeant," Sergei said, "then the whole platoon is going to the canteen to get blind drunk in honour of Karpin. Any questions?"

The Sergeant snapped to a smart salute. "No, sir!" He turned to the men. "You all heard the lieutenant colonel. Karpin's squad, you're on clean-up. The rest of you, get your shit together!"

Back in his office, Sergei pulled a bottle of vodka from the bottom drawer of his desk, sank a quarter of it in one go, then slowly laced up his combat boots. "Let's get this the fuck over with," he muttered as he stepped outside.

***

Kiev, Ukraine, 2003

The military was a distant, hazy nightmare as Sergei pounded his fist on the thin wooden door in the hallway, a nearly empty bottle of vodka clutched in the other. His blows echoed down the corridor.

"Lida, open up!"

He collapsed against the doorframe, patting down his hair, and grabbed the wall as he started to fall. The bottle escaped his clutch and rolled away. Sergei watched it with heavy-lidded eyes then turned back to the door. "Lida." His voice softened. "I need to talk to you."

Shuffling feet from inside signalled Lida's arrival. "Go away, Sergei."

"But I need to talk to you."

"If you bother me, I'll call the police. Again."

"How can I be bothering you? I'm your husband."

"You have to leave, Sergei."

"Just five minutes," he slurred. "Five minutes?"

"Go away."

"You think it's easy for me driving a minicab? I used to be—"

"I'm not going through that nonsense again. I'm calling the police."

"No! No!" Sergei leaned his ear against the door and heard the whirr of the phone's rotary dial. He exhaled deeply, then straightened up and staggered down the corridor.

The snow flurries had strengthened into a full-on blizzard. Sergei held up his hand to protect his eyes from the stinging snow, then paused, blinking. Something more was blurring his vision. He blinked again, but it was still there, a dark veil, like wearing sunglasses at night. A surge of pain shook his skull, vicelike, getting tighter and tighter. He beat at his head, staggered forward three steps, then collapsed in a heap on the freezing pavement.

***

Anya marched down the long corridor, her rubber-soled boots squeaking on the worn green linoleum as she tried to rein in her thoughts. She walked at a measured pace, torn between arriving as quickly as possible and delaying her entrance.

A nurse looked up as she reached the reception desk.

"Salenko!" demanded Anya. "Lieutenant Colonel Sergei Salenko."

"Family only, I'm afraid."

"I'm his daughter." Anya rummaged in her bag and pulled out her ID.

The nurse gave it cursory glance, then nodded to the door opposite her desk. "In there."

"Can I …"

"Yes. He's sedated right now."

Right now? He'd spent most of the past thirty years sedated. "Thank you," she mumbled, then turned and tugged on the door before she lost her nerve. She wanted to race back along the corridor and pretend this had never happened, that she didn't need to see him ever again.

Anya stepped inside the small room. Like everywhere else in the old Soviet Union, it betrayed decades of neglect and decay. Four metal-framed beds were evenly spaced, their cream paint chipped and worn. A sink was by the door, the tap dripping and the pale-blue tiles worn and grimy. In the far corner by the window, her father was hidden under a thin blanket, hooked to a small monitor that blinked slowly in time with his soft breathing.

Anya inched to his bedside. How could her father, who had once seemed almost superhuman, look so worn and grey? Grey skin, grey hair, grey sheets and blanket. His face was a mass of bruises from where he had fallen, and his left arm was in a cast.

Anya flinched, her eyes filling with sadness and pain as she quickly squeezed his right hand before dropping into a grey metal chair.

How could this be the same man who used to take her to the park on sunny days? She used to look forward to their picnics all week, to the solemn ritual of unfolding the blanket and laying it in the perfect place. Half would be laid in the shade for Anya, who didn't like the sun, half in the sun for Sergei, who would remove his shirt and lie basking while she unpacked everything. First the sandwiches — smoked mackerel for Sergei, Adygea cheese for Anya — then the pickled cucumbers, and lastly their dessert, pampushky — doughnuts filled with jam and dusted with powdered sugar.

Anya loved the routine of setting out the plates, pouring the drinks (fruit kompot, with a dash of vodka for Sergei) and unfolding the napkins. While they ate, Sergei would quiz Anya on the trees surrounding them — what type of tree, what type of seed, how to recognise them. Each time she got an answer right, he would reward her with a pat on the head or a kiss on the cheek.

As the vodka took hold, Sergei would drift off to sleep — "just for five minutes" — while Anya packed up everything and wandered to the lake to feed the ducks and swans with the leftovers.

She looked at his expressionless face, blotched and criss-crossed by broken veins, scored with deep contusions.

"I love you so much, Daddy," she whispered, as though afraid the walls might be listening. "You are forever in my heart. You know that, don't you?" She sighed and looked at the window, but all it revealed was a sky thick with clouds, as grey outside as it was inside. She started again, her voice stronger this time. "I'm part of you, you know? I can feel you even though you're barely alive."

She glanced at his impassive, unresponsive face. Only the monitor and the faint rise and fall of his chest showed he was alive. "I know you're with me; I know you know everything about me. I love you, do you hear? I love you," she sobbed. "And I will forever remain your most beloved daughter. Whatever happens, I'll find a way to be happy. You'll see. You'll see everything, even from above."

The thought of life without him gripped her heart, and tears washed her cheeks. "Can you see my tears, pouring like rain? They're a sign of my forgiveness. Forgiveness for you, forgiveness for me, forgiveness for everything you put us through …"

Her words caught in her throat and she paused. Over ten years ago, she had reached a point in her life when all she had known was behind her, and she had to let go of everything weighing on her soul.

She shivered and wrapped her mink coat tightly around her. She'd taken a step into the unknown while she still could. At the time, she thought she had everything: youth, beauty, self-confidence, time. She did not understand that the one thing she was missing, the void that lurked deep inside her, the sucking hole that spoiled everything she did, doomed her to another failed relationship, a confirmation of her father's prediction.

When had she realised it? She could still remember the day, sitting in her Manhattan penthouse, her total lack of desire to live this life filling the room, when she finally understood she couldn't do this anymore.

Her relatives back in Minsk wouldn't understand. They thought she had hit the jackpot, meeting a man with homes in London, New York and the Côte d'Azur, and being driven around in his Rolls-Royce. How little they knew, how little they would have cared even if she had told them she had no life. Anya was simply a toy, a trinket to be used and enjoyed, then cast aside when a new model or interest came along.

"Live for today!" That was the motto she and her girlfriends had lived by when they were younger, and what they would have undoubtedly said had they seen her wallowing in misery in the Manhattan apartment. But for Anya it was not enough. The more she was surrounded by the trappings of wealth and privilege, the emptier and disconnected she felt. Everything in her life had a price, everything was replaceable, including, she realised after yet another fight with her partner, her.

Not for the first time in her life, Anya had gone against general opinion, left her sugar daddy while her soul was still intact, and embarked on a journey to discover her purpose.

"Follow your heart," her father had told her, and in the most difficult moments, his voice had echoed in her head and guided her. So how could he have ended up like this?

Anya gazed at her father and tried to recall him the way he was before the booze completely took over his life. He'd been an educated man, a leader, a Soviet army colonel respected and revered. But nothing is perfect, and where there are pluses, there will always be minuses. In the Soviet army, honour and conscience go hand in hand with alcohol and a dissolute lifestyle. Nothing could prevent her father from going down that path — neither a strong-willed wife, nor three children, nor his duty to the motherland, a concept that was still important in those days. Not even the tear-sodden pleas of his beloved Anya, who was only five at the time. She did not understand what was going on, why the whole family was gathered in the living room, why Mum was crying again …

And then it all made sense. Daddy had got drunk once more, and Mum had said she couldn't do this anymore. It was either rehab or divorce; Mum had said those words a hundred times, and while Anya didn't know what they meant, she knew they were bad.

As usual, Daddy sat silently in his chair. If there were awards for being stoic, he would sweep the board.

As Anya watched, her mum and grandmother went from talking to crying, crying to desperate wailing, while her dad's seeming indifference fed the flames of their emotions.

Anya hadn't known what to do. She understood that when Daddy got drunk it was a bad thing, and that frightened her, but he wasn't drunk now, so why was she scared? She didn't know what to do. She wanted to run up and hug him; maybe he was just as scared as her. Despite the fear, she forced herself out of the chair, her legs carrying her towards him barely under her will. But, for some reason, when she reached him, she fell on her knees and started crying loudly like her grandmother and mother. The older women's cries reached a crescendo, and Anya had to shout to he heard. "Daddy, please get treatment! I love you, and I don't want you to leave!"

Sobbing uncontrollably, she wondered why the adults just looked at her, didn't try to calm her. Maybe what she was doing was right. Did the adults enjoy her grief?

And now, there he lay, closer to death than life. Anya roughly wiped away her tears roughly with the back of her hand, stood and gazed out the window at a brick wall across the street.

***

Don't leave!

Sergei wanted to cry out, but no words came. Anya had turned away; she might leave before he could say all the things he wanted to. Memories flickered, jagged, out of order, of nights when he'd kissed her forehead and lay at the foot of her bed, her breathing settling in time with the steady tick of his old Poljot Sturmanskie. That sound, once the measure of missions and flight hours, had become the metronome of her sleep. Now, those fragments of Anya were the only thing keeping his own heart tethered here.

20

He tried to force out the words, but the effort drained him. His eyes closed once more, slipping back into that drifting half-dream, only a slight blip on the monitor marking his brief emergence from his stupor.

He exhaled deeply, the habitual thirst dragging back memories of that day when Anya was five, pleading at his feet.

***

God, how his head hurt. He ached all over, and his heart was bursting out of his chest.

He needed a drink. His wife would probably hate him even more, but so what? She was really fat. After the third child she really let herself go, but she still blamed everything on him and his drinking.

Was he a drunkard? She needed to look at herself. Who would want to go to bed with her looking like that without a few shots of vodka? So he'd had a few drinks with friends, so what? And now it had begun, the moaning and crying. She'd even dragged the child in to try and guilt him.

Anya was crying bitterly. Was she really feeling that bad, or was she copying her mother? Maybe it was time to quit. He loved his children and wife, but did they love him? Or was it just for the "give, give, give" that they were with him? He fed them, gave them money; his eldest boy was at university, and the middle one was enrolled at the military academy. What more did they want?

Screw them. It came with the job.

He was desperate for a drink. For now he had to sit and take it, but he still had half a bottle of vodka hidden behind the TV. As soon as the circus was over, he'd quench his thirst without their irritating hysteria.

Maybe he was an alcoholic, but then so was Captain Mishka. He drank like a fish, and everything was OK. Sergei was a lieutenant colonel, after all, a Soviet officer, a squadron commander, with hundreds of people under his command. They had no idea about the pain, the burden he was forced to carry, how his life had changed him from the optimistic young officer he once was.

They were all young once, but then Afghanistan happened.

December 1979, in the middle of a freaking Afghan winter. What a time to choose.

Still, they arrived in triumph, rolled into the towns and cities like conquering heroes to support their Communist brothers. If they'd known what awaited them in the coming years, they'd have turned around there and then, headed back home while they still could.

How wise he was now.

How stupid he was then.

It was time to put an end to that nonsense and get a drink …

CHAPTER 2

"Afternoon." The nurse gave Anya a cursory nod as she appeared at the doorway of her father's room, the click, click of the nurse's knitting needles the only sound in the deserted corridor.

Anya softly closed the door and walked slowly to her father's bed. He looked at peace, serene even, with his eyes closed and slow breathing. But what was going on inside? Was there any meaningful brain activity, or was he already gone, with just his body clinging stubbornly to life?

How could someone, whose drinking had caused so much grief and turmoil, end his life in such tranquillity?

Anya slumped into the chair and gazed out the window. Heavy sleet was falling from a leaden sky, half-frozen slush that melted as soon as it hit the ground. The weather matched Anya's mood. It was a mood she was familiar with — a feeling of impending dread, knowing that the next incident, the next battle, could erupt at any moment, triggered by her father's return.

She stared at his face. *Did you know I used to flinch at the sound of your footsteps? Every time the elevator arrived at our floor, I prayed to God it wasn't you.* If it was, it always ended badly at best, and at worst…?

Anya's mind jumped back to when she was fifteen years old…

***

"Open it!" Her dad's voice echoed through the apartment, setting her nerves on edge. Without waiting for a response, he began to hammer on the front door. The sound was like a sledgehammer in her brain. "Open up!" he roared.

Anya glanced at her grandmother, cowering in the corner of the kitchen, her hands over her ears. Anya was going to have to deal with him alone.

She crept to the door. "No, Daddy," she told him, her voice tremulous. "I don't want to. You're drunk."

"Open up, girl!" he ordered, pounding on the door.

The sound of his fists thundered in her chest. "Please, Daddy," she begged. "Go away and sober up. You're scaring me."

"Open it, or I'll call the police!"

Anya's anger rose. "Go ahead. They'll lock you up until you're sober."

"Open the door, or I'll break it down!" he thundered. His fists continued to beat a ferocious tattoo.

"Daddy, don't, please. I'm afraid!"

"Open it!" He pummelled the door with renewed fury.

Sobbing, Anya reached up and unlocked the front door, then stood back as he burst into the apartment. His eyes burned with anger as he rushed at her, fists clenched. She pressed herself against the wall, shaking like a leaf, wished she were somewhere else, anywhere else.

He pinned her to the wall by her throat, growling, his face close to hers, his fists raised.

The fierce stench of alcohol and cigarettes was on his breath. She closed her eyes and waited for the blows to begin, but instead, he stumbled down the hallway and into the kitchen.

She heard breaking dishes and prayed softly. "Lord, when will this end? I can't do this anymore." Dry tears of inner pain and resentment filled her heart.

Sergei stood in the middle of the kitchen, swaying. "Is there something to eat in this stinking place?" he grumbled.

"Just take what's in the fridge," Anya said quietly.

He slumped into a chair. "You get it."

Anya hung back in the hall. "I don't want to."

"Get it!"

"No, Daddy," she whined, like a puppy expecting its next beating.

Her father grabbed a glass from the table and hurled it at her. It smashed against the wall, showering her with broken glass.

Her grandmother climbed to her feet. "Sergei, calm down. Can't you see the child is scared?" She moved tentatively towards him.

Sergei got to his feet and took a step towards Anya, still in the hallway.

"What are you doing?" Grandma cried, stepping between them.

"Out of my way," he slurred, shoving her aside.

She screamed in pain as she hit the floor.

Her cry broke the spell for Anya. She rushed to her and knelt beside her, brow furrowed. "Grandma, where does it hurt?"

She glared at her father, but he seemed oblivious to what he had done. He staggered into the bedroom, collapsed face down on the bed and began to snore.

"I landed on my hand," said her grandmother. "I think it's broken."

Anya helped her up and led her back into the kitchen.

Keys rattled at the door, and her mother, Lida, stepped into the apartment. Her eyes took in the broken glass and Anya helping her grandmother. She sighed deeply as she reached for the dustpan and brush. "Again?"

***

The apartment was calm. Sergei's heavy snoring from the bedroom was the only sound as Anya sat at the table with her mum and grandmother, sipping tea. Grandma's hand was wrapped in a crisp white bandage, and the broken glass was swept away.

Lida looked at Anya, frowning. "What do you want me to do?" she demanded. "Get divorced?"

"We can't continue like this," snapped Anya. "Sooner or later, he'll kill one of us."

"But if we get divorced, we'll lose our apartment," said Lida.

"If the choice is between a quiet life and an apartment, I choose life." Anya's tears were rising.

Her mother reached out and took her hand. "Please, little one, don't cry."

Anya wiped her face on her sleeve and forced a smile. "We need to take Grandma to the hospital."

The bedroom door opened, and her father staggered out. He glared at the trio sitting at the kitchen table. "It looks like a witches' coven," he snarled. "Are you three plotting against me?" His eyes settled on Anya's mother. "And where have you been!"

"Work! I came home to find my mother's hand broken." She glared up at him. "Aren't you ashamed to raise your hand against an old person?"

Sergei ignored her and began rummaging in the back of a cupboard. He slammed the door and turned round. "What have you done with my bottle?"

Anya's mother wrapped a protective arm around her daughter's shoulders. "It's gone. You don't need more vodka. There is a child and a sick old woman in the house, and you're still drunk."

Sergei was across the room in two strides. He grabbed Lida's shoulders and shook her. "Where's the bottle?"

Lida burst into tears. "Why are you treating me like this?"

"Where is the bottle?" he repeated, shaking her shoulders, his cold eyes boring into hers.

Lida visibly wilted. "Behind the stove …"

Sergei gave his wife a final shove, reached behind the stove and extracted a small bottle of vodka. He held it up with an admiring look, then unscrewed the cap and gulped it down in one go, his gaze never leaving the three women.

As the last drop hit his tongue, he tossed the bottle across the room, where it smashed on the polished red tiles, then he collapsed into a chair and began to sob loudly.

"Go to sleep already," said Lida.

Sergei looked up, bleary eyed, and peered into the shadows around the stove. "One, two, three, four …" He jabbed his stubby finger with each count.

"What are you looking at?"

Drawing his thick eyebrows together, Sergei swatted at something. "The little devils. Don't you see them, dancing around in front of me?"

Lida coaxed her mother out of the chair and took Anya's hand. "Let's get Grandma to the hospital." She glanced back at Sergei as she led them down the hall, gathering up coats, hats and gloves. "We'll get no more sense out of your father today."

***

How could so much cruelty and neglect be combined with so much love and care? Anya couldn't help but smile as she remembered the bedtime stories he had told her. Elaborate tales were woven from Ukrainian folk stories, featuring mythical villains like Koschei the Deathless, a malevolent sorcerer, or Baba Yaga, the evil witch, or Anya's favourite, Zmey Gorynych, the three-headed dragon. But whoever the villain was, the helpless villagers were always rescued by Anya the Beautiful, riding in on her white horse.

And he didn't just tell a story, he elaborated on it, spun it out over several nights, with each character having a different voice.

So much love, so much care, so much vodka...

***

Still as a corpse, Sergei stared at the ceiling.

They were back. The little devils had followed him to the hospital and were dancing above him. Their mangled limbs and contorted faces were a brutal reminder of something he had tried desperately to forget. Sergei had lived with them for so long, they barely bothered him. There was a time when they had almost driven him crazy, these strange, shadowy creatures that cavorted in front of him, always just out of reach, never fully visible, but now he barely registered them.

He would never forget when they had first appeared. It was after his division had been sent to mop up operations in that village in the mountains. What the hell was it called? All those places looked alike; they all blended in together. All except this one …

By the time his division had arrived, the tank boys had already done their dirty work. God, it was a mess. The Mujahideen had got one of them with a rocket launcher just as the tanks had rolled up, and the rest had gone crazy, blasting anything that moved.

Sergei and his troops had walked through the village in stunned silence, all the usual banter and bluster quelled by the horror. The streets were awash in blood, the contorted remains of men, women and children mixed with those of sheep and dogs, their remains scattered across the roads or in the crushed shells of their houses.

The top brass had labelled it a glorious victory against a rebel stronghold, but Sergei and his men knew better. It was a massacre, a killing frenzy, the worst kind of atrocity.

And after? No one said a word. Not one. What was the point? What was the point of anything? Pretty much all of them had done the same — sought oblivion at the bottom of a bottle in a vain attempt to erase what they had seen.

That was the first night the demons had visited Sergei. The shadowy figures remained just out of sight, their blood-soaked limbs recalling images from the village, half-glimpsed visions straight from Dante's *Inferno*, making sure he could never forget what he had seen, never be free from it.

His drinking worsened from that time, the bottle gradually consuming him, until he was finally alone, abandoned by everything and everyone he had ever loved.

No Lida, no Anya, no vodka. Just the demons and the memories.

He closed his eyes and let the darkness wash over him.

CHAPTER 3

Anya paced back and forth beyond the foot of the bed. She was finding her visits increasingly draining. What was the point of visiting an unresponsive patient clinging to the last threads of life before Death carried him away? Anya could almost feel Death hovering over the bed. What was keeping her father alive?

The doctor said his brain function was minimal, sporadic, and that by all rights he should have died weeks ago. "A stroke that massive usually results in sudden death," he had told Anya. "He must be a tough old bastard." It was said with grudging respect, a respect Anya struggled to feel.

She stopped at the foot of the bed. A tough old bastard. That just about summed him up. Tough love was the only type of love he could show to his family, which left each of them searching for love in other places. As Anya slumped into the chair beside the bed, she remembered her father in the kitchen ironing his shirt — he always wore a crisp white shirt when he saw one of his mistresses. The recollection threatened to overwhelm her already emotional state. It was something her mum knew about, but she no longer had the strength to take offence. She did, however, draw the line at ironing his shirt for these increasingly frequent visits.

And why should she be offended? It was already over; the divorce papers were on the table, and the apartment had been listed for sale in the newspaper.

It was already over for them as adults — all that remained was to try and part as civilised people — but for Anya, at fifteen years old, everything was just beginning. She could not imagine what lay ahead. She lacked dignity. Her life was controlled by fear, guilt and self-pity.

Anya stared at the bed. "You have no idea what you put me through, do you? Where my search for love — no, not even love, attention — led me?" She sighed as the bitter memories flooded back.

***

He was thirty-six, as I later discovered, though his bald head and dated clothes made him look older. He was waiting outside the school and fell in step beside me as I headed home.

"You're a pretty one," he said. "You have beautiful eyes."

It was the first compliment I had ever received from a man, and I was greedy for it. My knees trembled and my heartbeat faster. How should I answer him? What did he want from me? How should I behave?

"Thank you," I said, blushing furiously.

He grinned. "I'm Yuri. I like you. Give me your phone number."

One part of me was screaming that I should give him the brush-off, right now, but I didn't know how to. Mum had taught me to be polite.

With feigned bravado, I replied, "Why? Are you going to call me?"

Yuri grinned. "Of course I will! How could I not call such a beauty? I'll call you, and we can go out for a coffee."

"What if my parents answer?"

"I'll apologise and say I got the wrong number." He grinned at me. "It will be our little secret."

My upbringing battled my weakness and vulnerability. "But I don't know you," I protested, "and I don't have coffee with strangers." But I was thinking that keeping secrets is nothing new …

"How can we get to know each other if we don't go out for coffee?" He gave his eager grin again. "I'm not suggesting we have sex!"

I was shocked by his words but had no riposte. At least it's not sex, I thought, as I meekly gave him my phone number. The next day, Yuri was waiting for me outside school again. He gave me a huge bouquet of flowers and a big yellow teddy bear. "This is for you, baby," he said.

I had never received attention from a man before. He epitomised gallantry. For a young girl, it was a fairy tale.

He led me to his car, a shabby dark-red Vaz 9. "I'll drive you home."

The car was nothing special, but it was the first time I had been in a car alone with a man. It felt very daring.

On the way to my house, he pulled over in a quiet side street. "Let's talk."

Predictably, talk soon turned to kissing. I tried to resist — he kind of disgusted me — but his persistence was stronger than my willpower. He began to unbutton my blouse.

"Yuri, what are you doing?" I gasped. "I don't want to."

He softly stroked my face. "Come on, beautiful. You wouldn't have given me your phone number if you didn't want to."

I felt like I was about to vomit. I wanted to throw open the car door and run away, but the habit of enduring even when it hurt, of accepting everything as it is, was too strongly ingrained in me. Years of cohabitation with an alcoholic father had taught me I was only worthy of humiliation. It kept me in that car, in the clutches of a repulsive stranger.

When Yuri started to fumble between my legs, I sat up. "That's enough," I gasped. "Please, enough already."

I thought he was going to force me further, but he leaned back, leering at me and my exposed breasts. He reached for me again, but I quickly pulled my bra back up and began to straighten my clothes.

Yuri seemed unperturbed. "I can tell you're pleased. And don't forget the flowers and the bear; let them remind you of my kisses."

I nodded. "Yes, Yuri. And thank you for the gifts. I like them." Why was I so polite to him? Why did I crave his attention while simultaneously being disgusted by his thinning hair, the dandruff on the shoulders of his sweater, his cigarette-infused breath?

I climbed out of the car and stumbled towards home. My legs were weak, as though they were made of cotton. I felt dirty, defiled. I wanted to get home as fast as I could and wash the traces of his kisses from my body, but at the same time, it made me feel special, desired, more grown up. I had my own secret lover.

Yuri didn't call, and it was almost a week before he turned up at the school gates again.

When he saw me, he smiled and waved. "Did you miss me?" he said, taking my arm and handing me a box of fancy chocolates. "I missed your beautiful smile."

Once again, a simple compliment and a gift lowered my defences and allowed him to lead me towards his car.

"I'm happy to see you," he continued. "I have a surprise for you."

Why couldn't I say that I didn't want to go anywhere with him? I wanted to run away, but instead I climbed into the car, sitting mute as he drove us towards the city centre.

He parked the car outside a building, and, in a daze, I followed him up the stairs and into a small apartment. "My friend's away for a few days," he told me. "Said I can use his apartment."

I wasn't sure what to think, what to say. I had never been alone in an apartment with a man before. Was this a date? Should it even be happening? Maybe the fact it was happening meant it was supposed to?

The apartment was small with a scruffy kitchen, a worn fake-leather sofa and a couple of random paintings on the walls. We sat at the table.

Yuri poured me a glass of brandy. "Na Zdorovie!" He emptied his glass in one go.

I wanted to feel grown up and didn't want to look like a child, so I followed suit, gasping as the alcohol burned its way down my throat.

Yuri grinned. "Like a true daughter of the Soviet Union." He poured us both another glass and watched me carefully as we repeated the process.

By the time the second glass had gone down, Yuri didn't look so disgusting, his eyes seemed a warmer brown, and even his jokes sounded funnier.

After the third glass, I didn't resist as he took my hand and led me to the sofa. He began to kiss me, more vigorously than before, then he undressed me, his hands roaming all over my body.

"Yuri! What are you doing?"

"Don't be afraid, baby. I won't hurt you. This is what you want, isn't it?"

I don't know. Is it? Is he right? I said nothing, just gazed at the ceiling, all my barriers washed away by the cognac he had plied me with. After all, it had to happen sometime, so why not now? *But is this how it should be?...*

"You are so delicious, baby," he whispered. "I have never had such a delicious flower as you."

My mouth went dry, and I couldn't speak.

I didn't care what happened; I just wanted it to end.

I passed out.

"Wake up, beauty." His voice came to me as if through a dream. "It's time to leave. I'll take you home."

I sat up, groggy. My mouth felt full of cotton wool. "What happened? Did I fall asleep?"

"You passed out with pleasure," grinned Yuri. "That's normal. It happens to a lot of girls their first time." He was already pulling on his shoes, and he threw my clothes at me. "Come on, let's go. You're a woman now."

I began to dress in silence, trying not to think about what had happened. I knew one thing: I needed to go home, and I didn't ever want to see this man again.

He drove me home. I could think of nothing to say, and my brain was still in a fog from the cognac. When we reached my street, he pulled over and gave me a slobbery kiss.

"See you around."

Wordlessly, I got out of the car and rushed home. I craved a shower, even though I knew it would never be hot enough to wash the dirt from my body.

***

Anya studied her father's face. It was as impassive and unreadable as ever.

She stood and walked to the window, her stomach roiling at the memory, then turned back towards his bed. "If there was any innocence left in my life, it deserted me that day, in a grubby apartment with a grubby man, but a man who gave me the thing I was most lacking — attention. And for that, Daddy, I blame you."

***

He lost it all in the end. His wife, his apartment, even his mistress deserted him, throwing him out of the small apartment he had rented for her.

And for what? For booze? To be a good son of the motherland?

A good son of the motherland. Sergei had clung to that in Afghanistan, tried to convince himself and his troops they were on some glorious mission. As the months turned to years and the bodies piled up, it became harder and harder to peddle the lie. Eventually they lapsed into a sullen silence, all of them — from privates to officers — simply accepting the grim reality, hoping desperately it would soon end. But before it ended, it got worse.

As the Soviet mission stumbled and faltered, the Mujahideen grew bolder. They went from simply harassing the Soviet supply chains to directly attacking their bases.

Sergei's squad was stationed in the north-west, close to the Pakistani border, in Pashtun territory. The Pashtun fighters were a vicious bunch, utterly ruthless, completely at home in their barren landscape. What chance did Sergei's boys have? They dreaded each and every time they had to leave the security of their camp, a blasted stretch of barren ground encircled by barbed wire and craggy hills.

Sergei had pointed out to his superiors how vulnerable their location was, how ripe for an attack they were, but they didn't listen, didn't care. Someone in Moscow had decided they needed a base right there, so that was where the base was.

The attack came at dawn, when the camp was least ready. The soldiers were still sleeping, warm in their beds, suffering nightmares of frozen patrols, guard duty or endless drills on the rocky square that served as their parade ground.

Sergei was awoken by an ear-shattering blast as an RPG slammed into one of the barracks, swiftly followed by a second, then a third and a fourth.

He half-fell from his bed and started to drag on his clothes as Boris, his aide, stumbled into his tent, still buttoning his shirt. "We're under attack, sir!" he gasped.

"Tell me something I don't know," growled Sergei, stomping into his boots.

"Yes, sir!"

"Full situation report in two minutes."

"Yes, sir!"

Boris saluted and headed to the door, Sergei hot on his heels. The bitter wind grabbed the door from Boris's hand, throwing it wide open.

"Shit, Boris," began Sergei. He froze as something warm and sticky splattered across his face.

Boris crumpled to the ground, the back of his head blown out.

The second sniper shot smacked into the doorframe by Sergei's head. The third found its mark, blasting straight into Sergei's shoulder, in and out before he registered any pain.

The situation caught up with him: Boris's brains splattered across his face, the intense pain from his shoulder. Sergei dropped to his knees and came face to face with Boris's staring eyes. He retched, but his stomach was empty. He dry-heaved twice more, then looked up.

Several buildings were on fire, and the men were rushing around, some trying to quell the flames with rusted, outdated extinguishers, others simply trying to escape the sniper's bullets.

Sergei called to a captain hurrying past. The man dropped down beside him and pointed at the blood seeping through Sergei's combat jacket and covering his face. "You're hit, sir!"

"Fuck that," shouted Sergei. "Tell me what we know."

The captain tore his eyes from Sergei's bloody face. "Five rocket strikes, sir, and several snipers in the hills."

Sergei glanced at the rocky hills, hidden in shadow. "I said this would happen."

"Sir, yes, sir. The colonel did too."

Sergei scanned the hills more closely. There was a muzzle flash. "There's one of the bastards."

"Got it, sir."

"Send four three-man patrols out there, now. We need to get those snipers before they pick us all off."

"Yes, sir."

"And don't send them out the main gates," Sergei said. "They'll have something waiting for us that way." He nodded towards the darkness behind him. "Go through the fence to the north."

"Yes, sir!" The captain scurried off, leaving Sergei propped against the tent, waiting for it to be over.

The patrols made it out of the camp and soon cleaned out the snipers, none of whom attempted to run. The three bodies were dragged back to camp and thrown on the bare dirt of the parade ground — one craggy old man and two teenagers with fine facial hair. *Christ, they can't be much more than fourteen.*

"What shall we do with the bodies?" asked the captain.

Sergei looked round at his men, whose shocked, angry and frustrated faces told him they wanted to be anywhere else except this hell on earth. Their faces glowed red in the flames of the burning barracks as they stared at the bodies of their tormentors. "Burn them," he said.

Rough hands grabbed the Afghan bodies, hauled them up high and carried them towards the shell of a burning building. They were tossed into the flames to a loud cheer.

For a moment, Sergei's men were united in their hatred as they watched the bodies burn.

Was it savage? Brutal? Against the codes of war? Maybe, but so what? Almost twenty men had died in the attack, and the survivors needed an emotional release.

The motherland could go fuck itself.

The motherland. Even that old concept was creaking.

The Soviet Union was crumbling around them. More and more voices of dissent were being raised within the country, while Gorbachev and his glasnost were undermining the very foundations upon which the empire had been built.

And Sergei? He realised he had brought it all on himself.

Refused to face the truth.

Refused to change his ways.

Refused to do anything but stubbornly keep on drinking and driving away his loved ones until there was nothing left. Nothing but darkness and death, hovering over him as a reminder of his failures.

CHAPTER 4

The ward smelled strongly of urine as Anya stood by the foot of the bed. Her father looked worse than ever, his skin grey and sunken, the monitor recording the faintest trace of life.

Anya couldn't bear to look at him. She wheeled round and stared out the window, the grey nothingness pervading all she could see.

Her fingernails picked idly at the peeling paint on the window ledge, putting off the inevitable moment when she had to turn and look at her father, sit by his side and try to summon up the last vestiges of love for the shrunken shell that lingered in the bed.

He had taught her so much — how to swim, how to ride her bike — and now he was teaching her the hardest lesson of her life — how to forgive and move on. She pictured him strong, happy and smiling as he boosted her onto his shoulders to see the Pashka, the Easter procession, pass by, the candles flickering in the cool evening air. Then the image was gone, and Anya was alone in the hospital ward, with one thing left to do.

She buttoned up her coat against the unheated room then dropped into the chair. She made herself take her father's hand and look at his face.

His hand was cold and frail, its sagging skin covering withered bones.

She used to think he was the strongest man in the world. She loved to hold his hand and squeeze it tightly to show how much she loved him, then wait for the squeeze in response that meant he loved her too.

She wanted to beg God and the angels not to take him, but she knew it was too late for that. It was a question of time — a few more days, a few more hours, a few more minutes. She clung to her father's wrinkled hand, her soft sobs the only sound in the frigid room.

Tears rolled down her face, as life, like a movie, passed before her eyes, frame by frame. He'd let her jump in the puddles in her rubber boots on the way to kindergarten, argued with the judges at a dance competition because he believed she should have won, fed the ducks with her in the park on a Saturday morning. All these happy moments lined up in a chain called life, while time boiled away everything sad or unpleasant, exposing the residual good. Through everything that had happened, love still lived in Anya's heart, despite all the suffering she had endured because her father was an alcoholic.

She sat by her father's bedside and gazed at his grey visage, sensing that moment fast approaching. She closed her eyes and began to pray. She prayed for his life and his death, his honour and his disgrace, his love and his rejection, tears rolling down her cheeks.

***

The cold seeped through every fibre of Sergei's body as he looked around.

The forest was dark. The trees crowded together as though for company, their branches sagging, heavy with freshly fallen snow.

He looked at his bare feet, the skin red and raw.

So, this was it.

Sergei attempted to walk, but the snow was deep, and he was so, so tired.

He tried to lift his leg, but it was stuck tight. He stumbled forwards and fell face down in the snow.

He coughed, spluttered and forced himself to roll over and gaze upwards.

Between the canopy of branches above him, a small patch of sky was visible, where a single bright star was blinking at him.

Sergei sighed and allowed his body to settle back into the snow, which wrapped around him like a blanket.

He no longer felt cold, just calm and contented.

As if on cue, there they were — the little demons who had accompanied his darkest days and tormented him. But rather than grinning with their pinched, evil little faces, they were fluttering, drifting like the snow, caught on the wind and being slowly pulled towards the light.

Sergei smiled, a gentle smile that brought a youthful softness to his face.

The light was getting brighter, filling the sky, calling him home.

It was time.

He sighed deeply, folded his hands across his chest and closed his eyes.

The Jinn
(the Soul that blames)

46

A sinner died, and, as his coffin passed,

A man who practised every prayer and fast

Turned ostentatiously aside – how could

He pray for one of whom he knew no good?

He saw the sinner in his dreams that night,

His face transfigured with celestial light.

"How did you enter Heaven's gates?"

he said. "A sinner stained with filth from foot to head?"

"God saw your merciless, disdainful pride,

And pitied my poor soul," the man replied.

"A Sinner Enters Heaven"
(The Conference of the Birds)

PROLOGUE

Dear reader, I am Budoo. A Jinn. The daughter of King Barqan of the Marid tribe in the Qaf mountains. Unlike angels who are created from light and mankind who are created from mud, we, the Jinn, are created from the tip of the purest and hottest part of smokeless fire.

I have more power than you can ever imagine. I have lived a long life. I have seen all the wonders of the world. Yet now death and an eternity of darkness approach.

Why?

If you would understand why I now give up everything, I ask you to listen to my story.

CHAPTER 1

Yemen,

1969

The bus ground its way up the last hill then rattled to a halt, a cloud of dust momentarily enveloping it. As it cleared, Jean-Paul peered through the window.

A small village straddled the hillside to his right, the mud houses merging seamlessly with the terrain. Jean-Paul shook his head. It was 1969, man was about to step on the moon, yet the small Yemeni village looked just as it had for hundreds of years.

His eyes strayed to the left. A ragged river filled the narrow valley, spilling from the hills above town. The village women were washing their clothes and leaving them on the rocks to dry, as they had for millennia. Beyond that was nothing but the vast expanse of the desert.

The bus door creaked open, and the other passengers, wrapped in their djellabas, climbed down and dispersed into the shadows of the village.

"This is it, sir," said the driver, a wiry man with a scraggly beard, in heavily accented English. "We go no further."

"Thank you."

Jean-Paul hauled his backpack onto his shoulders and made his way to the front of the bus.

The driver looked up at him. "Are you sure this is where you want to go? There is nothing here but the Empty Quarter, and all you will find there is dust and death."

"And yet once there was a thriving city."

The driver narrowed his eyes then slowly nodded. "You seek Iram, the city of the Pillars? You are not the first." He followed Jean-Paul off the bus onto the hot, rocky ground.

Jean-Paul gazed at the empty expanse. "Do you believe it is out there?"

"Maybe once it was. But man is not meant to find it."

"Why do you say that?"

"Allah destroyed Iram for a reason. It was a place of wickedness and death. Should you discover it, that is all you will find there."

"Maybe that is what I seek..."

The driver gave him a wary look. "Be careful what you wish for. When a man travels with death in his heart, that is what he will find."

Jean-Paul tightened the straps on his backpack and squinted in the harsh light.

"You should go back to Aden, to the beaches, the sunshine," said the driver. He peered at Jean-Paul's resolute face. "I'll be back next week. See you then?"

Jean-Paul nodded. "Until then." The heat of the sun hit him as he stepped from the shadow of the bus. Hot days, cold nights and utter solitude. That was what the desert offered, what he craved. He watched as the bus turned around. Then with a final wave from the driver, it started back up the hill, a black cloud of raw diesel fumes spewing from the exhaust and stinging his eyes. Jean-Paul pulled his hat low over his face. He kicked the toe of his boot into the hard ground and watched the tiny puff of dust envelop his foot, covering the shiny leather. By the end of the day, his new boots would have rubbed half a dozen blisters into his soft feet, but that was all part of the process, right? The cleansing power of pain and suffering. Jean-Paul checked his compass then scrambled down the loose gravel and crossed the river on a narrow path of rocks. He glanced back at the village. The women had paused in their relentless scrubbing and were watching him, some with curiosity, others with concern. One by one, they returned to their clothes, to the river, to the gentle rhythm of their lives, unchanged, unchanging.

Jean-Paul faced forward and headed into the desert.

CHAPTER 2

There are two great tribes in the Jinn world: the Marid and the Ifrit. My father was the king of the Marid, the greatest of them all. The Ifrit, however, were the most ambitious, wishing to lure mankind away from the Light to prove to God that Jinn were more worthy than humans. Recognising the Marid were the most powerful of the Jinn, the Ifrit sought to secure their loyalty, thus ensuring the other Jinn tribes would join their crusade. The Marid are as proud as they are powerful and would never willingly follow the Ifrit into battle. The Ifrit king sought to create a situation that would leave my father with no choice but to join forces.

The Marid controlled the part of the Qaf mountains that the Ifrit claimed was used to create Adam's soul, the very ground that Shaitan spoiled by stepping on it, ensuring his attributes would also reside within mankind. Using their claimed direct lineage from Shaitan, the Ifrit declared this land was their blood right and challenged my father to surrender it. My father, knowing the lying and manipulative nature of the Ifrit, did not wish to be drawn into a pointless war. That would further the rift between tribes and force them to take sides, ultimately resulting in countless deaths.

Both kings knew the ground Shaitan soiled was on Earth, not Qaf as the Ifrit claimed, but both also knew the truth was irrelevant and propaganda would be the determining factor in luring other tribes into the war. My father asked the Ifrit king what terms would avoid such a calamity. The king replied that joining the families, by marrying me to his son, would avoid bloodshed. Such a marriage, however, would imprison the Marid into an allegiance that would leave a torturous legacy for our people.

My father, wise and cunning, agreed to the marriage on two conditions: that I agree to the union out of free will and that the most fertile of the Ifrit farming land be immediately presented to the Marid as proof to the other tribes of the sincerity of the Ifrit's intention. The Ifrit king agreed, pleased that all was going to plan, but his pride needed to stipulate a condition: a human sacrifice. Knowing my disgust of pointless killing, even of humans, he wanted the tribes to see the Marid were bending to his will. The choice of sacrifice was to be jointly decided by the engaged couple. I saw the revulsion in my father's face, but before he could react, I held his hand and blinked as we looked into each other's eyes. In this instant my plan was transmitted, and he gave a slight nod of acknowledgement. Both kings agreed to the terms, the farming land was transferred to my father's control as promised, and the news spread amongst the Jinn tribes.

CHAPTER 3

Heat and thirst. Jean-Paul told himself to ignore them. His five years in the Legion had taught him they were mere physical manifestations, signals from the brain to warn us, like the red light on a car dashboard. Embrace them. Keep walking and keep moving, that's what their cadres had taught them. Allow the repetitive physical motion to numb the brain, to wipe away the misery and the torment, the memories and the pain.

As the sun rose higher and his shadow crept behind him, Jean-Paul found his rhythm.

The steady tramp of his feet across the sand.

The creak of his pack nestling against his shoulders.

The blaze of the sun on his back.

Life was reduced to its essentials — walking at a steady pace for an hour, then a brief stop to check his compass and drink some water.

Hour after hour he repeated the same rhythm, each step affirming his commitment to his quest. Each hour took him further from the village, further from safety, like a boat heading into the open ocean in hope of finding dry land beyond the horizon.

Was the bus driver right? Was he seeking death? Was his quest to find Iram a thinly veiled suicide attempt? Many before him had attempted in vain to find it, most were vastly more knowledgeable than Jean-Paul. Why did he think he could succeed where others had failed?

Don't question it. You have your pain. You have your reasons. And whether you succeed or fail, whether you live or die, in the end it is all the same.

Step by step, breath by breath, the weariness built. Just when he thought he couldn't continue, the golden hour came, the brief interlude as the sun raced towards the horizon. The heat dropped, and the walking became easier. Darkness enveloped him within minutes, and Jean-Paul collapsed onto the sand, eased his arms out of the straps of his backpack, and revelled in the stillness as the sweat cooled on his skin.

Night-time brought new wonders as he lay in his sleeping bag gazing at the sky, a blanket of stars for company. Thousands, millions, billions, more stars than Jean-Paul could ever have imagined, and a brief shower of shooting stars to lull him to sleep.

As his eyes closed and his mind drifted, she came to him. Émilie, as he had last seen her, her dark eyes smiling at him as she perched on the end of the bed and laced up her boots.

"It's so early," Jean-Paul had protested from the warmth of their bed.

"I want to get a walk in before breakfast." She stood, leaned over and kissed him.

He looked up at her. "Be careful."

"Of course. See you at breakfast."

Why hadn't he stopped her? Why hadn't he gone with her? Why hadn't he dragged her back into bed and made love to her one last time?

Jean-Paul sat up, tears streaming down his face, and looked around. The dunes rose around him in the soft starlight, their ridges seeming to move, like waves on the ocean. The stars arced above him. Everything was unchanged, as it had been, as it would be forever, including his pain.

He lay down, forced his eyes closed and tried to go back to sleep, but he knew it was futile. Every night Émilie visited him, and every night, after her visit, he was wide awake. There was nothing for it but to accept the inevitable, pack up his meagre camp and begin walking while it was cool. Jean-Paul chewed on a piece of dried bread and some dates, swigged some water and shoved everything back in his pack.

After a quick check of his compass, he resumed his steady march, heading towards the dawn and the rumoured ruins, three days march away across the desert.

CHAPTER 4

The Ifrit prince had a repugnant stench of arrogance about him, of privilege and blood, and a reputation as a sociopath, even by Ifrit standards. Despite his education, wealth, power and numerous opportunities to further Jinnkind, he relished perfecting the art of torturous death at the cost of human and Jinn lives. He worshipped Shaitan, seeing himself as a younger version, and tried whenever possible to emulate the legends we had grown up with.

We met in the gardens of my father's palace, and the discussion quickly turned to the best way to choose the human sacrifice which would bind the marriage. His distaste for your kind was far greater than mine, and he would have happily performed the kill himself had the task not fallen to me. He drew up a shortlist of candidates, none of whom deserved to die for a marriage I had no intention of allowing to take place.

Sensing my hesitation, he picked a poor peasant family with a disabled son. You would be doing them a favour," he said with a smirk. "He's already damaged, and the parents would be released of their pointless burden and worthless human moral obligations. Can't you see the parents are overwhelmed and close to breaking point?"

He paused and smiled ever so slightly, his eyes becoming increasingly intense as he lent in and sniffed my perfume. "I wonder how little it would take to break one of the parents?"

Before I could intervene, he placed the mother of the child in a trance-like state and watched in delight as she threw herself beneath the wheels of a passing ox cart. As the cart crushed her skull, he turned to me calmly. "Not much, apparently."

I fought to keep the horror from my face.

"That worked rather well," said the Ifrit prince. "Your turn."

Seeing his pleasure in killing, I realised he would continue until I fulfilled my obligation. But I could not, would not, kill an innocent child.

As repulsed as I was at his complete lack of respect for life, albeit only human, I needed to remain calm and buy time to find a way to save the child's life. "Suicide?" I said, unimpressed. "A little predictable and overdramatic don't you think? I'd like to come up with something a little more … impressive … as my wedding gift to you. Give me some time, and I'm convinced you'll be pleased with my creativity."

The Ifrit prince grinned. "Creative killing? I like that in my future bride." He brushed his hand across my cheek. "One week," he said as he strutted away. "One week and I will expect to see your choice."

As soon as he had gone, I set out to find a magician.

CHAPTER 5

By the end of the second day, Jean-Paul was in trouble. His water supplies were running low, despite having eked them out, his parched swollen tongue was a constant reminder of his plight, and his feet were raw, making every step agony. And then there were the dunes, which seemed to conspire against him, forcing him south to avoid the big ridges, making his journey longer by the hour. He kept forcing himself to take one step after another, but eventually he ground to a halt, standing like a docile donkey awaiting instruction.

Jean-Paul lifted his head and looked at the ocean of dunes around him. It was hours since he had last checked his compass, so he had no idea where he was. The fading light softened the contours of the sand, disguising the cruel environment with a gentle façade that belied its brutal intent.

He opened his mouth to roar, "Is that all you've got?" and hear his words echo off the indifferent dunes, but all that came out was a weak, croaking gasp of despair.

Jean-Paul gave a bitter smile as he recognised his pitiful condition. He slumped onto the soft sand, his pack weighing on his back.

As he gave in to exhaustion, he pictured his Legion cadre, Sergeant Lemare, two hundred pounds of muscle, bristling moustache and attitude, leaning over him, his cigarette-soured breath in Jean-Paul's face as he roared his disapproval. "That's it? You're quitting? Even a fucking dung beetle has more determination than you, you pathetic piece of camel shit!"

Jean-Paul smiled again, in spite of the pain and torment. How was it possible to miss someone like Lemare?

The memory faded, leaving him with the gaping wound that Émilie's disappearance had left, the hole he was trying to fill with his desert quest.

Jean-Paul looked around. Yesterday he'd called this the golden hour. Now it was a reminder of how much he had deteriorated in one day. How much closer he was to facing his own mortality. And the strange thing? He didn't care. In fact, he welcomed it, welcomed the knowledge that one way or another he was closer to his destination. An image flashed into his mind, the tattoo that one of his fellow legionnaires had on his left shoulder — a skull and crossbones and the words, 'Death or Glory', the motto of the Royal Lancers. He had embraced the concept then, and he embraced it now. He would either find the Jinn or die trying. Either outcome was acceptable.

He had not previously contemplated death in this way, but now, with it lurking close by, he was indifferent to it. The sooner it came, the sooner the pain would be over, and the sooner he would be reunited with Émilie. As the sun dropped behind the dunes, Jean-Paul rolled onto his side and lost consciousness.

***

"Wake up, sleepy head!"

Jean-Paul opened his eyes. Émilie leaned over him and gently kissed him. "Are you going to sleep all day?"

"I was having a nightmare," murmured Jean-Paul. "You were gone, and I was alone in the desert."

Émilie's expression dropped. "That's why I woke you. You have to wake up, now."

Jean-Paul stirred, the straps of his backpack digging into his shoulders. "Don't make me."

Émilie shook him. "Wake up, my love. You have to wake up now."

She stood, but when Jean-Paul reached for her, his hands found nothing but air and the bitter isolation of loneliness. "Come back to me, my love," he gasped.

Nothing.

"I have consumed all I can from this world, Émilie. I have fought for my country, travelled to the furthest reaches of the earth, drowned myself in alcohol and drugs, yet still I miss you so much. Nothing can replace the void you've left …"

The silence was overwhelming — a dark and endless pit, like death itself.

He rolled onto his side and blinked, his eyes crusty and swollen. He was more afraid than he had ever been in his life.

He just wanted to sleep and find Émilie once more, just find her and be with her, but at the same time there was a darkness, a deep sense of horror lurking just out of reach that he didn't want to disturb.

He had come seeking the lost city and the Jinn, looking for solitude and death. Now he had found this, it clawed at his guts like a rat trying to escape a narrow culvert. It was not a thing of peace and comfort, as he had imagined, but profound loneliness and despair, an eternity of death, decay and gnawing terror.

Dancing lights shimmered on the horizon.

Jean-Paul forced himself to sit up. He was not alone! There was hope, life. Was it a mirage? Maybe. Who cared? Jean-Paul's survival instinct kicked in, and he tried to shout, but his cracked, swollen tongue filled his mouth, and only a faint squeak emerged.

Attempting to stand was too much effort, and he fell back onto the sand. He gazed at the dancing lights for a moment longer, then closed his eyes.

CHAPTER 6

Human magicians have the ability to trap Jinn and get them to do their bidding. I found one and asked him to order his Jinn slave to kill the Ifrit prince. In return, I agreed to grant a wish of the magician's choice. The magician's enslaved Jinn followed the orders of his master and set out to kill the prince. Jinn fight by changing their shape into different animals at dizzying speed, attempting to gain the advantage. The battle raged back and forth, but ultimately, in an attempt to escape, the prince turned into a horse and was consumed by the enslaved Jinn, who had just transformed into a tiger. When the Ifrit king heard of his son's death, he reluctantly relinquished the bind on the Marid, turning his attention to the pursuit of his son's killer.

The enslaved Jinn, for his part, was freed from a life of servitude to a vicious master. The magician, realising the Ifrit would come to interrogate him and demand why his enslaved Jinn had killed their prince, turned himself into a mouse to escape the Ifrit's wrath. He was promptly eaten by a hungry cat as he scurried away between market stalls.

With war between Ifrit and Marid averted, I turned my focus to the peasant and his son. As I watched him, I was struck by the father's devotion to his wife and God. I vowed to do whatever I could do to make up for the tragedy that had befallen them. I appeared to the father and offered to grant either complete health for his son or endless money for the best medical care. To my amazement, the father refused my offer. He accepted his situation and its hardship as a blessing from God, quoting the Quran: "My Lord! Truly, I am in need of whatever good that You bestow on me." I pressed him once more, but he was resolved. I could not sway him.

His refusal intrigued me. I pondered the human condition for the first time, reflecting on how this man chose to live his life. Why would he deny himself? Why would he live a hard life when an easier one was in reach?

In an effort to understand, I appeared to him one day as his dead wife. He was initially furious at me for desecrating her memory and reopening wounds not fully healed. I apologised, but when I started to leave, he begged me to stay. As we talked, I revealed that not only could I look like her with the exception of her eyes, but that I also had access to her memories and could be exactly like her. In his desperate longing for his wife, he agreed to us being together, on the condition that I did not appear in front of his son in that form. Neither of us knew what to expect, and we couldn't possibly guess how it would end.

CHAPTER 7

Faces hovered over him, speaking in a language Jean-Paul couldn't understand. Rough hands moved him and peeled off his backpack. Probably robbers, the final indignity. Then he remembered no more.

"I thought you would sleep all day."

Jean-Paul slowly opened his eyes.

He was in a large tent, its open entrance revealing the soft afternoon light dappling the curves and contours of the dunes.

As he forced himself to sit up, an old man peered at him, his face creased from years of exposure to the desert winds and sun. "We thought you were dead."

Jean-Paul looked around. His boots had been removed, and his feet were bandaged in soft muslin soaked in aloe vera. One of his aluminium water bottles was by his side.

The old man pointed to it. "You should drink."

Jean-Paul picked up the bottle and drained it. He had a splitting headache, every muscle in his body ached, but otherwise, he seemed all right.

The tent was lavishly decorated, woven rugs covering the floor and cloth-wrapped poles supporting the roof.

"Welcome to my home," the old man said, still peering at him.

Jean-Paul nodded, forced his lips apart and tried to move his tongue.

"You are a long way from home." The old man sipped a small cup of mint tea, poured one for Jean-Paul and handed it to him. "This will revive you."

With shaking hands, Jean-Paul took the tea. "Thank you," he croaked, "for everything."

The old man smiled, revealing sparkling white teeth. "My daughter said you were dead, that we should leave you, but no, here you are." He touched his chest. "I am Nabil."

"Jean-Paul."

"French?"

"Originally. But now I live in New York."

Nabil gave him a knowing look. "Did you come here to die, or are you just stupid?"

Jean-Paul laughed despite himself, a dry, crackling sound like autumn leaves underfoot. "Maybe a little of both," he admitted.

He took a sip of the tea. The sweet, warm liquid slid down his throat, and the sugar rushed through his body. He was alive. Jean-Paul wasn't certain if he was pleased or disappointed. Even though he had putatively come to the Empty Quarter to seek the fabled lost city of Iram, Nabil's words had a strong ring of truth. His actions were not those of a rational man with a lust for life. Was it possible to fear and welcome death at the same time? He had questions that needed answers, but he dreaded knowing the answers. He had thought that coming to the desert, exposing himself to its fierce and merciless purity, would help him see things more clearly, but he was as confused now as the day he had left New York.

Nabil watched him closely. No sooner had Jean-Paul emptied the glass than Nabil took it from him, dropped a lump of rock sugar in it and refilled it from a small brass pot. He handed it back and gestured to drink.

Despite Jean-Paul's weariness, there was something in the old man's eyes that made his request hard to refuse. He dutifully forced down another glass of the sweet mint tea and collapsed back on his pillows.

***

When he next awoke, it was dark. For a moment, Jean-Paul forgot where he was; he imagined himself back in his New York apartment, Émilie by his side. He lay still for a moment, enjoying the illusion, even as his brain told him he was deceiving himself. Finally, he could stand the deception no longer and forced himself to sit up. Outside the open entrance of the tent, a small fire was burning and several figures were huddled around it.

Jean-Paul climbed slowly to his feet and tottered outside.

Nabil looked up at the sound of Jean-Paul's shuffling feet and indicated that he should sit next to him.

Jean-Paul took his place on the blanket.

"You are feeling better?"

Jean-Paul nodded. "A little stronger."

Nabil picked up a plate of food. "This will get your health back."

Jean-Paul looked around for utensils then realised he was expected to eat with his fingers.

Nabil put him out of his misery. "Eat with your right hand," he told him. "Always the right. Never the left." He handed him a small bowl of water and a cloth, watched as Jean-Paul carefully washed and dried his hands, then handed him the plate.

Jean-Paul dug into the food with his right hand. As soon as the first taste hit his tongue, his hunger returned, and he began shovelling the food in.

Nabil laughed and patted him on the back. "Now you will start to feel stronger."

It didn't take long for Jean-Paul to clear his plate, and no sooner had he done so than one of the women hurried forward to refill it. As Jean-Paul ate, he looked around. "What brings you and your family so far into the desert?"

"My calling," answered Nabil.

"Your calling?"

Nabil gestured to a huddle of young children half-hidden in the shadows on the far side of the fire. "My tribe upholds a tradition that has been a part of our culture for centuries, sending their young children to me to be raised in the old nomadic ways until they are six years old," explained the old man. "Here I teach them not only about the desert but also the scriptures, the local languages and our tribal laws." He gestured to the children. "For them, I am part teacher, part father, part peacemaker, and this harsh, hostile wasteland into which you came to die is my home, my garden. I have lived and travelled here since I was born. I know every dune, every grain of sand as though it were part of my body."

"Interesting," said Jean-Paul, fighting back a yawn.

"The food has made you sleepy," said Nabil with a laugh. "That is good." He took Jean-Paul's empty plate. "Surrender to it, and in the morning you will feel refreshed."

Jean-Paul gazed at the clear, star-filled sky. "I don't think I could stay awake if I tried," he said, climbing to his feet. "Thank you for the food; it was wonderful."

"Sleep well."

***

The bustle of the family woke Jean-Paul the next morning. He emerged from the tent, walking more easily than the night before, and found Nabil sitting drinking tea.

Nabil beckoned to him. "You are looking better. Now we have to get you moving." He glanced at the sky. The sun was kissing the horizon, painting the dunes with a rosy blush. "Come, let's walk before the day becomes too hot."

Nabil led him in silence at a gentle pace along a shady ravine. Little by little, Jean-Paul's muscles came to life. His feet were sore, but the soft bandages enabled him to walk, albeit slowly.

Beside him, Nabil moved with an easy stride, looking around as though seeing everything for the first time.

As they emerged from the ravine into the sunlight, a ruined castle revealed itself on the hill above them, the red-brick walls blending with the surrounding hillside, the broken turrets like ragged teeth. Nabil stopped, whispered to himself, then turned and resumed walking.

Jean-Paul stared at the ruins in disbelief.

Nabil glanced over his shoulder. "Come."

Jean-Paul didn't move. "What is that place?"

"Old place. Bad place."

"Is it an old city?"

"Old city, yes."

"Iram?"

Nabil furrowed his brow. "You know of this place? That is why you are here?"

Jean-Paul nodded, his eyes fixed on the ruins. "What did you say when you saw it?"

"A prayer of protection. From the Jinn."

"A Jinn lives there?"

"Better not to know of this creature. She is dangerous." Nabil turned and stomped away.

Jean-Paul hurriedly followed, his battered feet struggling to keep up. "What did you say? The prayer."

"I seek refuge in the Perfect Words of Allah from the evil of what He has created," Nabil said.

Jean-Paul looked towards the ruined tower, trying to imagine what the Jinn might look like. "And this is to protect you from the Jinn who lives there?" he asked.

The old man said nothing and kept walking. "Not a good place. Better to get away."

Jean-Paul bit his tongue and fell in step. There would be a time to pursue this, but it was not now.

***

Later that evening, as the fire burned low, Jean-Paul broached the subject once more. "When we were walking today ..." he began.

"You want to know about the Jinn?" Nabil asked.

"Yes. To us in the West, they are magical figures from children's stories."

Nabil fixed his dark eyes on Jean-Paul and shook his head. "What little you know."

"You believe in them, as real things?"

"Of course. Jinn are as real as you and me but much more dangerous," said Nabil.

"That's why you said a prayer?"

Nabil nodded, holding Jean-Paul's gaze. "You want to know about the Jinn?"

"I do."

He studied Jean-Paul for a long time. "You have a deep tragedy within you."

Jean-Paul shrugged, the tears rising.

"Something you think the Jinn can help you with?"

"I have read that if you meet a Jinn, they know everything about you."

Nabil looked pensive. "And there is something in your life you wish to know the truth about?" His dark eyes bored into Jean-Paul. "This is why you are here? To find the city? To find the Jinn?"

"To find an answer," Jean-Paul whispered.

Nabil poured them each a glass of tea and set the drinks on the rug in front of them. The fire's red glow lit his face, emphasising every line, every crevice. He looked immeasurably old, immeasurably wise.

"You will tell me your story," he told Jean-Paul, "and then I will tell you about the Jinn." He picked up his tea. "Are we agreed?"

"Agreed."

The old man sipped his tea and tilted his head towards Jean-Paul. "Proceed."

Jean-Paul swallowed hard. He had just committed to talking about the one thing he had avoided for the past five years, the thing he had come to Yemen to escape. He could feel his eyes stinging even before he began to speak, but waves of calm washed over him from Nabil, comforting him.

"My story is short but bitter," he began. "I met a girl — Émilie — we fell in love, got married. It was one of those magical all-embracing relationships; we had no need of other people. We could spend every minute of the day together and still not want to go to sleep because it was not enough." His face softened. "For our honeymoon, we forsook the beaches and the big cities and went to Norway, to walk and enjoy the solitude."

Solitude. The bitter pill that Jean-Paul had been swallowing for the past five years.

"On our second day, I'd had a bit too much wine the night before, so Émilie went for a walk by herself while I slept in."

Jean-Paul pictured her smiling face as she leaned over and kissed him, bundled up in her sweater and parka.

"Be careful," he had told her.

Émilie smiled her soft smile. "Of course. See you at breakfast."

Jean-Paul eyed a few grains of sand that had lodged themselves between the threads of the rug. He exhaled and turned back to Nabil. "I never saw her again. The police searched for days but found no trace of her — no sightings, no body, nothing."

Nabil nodded. "And you want to know what happened to her?"

Pain creased Jean-Paul's face. "The longing for her has taken over my life for the last five years. Was she abducted and murdered? Or did some freak accident befall her when she was out walking?" He stared into Nabil's eyes. "A Jinn would know, right? A Jinn could tell me?"

"The Jinn claim to know everything that has happened in our lives," Nabil said. "But maybe you wouldn't like the answer."

"My wife is gone. There is no good answer. The only good thing would be to finally know the truth."

Nabil sat silently for a long while, staring into the flames. When he spoke, his words seemed to come from far away, another time, another place.

"According to the Quran, the Jinn are said to be creatures with free will just like us," he said, "created from smokeless fire by Allah, and their leader used this freedom to defy our Beloved, refusing to bow to Adam when commanded to do so. For refusing to obey Allah's order, he was thrown out of Paradise and called Shaitan, the one you call Satan."

"So they are like us? Sinners and dreamers? Wise and foolish?"

"Yes and no. Some of the Jinn are believers; others are unbelievers. Some Jinn marry and have children. Sometimes Jinn even fall in love with humans."

"They're solid? They have real bodies?"

Nabil shook his head. "Only if they wish to. Some have mass and live in one place, others have no physical mass; they can choose to fit into a small space, or appear larger than a mountain." He glanced at Jean-Paul. "You say you want a Jinn to tell you the truth about what happened to your wife?"

"Yes."

"Then know this. It is said Jinn are perpetual liars, and that for every ten things they disclose to you, nine will be lies. They love to deceive humans, not because they hate us, but because they take great pride in deceit and manipulation."

Jean-Paul thought for a moment. "You said a prayer when we passed that ruined castle. Do Jinn always live in such places?"

Nabil shook his head. "A Jinn living thus is in torment, hiding away from something — a kindred spirit for you, no?" He glanced at Jean-Paul. "Most Jinn live in communities, much like humans. They eat, marry, die; some follow religions. They have armies with ranks and rules. They can choose to settle anywhere, from a vast area to a tiny hole, as they are massless creatures and can fit into any space they find sufficient." His eyes shone. "They are invisible to humans, but they can see us. Sometimes they deliberately come into view or contact with humans, often with tragic consequences."

"How long do they live?"

Nabil shrugged. "Who knows? Jinn are believed to live much longer than humans. Some are said to be still alive having seen the prophet Muhammad in the seventh century, but they are skilled at blending into the human world when they wish to do so, and in many cases live unnoticed among people."

"But they can be summoned by people, yes?"

Nabil knitted his brow. "Often this is done by humans attempting black magic, who call on Jinn specialising in dirty deeds to perform the magic for them, agreeing a contract that binds them until it is fulfilled, but a Jinn will never do anything without a heavy price or sacrifice in return. Such black magic on humans can only be undertaken by dark Jinn — Ifrit or Marid."

"What types of black magic?"

"Usually cursing other people," Nabil said, "or influencing a marriage — make it end it in divorce, for example." He scowled. "But such acts are forbidden in Islam and considered a major sin in Islamic teaching."

Jean-Paul silently processed Nabil's words. He knew what Nabil was telling him should have given him pause for thought, but he was long past caring. He had come to the desert seeking death or answers and couldn't back out now.

"You know how to summon a Jinn?" he said finally. "You could show me how to do it?"

The old man refilled their glasses with steaming tea and tossed more wood on the fire, which flared, lighting up his face. "Would you like to hear about the first and greatest love story ever?" he asked.

Jean-Paul shook himself out of his trance. "Sure."

Nabil coughed and sipped his tea. "You know about Iblis being cast out of Heaven to become Shaitan, but do you know how his betrayal by his one true love still burns inside him?"

Jean-Paul shook his head.

"Long before our kind were created," began the old man, "the earth was populated by the Jinn. For thousands of years, they built empires, produced technical wonders, made great advances in science, alchemy, culture and the hidden knowledge — the occult. Combined with their God-given ability to travel great distances in the blink of an eye, take the form of any living creature and influence the minds of lesser creatures, this was the golden age of the Jinn. Remnants of their technical and architectural achievements are only now being discovered and mistakenly identified as alien artefacts. Empires that lay in Earth's oceans were created by the Jinn, only to be washed away during the great flood."

"Like Atlantis?"

Nabil nodded as a chill breeze washed across them, and he reached his hands towards the fire. "But their hunger for more consumed them, and all that they created to further Jinnkind ended up imploding it. Energy sources and medical wonders were weaponised, natural resources cut off to suffocate and starve each other, systematic raping and killing, all in the name of pride, power, greed and control. The Jinn perfected their expertise in manipulation and destruction during these millennia, and these remain the tools of their trade today.

"When Allah saw this, He summoned Iblis. Iblis was not an angel as some believe, but a king of the Jinn who ruled with an iron fist. Allah knew of his reputation, how ego ruled his ambition, and tasked him with cleansing the earth of those who had lost themselves in base depravity and ingratitude.

"Iblis carried out his duty diligently, killing his own kind to purify the earth in the name of Allah, and was rewarded by being the only Jinn allowed to sit in Heaven with the angels. In return, Iblis loved Allah like no other. Iblis's devotion was unwavering and blind, and his love for his Lord guided his every action. Even the angels recognised his beauty and magnificence, so great were his accomplishments and dedication to his Lord, his one and only Love."

Nabil glanced across the fire. The children had come out of their tents and were huddled on the far side of the flames, listening intently. He ushered them back to their beds. "Some things are not for young ears," he said as he settled beside Jean-Paul. "Now, where was I? Ah yes, all was well until Allah created a new kind."

"Humans?" said Jean-Paul.

Nabil nodded. "When he saw the new creations, Iblis feared losing his position in Allah's favour. Knowing this new creation would be made of the earth itself, Iblis trod on an area of sacred ground that would be used to create mankind's soul, to taint it with the essence of the Jinn.

"When Allah presented His creation to Iblis and the angels, He commanded them to prostrate themselves before His new creation. All the angels lay down in acknowledgement of this new wonder, brought to life by Divine Breath. They knew of mankind's fallibility but also saw reflections of their own light, beauty and the ability to achieve great good combined with compassion that could propel mankind to achieve what the Jinn would never be able to.

"When Iblis gazed upon the new creations, he saw only pride, selfishness and ingratitude, but without the powerful traits of the Jinn. In his eyes, they were a mistake, an abomination, less than Jinnkind; creatures who would live significantly shorter lives but still be susceptible to all the shortcomings of the Jinn. He refused to prostrate himself before such inferior beings.

"When Allah asked why he had refused, Iblis questioned mankind's devotion and reminded Allah of his own loyalty in fighting Allah's wars on Earth, even killing his own kind. Could mankind match this devotion and magnificence? But even as he spoke, Iblis knew his remarks would guarantee his expulsion into an eternity of hellfire. He added, 'My Lord, my one true Love, spare me from hellfire until the day of judgement, and I will prove the weakness of mankind to you by turning them away from the Light, by them committing more sins than the Jinn.'"

"Allah replied, "I will keep forgiving them should they ask for my forgiveness. To return to my favour, you need only to bow to my creation."

"But Iblis's pride would not allow him to bow before a human. "Never!" he screamed, as he was hurled out by the angels, initiating his transformation to Shaitan."

Nabil looked at the dark sky. "It is believed that when you see a shooting star, it is a Jinn who has been caught trying to listen to the angels and has been thrown back to the Qaf mountains."

He turned to Jean-Paul. "And to this day, the ground-shaking screams of Shaitan's pain can be heard across the mountains as he mourns his loss, yearning to be in the presence and favour of his one true Love, the Giver of purpose to his life. But his pride will not allow him to prostrate to such a creature as mankind."

The fire had burned low to no more than a handful of orange coals. A cold shiver ran down Jean-Paul's spine, and he edged closer to the embers.

"You felt that?" asked the old man.

"It was just the wind."

Nabil gestured to the desert around them. "Or could it be the Jinn, watching us even now."

Jean-Paul looked around. The darkness was all encompassing, hiding the shapes of the nearby dunes. An entire army of Jinn could be watching them, and they would be none the wiser. For the first time, Jean-Paul felt the sheer size and solitude of the desert pressing in around him; he felt afraid of the Jinn.

Nabil watched him shoot uneasy glances into the darkness. "Now do you understand the power of the Jinn?"

Jean-Paul nodded.

"And do you still want me to take you to the ruins and summon the Jinn who lives there?"

"As long as it doesn't endanger you," replied Jean-Paul.

"My faith protects me," Nabil said, "but you won't have the same protection. She is a powerful Jinn princess. She could strip the flesh from your bones with one look, if she desired."

"How do you know so much about her?" asked Jean-Paul. "Have you encountered her before?"

Nabil exhaled slowly, looking intently into the distant dunes. "I told you, this desert is my home. I have grown up knowing of this creature. I have learned to respect her and her powers."

"Given everything you've told me about Jinn," Jean-Paul said with a shrug, "it seems strange that a creature of such powers would hide in an abandoned ruin in the desert. What is her story?"

Nabil shuddered and gazed at the flames. "I will not tell of it, especially so close to her, and at night."

"But will you take me to the ruins and show me how to summon her?"

Nabil hunched his shoulders. "It would not be my pleasure to do so."

"But if I wanted it, more than anything else, would you take me?"

Nabil fixed his dark eyes on the coals and took so long to answer, Jean-Paul thought he wasn't going to reply. Finally, he looked up. "If you are resolved to do this, if I cannot turn you away, I will take you." He stood, stretched his back and looked down at Jean-Paul. "Sleep now and gather your strength. Tomorrow, at first light, I will take you to her, and perchance she will tell you her story herself."

CHAPTER 8

At first, it appeared to be working. The man seemed happier, and I was living as a human, finally having the chance to learn more about them and understand why God had blessed them so. However, in time, we realised we could neither continue to live in secret together nor present me to his community as his dead wife. To my surprise, he declared his love for me and said he wished to continue sharing his life with me, accepting me as Jinn and not human. I was intrigued. Why would he do that? Was his love so great, so pure, that it saw past our differences to something formidable that bound us together? How could a simple human live by the code of such wisdom, not understanding but just "knowing'?

I have to admit, I fell in love for the first time in centuries. I became consumed with his love, his care, his attention. These qualities permeated every aspect of his life — his worship of our Beloved, his constant care for his son, always protecting me from the gossip of the village, even to the point of being ostracised by parts of his community. We knew our love was not conditional on him being able to provide for me, and this intensified all we felt for each other. His son carried the same wonderous qualities and saw beauty in me that I had long forgotten existed. For the first time in my life, I felt complete, loved, accepted, not as a Jinn or human, but as a soul on a journey.

But the nature of the Jinn has a way of destroying all that is beautiful in its selfish need to be idolised. Before long, he wished to marry and create a home for our love. He did not ask me to bow or be subservient to him, only to treat him as an equal. I had now experienced first-hand the virtuous qualities that angels recognised in humans when they bowed to Adam, but my nature wouldn't allow me to accept him as an equal. To me, he was nothing more than an impressive novelty. I was a Jinn princess, worthy of a partner of equal stature, not a simple peasant. Jinn are elemental creatures, and despite him pleading with me to stay, my hubris pushed me out of the home of love and into the wilderness again.

As I wandered the trackless wastes, days turned to weeks and weeks to months, and my selfish pain and longing outgrew my vanity. The pain of missing him — this wonderful, caring soul who gave without asking for anything in return other than to be treated as an equal — wormed its way into me, and the wound it created would not heal. Echoes of his love whistled through the opened door of my heart, and I could not close it again.

On realising I would never find another soul as rich as his, I rushed back to his hut and peered through the shutters. There he was, helping his son to get ready for bed, with the same loving look that would take me to places in my heart only he could touch.

I waited until the next morning to speak with him alone, but as I appeared to him, his joy at seeing me quickly turned to sadness. But it was not sadness because of what had happened. The same faith that gave him the strength to be grateful for all he saw as part of life's blessing had given him the strength to accept we couldn't be together. On pressing him for a reason, he simply said, "To understand the rare blessing of love, one must let go of pride." He thanked me for my visit and offered a prayer that I would one day find true love once more. To this day, I cannot say his name aloud; it reminds me of my shame and loss at my own hands.

Stunned by his love and devotion, and by my failure to find someone to truly love me, I retreated to this forgotten place and hid myself away from the world of Jinn and the world of men, to pass away the endless centuries of my life in dreamless sleep.

And woe betide anyone who dares to waken me.

CHAPTER 9

Nabil nudged Jean-Paul from his slumbers and forced a glass of hot tea into his hand. "It's time."

When Jean-Paul emerged from the tent, the sun was still below the horizon, soft pink light barely painting the tops of the dunes.

Nabil was jittery as he hurried with Jean-Paul towards the ancient fortress, still deep in shadows. "This is not good," he murmured. He glanced at Jean-Paul. "You are resolved on this?"

"I am."

Nabil nodded curtly and, with a stern expression, began marching at a fierce pace that Jean-Paul struggled to match.

The rising sun painted the dunes with soft golden light as the two men marched in silence. Soon, they stood in the shadow of the ruins. Nabil led Jean-Paul between the piles of rubble from the crumbling towers and through an arched doorway into the heart of the ruins.

It was dark; the far side was completely hidden in shadow. A shiver ran up Jean-Paul's spine.

Nabil glanced at him. "You can feel it, eh? We should not be here. She does not want us here."

"Please understand this is not something I want to do," said Jean-Paul, "but something I have to do."

Nabil nodded. "I see the torment in your soul. We each of us have burdens that we must bear. This is yours."

Jean-Paul's eyes were drawn to a deep void in the shadow of the ruined castle, a broken, leaning tower with an open archway that led into the belly of the building. He sensed something was lurking there, something darker than his own emptiness.

"Is she there?" he whispered.

"You don't need to ask me," said Nabil. "You can feel it, no?"

"I feel something," admitted Jean-Paul.

"Will you not leave with me now while you still can?" pressed Nabil.

Jean-Paul shook his head. "I can't. I've come this far. I have to see this through."

"Very well."

Nabil turned back towards the tower and, in a low voice, began chanting a repeated prayer that rose and fell. Nabil's words were carried away on the gentle breeze. When he had finished, Nabil turned towards Jean-Paul, pressed his hands to his own heart, then touched Jean-Paul's chest to transfer the blessing.

Before Jean-Paul could thank him, he turned and hurried away, calling over his shoulder, "She is in there, waiting for you. May merciful Allah guard you and protect you."

Jean-Paul stood staring into the broken tower, into the very heart of darkness. It was done. There was no turning back.

The sound of Nabil's scurrying feet faded, leaving Jean-Paul alone in utter silence. He peered into the darkness at the back of the tower, willing something to happen, something to appear, yet terrified in case it did.

Silence.

A gentle breeze stirred the dust at his feet, then ceased.

The sun continued its journey over the horizon, but no light penetrated the ruined tower. Somewhere in there was the Jinn. She had been awakened; her presence was palpable. All Jean-Paul had to do was summon the courage to find her.

Jean-Paul had to force himself to step forward, over the tumbledown stones towards the entrance, each step bringing him closer to the source of the dread that threatened to engulf him. One part of him wanted nothing more than to turn and flee, catch up to Nabil and forget he had ever been there, but despite his dread, he kept moving forward until he stood in the entrance to the tower.

Blackness seemed to creep from the tower and wrap itself around his feet as he stepped over the threshold into the heart of the darkness. With each step, the faint daylight behind him faded, until he stood in utter blackness. His heart was hammering.

"Hello? Hello? Is anyone there?"

Silence greeted him.

He waited a long moment before repeating, "Hello? Jinn, I need your help!" It sounded stupid even as he said it, his words falling into the silence.

Nothing.

Jean-Paul had no idea how long he stood waiting, wondering what was going to happen next. Minutes? Hours? Days? He felt held, as if under a spell, which broke when he spoke, the sound of his own voice startling him.

"This is a waste of time," he said finally. He peered into the darkness, wishing he had asked Nabil more. "Is this it?" Anger and frustration rose to his chest. "Are you even there? Do you exist?"

His words fell into silence.

"Show yourself!"

He could feel tears stinging his eyes, and he wiped them away with his rough sleeve. "Do you even exist?"

The utter indifference of the universe weighed down on him.

The Jinn was a myth.

He would never find out the truth about Émilie. The aching void in the deepest part of his heart would never be healed.

He had come seeking closure but instead had found further frustration, the sheer indifference of the universe bearing down on him.

An icy chill gripped his spine as he turned to leave. Halfway to the exit, he stopped dead, frozen to the spot, sheer terror coursing through his veins.

He turned back slowly, not of his own volition, but as though under the power of another.

The darkness seemed deeper than ever, an inky black pool filling the far end of the room. He could see no form or shape, yet knew with certainty something was there — something old, powerful, vindictive.

He shivered, finding it hard to breathe; his diaphragm unable to expand. Then an almighty shove lifted and landed him outside the ruins. As he lay on his back, trying to comprehend what had happened, the breath slowly returned to his winded lungs.

The Jinn had happened! She was real! Real — and powerful.

Jean-Paul slowly sat up. The sensible thing to do would be to turn and run — the Jinn had demonstrated not only that she was immensely powerful but also that she didn't want to be disturbed by him. But he hadn't travelled this far and endured all his hardships to give up now. He slowly climbed to his feet and marched back in, only to be met with the same response.

He hit the ground harder this time, his head striking a small rock. It took him longer to recover, but as soon as he caught his breath and steadied his spinning head, he marched back in. "Don't throw me out!" he shouted as he entered the tower. "I need your help!"

The reaction was different this time. Rather than hurling him from the tower, the Jinn threw him to the floor, pressing down on him and slowly squeezing the air from his lungs.

Then it began, softly at first, then louder and louder — the howl of a banshee, filling the room, assailing his ears. At the same time, an acidic stench washed over him.

Gradually the scream revealed itself as words, unintelligible at first, and then, to Jean-Paul's amazement, resolving into English.

A figure appeared above him — a woman with wild hair, piercing eyes and a lascivious look. She stared down at Jean-Paul. "Did you come here to die?"

"No, I came for your help," he gasped.

"Then you came to be damned, for I am Budoo, a Marid, a Jinn daughter of King Barqan of the Marid tribe. Who dares to awaken me?"

The cold seeped into Jean-Paul's bones, leaching the life from him. He forced out an answer through trembling lips. "I can't breathe." The tension in his chest eased and he gasped for air, sucking it in with a wheeze that caught in his throat.

Part mist, part corporeal, the woman swirled around him, the beams of light that crept through the cracks in the ceiling bringing her in and out of focus.

Jean-Paul gathered himself, controlling his trembling. "I was told you were a Jinn of the utmost powers, the highest rank."

"You are well versed in flattery."

"I mean no offence. I was informed that only you could help me."

The figure settled in front of Jean-Paul and materialised into visible human form. "What do you seek?"

"I am told that you, and only you, can tell me something about my life, something that has haunted me for years."

The Jinn studied him. "You want to know about your wife?"

Jean-Paul gasped. "Yes!"

The Jinn's form seemed to soften as she settled in front of him. "I can do that," she told him, "But there is a price to pay."

"Name it."

A smile creased the corners of her mouth. "That is a dangerous thing to say to a Jinn."

"I have nothing else to live for."

The Jinn held his gaze. "Very well. If I tell you about your wife, you will agree to let me live with you for a year, with you as my guide. I wish to understand the power of human love, the capacity for such blind devotion."

Jean-Paul gave her a curious look. "That's a strange request. I had understood that Jinn regarded humans as weak, inferior creatures?"

"And yet God does not; He wanted us to prostrate ourselves at Adam's feet. I would like to understand why."

"Have you not been among humans before?" asked Jean-Paul.

"I have."

"And that did not help you understand our capacity for blind love and devotion?"

The Jinn's eyes flashed, and Jean-Paul feared he had pushed her too far, but the anger faded.

"Maybe you will understand me better, and what you are committing to, if I tell you my story. After that, if you still wish to proceed, I will tell you what you wish to know."

Jean-Paul nodded. "Very well..."

A faraway look washed over the Jinn's face.

Jean-Paul listened with fascination as Budoo told him of her marriage, the poor farmer and the spell she had cast on her husband.

When she had finished, he nodded slowly. "If you've lived among humans before, why would you wish to do that again?"

"My motives are my own," she told him, "And you would be advised not to question me if you wish to survive our time together."

"I shall remember that," replied Jean-Paul.

"You have listened to my story," said the Jinn. "Do you still wish to proceed?"

Jean-Paul paused. It was not too late. He could offer polite thanks and withdraw, his skin and soul intact. But then what? He would still be haunted by his wife's unexplained death and would know he'd had the chance to discover her fate but had refused it. The Jinn's offer was dangerous, but it was the only one he would ever get.

"I wish to proceed," he said in a cracking voice, his eyes wide.

The Jinn nodded. "Very well. Ask what you will."

Jean-Paul took a deep breath. This was the moment. "What is my name?"

The Jinn's dark eyes bored into him, as though seeing his very soul. "Jean-Paul Deschamps."

"Where was I born?"

"Paris. But now you live in a place called New York."

"Where did I go to—"

"You dare to test me?" the Jinn bellowed. "Did I not just warn you about that?"

"I'm sorry, Your Majesty," Jean-Paul replied quickly. "I just wanted to be sure that what you tell me is the truth."

The Jinn smiled. "Do you remember your first day at school? You were too scared to ask the teacher if you could visit the bathroom and ended up peeing your pants? What was it the other kids called you? Jean-Pee? Then there was the time you tried to kiss that red-headed girl, Gloria, and she slapped you?"

"Why do you only seem to recall my most embarrassing moments?" said Jean-Paul.

"It is my nature," she replied. "I prey on weakness. Go ahead. Ask what you want to know."

Jean-Paul's legs were trembling. After five years of uncertainty and fear, he was about to get closure, maybe even peace. "My wife, Émilie," he began. "She disappeared. I need to know what happened."

The Jinn said nothing. Jean-Paul feared she was going to renege on the deal, or maybe she didn't know this one thing, then an image appeared in his mind. It was Émilie as he'd last seen her, blowing him a kiss as she left their hotel room.

The images came thick and fast. It was like watching an old cine film.

Émilie was leaving the hotel, the sun on her face as she strode along, peering in the shop windows.

The scene quickly changed to Émilie striding along a path in the hills, grey craggy peaks towering above her. She stopped, her eyes drawn to a long glacier as it snaked down the valley, scored and creased by a tangle of crevasses.

"Stay on the path!" Jean-Paul told her, but, even as he said it, Émilie abandoned the trail, stepped out onto the uneven icy surface of the glacier and began picking a path towards a deep crevasse.

Jean-Paul's chest tightened as she approached the yawning chasm, and his hands rose to his face in horror. "Why?" he groaned. "Why would she do that?"

The blue ice gleamed beneath the bright sun. Closer and closer Émilie crept, as though pulled by some mysterious force, until she stood on the very edge of the crevasse, gazing into the dark, icy depths.

"Move away, Émilie!" cried Jean-Paul. "Move away, please!"

But no matter how much he shouted, Émilie stayed teetering on the edge. In an instant she was gone as the lip of the crevasse broke away, carrying her into the deep darkness of death.

Jean-Paul gasped as the vision disappeared. Silent convulsions gripped him and exploded into great gasping sobs that shook his whole body. He had hoped that finding out the truth would give him relief, but it felt like it had cast him into a pit of despair, a place of endless sorrow and regret.

The Jinn's voice cut through his cries. "Not the relief you were hoping for?"

He scrubbed at his face as he fought to hold back the tides of despair and opened his eyes to find the Jinn staring at him with fascination.

"Such love at such a young age. Such devotion. Such loss. And yet you have endured and not given in to your despair. How can such a weak, feeble race find such strength?"

Jean-Paul said nothing. His pain overwhelmed him to the extent he felt numb. He staggered out of the ruined fortress and back out into the desert.

***

As he stumbled away, the Jinn smiled to herself. "See you soon," she said softly.

***

Somehow, his feet led him back to the nomad's camp.

Nabil looked up as Jean-Paul lurched towards the fire and slumped onto the sand, his sightless eyes held by the dancing flames.

"You saw her?"

Jean-Paul nodded.

Nabil reached for the teapot, poured him a glass of sweet mint tea and forced it into his hands.

Jean-Paul continued to stare into the flames, his tea untouched.

"Drink," said Nabil.

Jean-Paul took a sip, then another. Little by little, it worked its magic, and he began to return to the present.

"You met the Jinn and survived," said Nabil. "That's more than many people manage." He studied Jean-Paul's distraught face. "Did she tell you what you wanted to know?"

Jean-Paul nodded.

"Remember what I said," said Nabil with a wag of his finger. "Jinn love to tell lies, just for the sheer mischief of it."

"She told the truth."

Jean-Paul caught his reflection in the polished tea serving tray. He seemed to have aged ten years. His frame had shrunk, his eyes had sunk deep in their sockets and his skin sagged from his bones.

"What now?" asked Nabil.

Jean-Paul dragged his eyes from the tray. "Now I must fulfil my end of the agreement."

Nabil looked at him as though he were looking at a dead man. "You struck a deal?" he said in horror.

"We each got what we wanted," replied Jean-Paul. He turned to Nabil. "You have been too kind, thank you. My time here is done."

CHAPTER 10

The Jinn watched in fascination as Jean-Paul said his farewells to Nabil, climbed wearily aboard the bus and slumped in his seat. She had seen enough men on their way to the gallows to recognise the sight of a dead man walking. After centuries of slumber, she was fascinated to see if Jean-Paul's will to live was completely gone, or if he had the strength to climb out of the hole and rebuild his life.

As the bus coughed its way up the hill and out of the village, trailing a plume of black smoke, she drifted along behind it, filled with voyeuristic curiosity. This man owed her a debt, and she was determined to collect it before he died.

***

The bus fought its way through the narrow streets of Aden and ground to a halt at the central bus station. It coughed once more then settled, like an asthmatic at the end of a long hike. Jean-Paul stepped out into the babble and bedlam of the city, instantly overwhelmed by the noise, crowds and avaricious eyes of the touts and sellers as they zeroed in on vulnerable tourists. It was a sharp contrast to the peace and solitude of the desert.

His encounter with the Jinn had left him feeling even more bereft than before. Learning about his wife's death had thrown up as many questions as it had answered. Why had she stepped onto the glacier? Émilie knew the dangers; what had impelled her to leave the path? And why had she stood so close to a crevasse? Jean-Paul imagined her terror as she plummeted into its icy depths, the pain and horror as her battered body tumbled and fell to the bottom, shattering bones on the way. He only hoped the fall had killed her, and that her death had been quick and merciful. He couldn't bear to think of her suffering a long, lingering demise as she lay in agony, begging the cold to take her.

Jean-Paul pushed his way through the mass of humanity, his feet carrying him into the maze of dark streets and alleyways forming the seamier side of Aden, home to hash houses and drug dens.

A scruffy man with a scraggly beard spotted Jean-Paul. "Hello, my friend," he said, falling in step. "What are you looking for? A rug? Some leather boots? Or some fun?"

Jean-Paul stopped and stared at the man. What was he looking for? The answer was simple — oblivion, either temporary or permanent. He had come to Aden to discover what had happened to Émilie, and now? There was no reason to continue living. Jean-Paul met the man's shifty gaze. "Something to free my soul," he told him.

The man smiled, revealing a row of broken, blackened teeth. "Good choice, my friend." He took Jean-Paul's elbow and led him even deeper into the medina, through a twisting labyrinth of alleyways so narrow, the two men could not walk side by side.

The guide stopped outside a nondescript door and rapped three times.

A bolt trundled across and a half-hidden face peered out, assessing Jean-Paul at a glance. "Twenty dollars."

Jean-Paul rummaged in his pocket and found a twenty-dollar bill. "Here."

The door opened and Jean-Paul's guide pushed him inside.

The man who had opened the door handed him a dirty syringe and a rubber tourniquet and pointed towards a room strewn with torn, stained mattresses.

"Anywhere you want. And if the police come, you're on your own."

Jean-Paul peered at the syringe. "I want more."

The dealer was young, maybe twenty, with a thick mop of curly hair. His eyes gleamed in the light of a yellow lantern. "It's strong stuff..."

Jean-Paul pulled another twenty-dollar bill from his pocket and thrust the money at him. "My money, my choice."

The man shrugged. "It is." He took the note and handed Jean-Paul another syringe. "It's your funeral."

Clasping the syringes, Jean-Paul stepped into the darkened room, gagging at the stench of faeces and decay. Several mattresses were occupied by cadaverous bodies in varying states of consciousness, their limbs splayed out like discarded rag dolls.

Jean-Paul found a mattress in the corner, slumped down and examined the paraphernalia he'd been given. He'd smoked dope on numerous occasions and tried LSD a few times, but had never used heroin. How hard could it be? He rolled up his sleeve and examined his veins.

He hesitated and thought of Émilie. What would she feel if she saw him now? Shame? Pity? Revulsion? Pushing the thought aside, he wrapped the rubber tourniquet tight above his elbow and lined up the two syringes on his leg. He knew the effects would come fast so needed to be sure he got both shots in while he was still capable.

Calmly, methodically, he injected both syringes into his arm, one after the other.

The rush was almost instant. A feeling of euphoria washed over him, accompanied by an extraordinary sense of well-being, as though he were in his favourite place or wrapped in the world's most luxurious blanket.

Jean-Paul smiled.

This was it.

This was good.

He would soon see Émilie, and she would understand.

He smiled, closed his eyes, twitched once, twice, then passed out.

***

The Jinn mirrored his smile as she looked down on the horrific tableau.

"Not yet, my friend," she whispered. "We have an agreement."

***

The thin cotton curtains moved gently on the breeze, diffusing the bright sunlight onto Jean-Paul's face.

His eyes drifted open then closed again.

Scraps of dreams fought with nightmarish visions of an attack.

His ribs ached as he rolled over in the small bed, seeking a comfortable position, wanting nothing more than to drift back into the dream.

The dream.

Just out of reach, but always there.

Émilie leaned over him, gently wiped his fevered brow with a cool, damp cloth and kissed him on the cheek. "Sleep, my love, sleep," she whispered.

Jean-Paul sank gratefully back into the pillow.

***

Jean-Paul sat up with a start. The room was dim, with just a small table lamp in the corner casting long shadows that hid more than they revealed.

"Where am I?"

A young woman was perched next to the lamp, her nose buried in a book. At his words, she jumped up and ran from the room. "Grandmama! He's awake!"

An older woman hurried into the room and moved swiftly to Jean-Paul's bedside. She was in her mid-sixties and wore a careworn expression and a dark, floral cotton dress. She pressed the back of her hand to Jean-Paul's brow with a familiarity that suggested she had done it many times. "Your fever has gone; that's good."

Jean-Paul looked up at her. There was kindness and concern in her eyes. "Where am I?"

"Aden."

He absorbed that for a moment. The last thing he could remember was climbing onto the bus. "How did I get here?"

"Rest easy. I'll bring you something to eat, then you can sleep some more."

Lacking the strength to protest, he settled back into the bed under the watchful eyes of the young woman.

By the time the grandmother returned, he was asleep.

***

When he awoke, it was morning. The sun was shining with the just-washed brightness that follows a rain shower. Jean-Paul looked around the room. His clothes were laid out on a chair, freshly laundered, and a walking stick was propped beside them. As he climbed from the bed, he discovered the reason for the walking stick. His leg was bandaged from shin to mid-thigh, as were his ribs. He dressed slowly, then limped out of the room, leaning heavily on the stick. He found his way to a small, sun-drenched courtyard.

The young woman was sitting on a wooden bench with her nose buried in a book. She looked up as he approached, set her book down beside her and helped him into a wicker chair piled with cushions.

Jean-Paul looked around the courtyard. It was at the centre of a well-tended single-storey house. "Where am I?" he asked as the woman settled back onto the bench. She looked around twenty and was slim, with strong features and long, dark hair.

"My grandmother's house."

"How did I get here?"

"The lady brought you," said a voice behind him.

Jean-Paul turned to see the grandmother standing behind him.

"You were in a bad way," she explained. "The doctor said you had been attacked, beaten and robbed. You had several broken ribs, a sprained ankle and a concussion."

"Why am I here?" said Jean-Paul. "Why not in a hospital?"

The grandmother gave a wan smile. "Clearly you have not had the pleasure of visiting one of our hospitals." She sighed. "Believe me, you are safer here."

"And my grandmother is a nurse," added the young woman. "You are in good hands."

Jean-Paul took a moment to absorb all this. "And the woman, the one you said brought me here?"

"A friend of yours, we assumed."

Jean-Paul had a momentary flash of Émilie leaning over him, kissing him. "Where is she now?"

"She said she will be back in a few days. You should be fit enough to leave by then." She gestured towards the house. "Now, let me get you some breakfast. You must be starving."

"And might I ask your names?"

"I'm Maryam," the grandmother said, "and this is my granddaughter, Yasmine."

Jean-Paul nodded. "Thank you, Maryam, Yasmine, for looking after me."

***

A short while later, Jean-Paul eased himself back in the chair, taking care not to put too much weight on his aching ribs. Despite the pain, he felt full and contented. He and Yasmine had devoured a mound of fresh pancakes soaked in butter and honey, washed down with freshly squeezed orange juice. As soon as they had finished, Yasmine returned to her book.

"You spend a lot of time reading?"

Yasmine looked up. "Grandma says reading is the door to another world."

"Another world?"

"The world you want to live in."

Jean-Paul absorbed that for a moment. "What are you reading?"

He didn't expect to see the medical textbook she held up and was intrigued. "What kind of world do you want to live in?" he asked.

"One where I'm a doctor."

"A doctor? I'll bet there aren't many female doctors in Yemen."

"Not yet." She peered intently at Jean-Paul. "What type of world do you want to live in?"

"I … I … don't know …"

The question flummoxed him. For the past five years, he had not thought about the future; he had lived — wallowed — in the past. How could he answer the question? He didn't even know if he wanted to live.

Jean-Paul studied Yasmine's face. Such relentless determination and lust for life shamed him. He had spent five years floundering in his grief, wasting his talent, his education. And for what? To wind up beaten half to death in an Aden alleyway, relying upon the kindness of a stranger to save him. What kind of memorial was that to the memory of Émilie?

He unstrapped his Omega Chronostop and handed it to Yasmine. "For you."

She shook her head. "You're very kind, but we need no payment. Charity, freely given, is our blessing."

"This is not for your care," explained Jean-Paul. "Your words and eyes have a sincerity I'd long forgotten existed. I want to return your inspiration with a gesture of my belief in you as a doctor. See, it helps you measure someone's pulse." He showed her the pulsometer scale and hung the watch on her slim wrist. "Deal?"

Yasmine nodded solemnly. "Thank you."

As he settled back in his chair, his mind drifted back to the desert and his time with Nabil. Had it all been a dream? The ruined castle? The Jinn? Had he left Aden, or had he imagined the whole thing? Was it all a drug-soaked fantasy that had ended when he was mugged and left for dead?

Exhaustion washed over him. "I'm going to lie down," he told Yasmine.

"Grandma says rest is the best thing for you."

Jean-Paul gave a weary smile. "How can I disagree with Grandma?"

***

The murmur of soft voices woke Jean-Paul from his deep, dream-filled sleep, a world where Émilie and Nabil, Yasmine and the Jinn all swirled around him in a confusing blend of reality and fantasy.

The voices stopped outside his room. "I'll leave you here," said Maryam.

Jean-Paul didn't catch the reply but could hear footsteps disappearing down the hall.

He gasped as the door opened and his dreams seemed to return. Émilie stepped into the room.

"Are you feeling better?"

Jean-Paul stared at her, open-mouthed. "Émilie?"

"I think it's better if you don't call me that."

Her voice dragged Jean-Paul back through a vortex of dream and fantasy, until she once more stood before him, her power washing over him. Like a man gathering in a fishing net, he pulled on the threads of his thoughts and dreams, and gathered them back in. When he looked at her again, he saw past the exterior to glimpse the creature within. She was a perfect copy of Émilie in every way except for the Jinn's dark and brooding eyes.

"Why did you choose her?" asked Jean-Paul.

"It is the strongest image in your mind, the image you most wanted to see," the Jinn said.

Be careful what you wish for. "What should I call you?"

"Anything you want — except your wife's name."

"How about Sophie?"

The Jinn scowled at him. "Your cat's name?"

"It was the first one I thought of."

"Fine." Her gaze felt more penetrating than the most advanced X-ray. "You've been here some weeks. You look ready to leave."

He nodded. "I'm ready."

She turned to the door and paused. "Just one thing. If you try to kill yourself again before our agreement is finished, every member of your family will suffer the consequences. Understood?"

A shiver ran down Jean-Paul's spine as he gazed into her dark eyes. "Understood," he croaked.

CHAPTER 11

The apartment was light and airy, on the top floor of a modern building with a view over the city. Jean-Paul limped to the window and took in the view of Central Park sprawling out below them. "How can you afford this place? You've been living in a ruined castle for the past five hundred years."

The Jinn gave a wry smile. "I am Jinn. You think anything in this world is beyond me should I choose it?"

"Clearly not. But how—"

"That is not your concern. Show me your world, explain the strange and the random, and in return I will take care of the details. As to my methods? If there is one thing that has not changed in the past five hundred years, it is human needs and human greed."

And so, Jean-Paul introduced the Jinn to the modern world. After five years avoiding it, Jean-Paul felt like a man reborn. He loved the role of teacher as his student soaked up the sights and sounds of a world that had grown vastly more complex during the five hundred years she had been in hibernation.

They went to restaurants and cafés, discos and clubs, movies and the theatre.

They drove in cars, rode a motorbike and even took a flight across the Atlantic to Europe.

The Jinn was eager to understand the world and the roiling currents raging through Europe and America — the Vietnam War, the Paris riots, and the assassinations of Martin Luther King and Bobby Kennedy.

They made love regularly at first, but any idea that Jean-Paul might have harboured that he would fall in love with the facsimile of his wife was quickly shattered. While Budoo had the face and body of his beloved wife, her nature was very much her own. Their lovemaking, rather than being an intimate language that only two people in love can share, as it had been between Jean-Paul and Émilie, was fierce and tempestuous, led by the Jinn's wants and desires. Within a few weeks of reaching New York, she abandoned their "marital" bed and began going out alone at all hours, then returning home smelling of different perfumes. Initially she made the effort to reappear as Émilie, but as time went on, she retained the shape of her current lover's desire.

Jean-Paul and Budoo still connected at times, none more so than over the moon landing. Budoo stared in fascination at the flickering black-and-white images, from the moment the Saturn 5 rocket blasted off the launchpad until splashdown in the Pacific Ocean when the three astronauts emerged safely from the command module. She didn't move from the television the whole time, oblivious to the need for food, sleep or any other basic human demand.

Each day, as the moon mission progressed, Jean-Paul would emerge bleary-eyed from his bedroom to find her sitting on the living room floor, eyes fixed on the flickering monochrome images being transmitted from space.

"How can you not be watching this?" she chided him. "I've been alive over a thousand years, and I've never seen anything like it, never even conceived such a thing." She watched as Jean-Paul made himself a cup of coffee and lit his first Gauloise of the day. "How can humans be so useless for so much of the time, then envisage and achieve something like this?"

Jean-Paul shrugged. "We aren't all cut out to be astronauts."

Budoo gave him a final scathing look before returning her attention to the television. "Clearly."

Jean-Paul shuffled over and slumped on the sofa behind her. "How can you still have such a low opinion of humans after all you've seen? Not just the moon landing, but the Empire State Building, jet planes, Mozart, the Renaissance?"

Budoo answered without turning around. "You humans have a saying — the exception that proves the rule. The examples you just quoted? As dazzling as they are, for me, they are overwhelmed by the sheer weight of stupidity and sloth that I witness on a daily basis." She turned to face Jean-Paul. "How can a race capable of reaching such dazzling heights spend so much time wallowing in the dirt like pigs snuffling for scraps?"

Jean-Paul shrugged again. "It's our nature, I guess. So many people clawing their way to the top on the broken bodies of those they no longer need."

"Exactly. A pitiful, spiteful race who, despite reaching occasional heights, will never amount to much." Budoo turned back to the television. "Now go away and leave me to enjoy a rare moment of real achievement."

***

"What the hell is Woodstock?"

Jean-Paul and Budoo stared at the brightly coloured poster taped to the door of the Greenwich Village coffee shop they often frequented.

"Three days of peace and music," read Jean-Paul. "It sounds awful."

A young man stopped behind them and peered at the poster. "Groovy!"

"And that," said Jean-Paul, as they continued down the street, "is why I don't want to go."

Budoo gave him a sly look. "And that is another fascinating thing about humans."

"What?"

"You're capricious. You change so quickly, yet each generation despises the next, their fashion, their music, their lifestyles, forgetting they were once young, once embraced change."

Jean-Paul frowned. "You want to spend three days in a field in upstate New York, surrounded by a bunch of hairy hippies, listening to their excuse for music?"

Budoo took his arm in a passable impersonation of a loving girlfriend. "I do. And you're going to take me!"

***

Woodstock turned out to be everything Jean-Paul had feared, but everything Budoo had promised. The music was loud, the crowds immense, the toilet facilities rudimentary at best, and yet he enjoyed every minute of it. Budoo left him shortly after they arrived, disappearing into the tent of a long-haired Adonis to indulge in her favourite activity, leaving Jean-Paul to fend for himself.

If he left the festival, Budoo would know. She would track him down and drag him back, so he found a quiet place on the outskirts of the crowd where he could sit and watch events unfold without being overwhelmed by the music. The rain had stopped, and though the ground closer to the stage was a quagmire, where Jean-Paul sat was pleasant and grassy, if rather damp.

As he observed the melee around him, he found himself starting to enjoy the music. And why shouldn't he? Just because he was ten years older than most of the crowd, there was no reason he shouldn't enjoy it. Their hair may be longer, they may dress differently, but none of that mattered when it came down to it.

And it wasn't just the music. There was an atmosphere he had never experienced before, of love and acceptance, of happiness and joy, enhanced by the sunshine and a plentiful supply of marijuana. It was something Jean-Paul was familiar with from his youth in the jazz clubs of Greenwich Village, but never had he seen it in such quantities, being smoked so openly. A mist hung over the horde, drifting on the wind towards Jean-Paul sitting on the gentle slope.

There was no need to walk around. From where he sat, Jean-Paul could see two women tie-dyeing T-shirts in a riot of psychedelic colours, a group of dancers lost in the movement as they swayed and twirled to the rhythm of a ney flute, and a dozen others gathered round an impromptu pit barbeque.

Jean-Paul couldn't recall the last time he had felt so relaxed. He pulled a cigarette from the packet, lit it, then closed his eyes and lay back, allowing the sun to warm his face, the music to draw him in and the mix of odours to waft over him.

"Have you got another one of those?"

Jean-Paul opened his eyes. A young girl in her early twenties was looking down at him.

"I smelled your cigarette," she said, nodding towards his Gauloises. "I spent last summer in Paris and smoked more of those than I can remember."

"Of course." Jean-Paul reached in his pocket, pulled out a crumpled pack and tapped one out.

To his surprise, she sat down next to him and smiled. "Light it for me?"

Jean-Paul put the cigarette to his lips, lit it and handed it to her.

She closed her eyes as she took a big drag. "The taste of Paris."

"Where did you stay?" he asked.

The girl smiled again. "I love that French accent."

"Merci." He held out his hand. "Jean-Paul."

The girl took his hand; her skin was soft and warm. "Clara. I lived in the Latin Quarter. It was a magical time." She smiled at the memory. "How about you?"

Jean-Paul studied Clara as they talked. She was slim, with a tangle of dark-brown curls and delicate features. Her orange tie-dyed tank top picked out the tangerine hues in her long, multi-coloured, flowery skirt.

She wore no bra, of course, and Jean-Paul couldn't help smiling at how outraged his mother would be if she saw how young women dressed.

Clara smoked the cigarette down to a nub, then reached behind her ear and produced a joint from somewhere amidst her tangled hair. "Want to share mine now?"

Jean-Paul hesitated. He'd only smoked marijuana a couple of times, at a party, surrounded by people he knew and trusted. He looked around. Almost everyone seemed to be smoking weed; there were no cops waiting to bust you. It was, quite simply, the thing to do.

He smiled at Clara. "Sure, that sounds great." He watched as she lit the joint, took a deep drag, then handed it to him.

As he inhaled, Jean-Paul was sure he could taste Clara's lips, sweet and fresh, on the paper. He wondered what it would be like to kiss her. He started to smile, but Émilie's face appeared in his mind. Just thinking of another woman felt like betrayal. He hurriedly handed the joint back to her.

Clara gave him a curious look. "Don't like it?"

"No, no, it's fine."

"I've never seen someone's face change so quickly," she said.

"Sorry. This probably isn't a good idea," muttered Jean-Paul.

Clara gave him a searching look and held up the joint. "This?" She reached down and lifted up his left hand, his gold wedding band glinting in the sunlight. "Or this?" She dropped his hand back into his lap.

"It's not what you think," mumbled Jean-Paul.

"I don't care if you're married," she told him. "I figure if you're here without your wife, you've already made your peace, right?"

Jean-Paul took a long time to answer. "Yes and no." He sighed. "It's complicated."

Clara lay back on the grass, closed her eyes and took another long drag. "I'm not in any rush."

Jean-Paul looked down at her. She puzzled him. They had only just met, yet she was pretty much inviting him to tell her his life story. As he looked at her serene face, he was gripped with an overwhelming urge to tell her everything — not just about Émilie, but about the Jinn and his deal. In short, everything that had led to him sitting in a field at Yasgur's farm smoking a joint and listening to Richie Havens.

And so he did, beginning with meeting Émilie, through their marriage and her death, and finally on to his time with the Jinn. After years of silence, he found the words just flowed, spilling out in a torrent as Clara patiently listened to him, not commenting, simply absorbing everything he said. He found it easy to talk to her — such a contrast to his time with Budoo, when he felt he always needed to think about what he was saying to not arouse her volcanic temper.

When he finally ground to a halt, Clara looked at him with her alluring dark brown eyes for a moment, then gazed at the sky which was beginning to darken as the clouds rolled back in.

Jean-Paul stared her. "You probably think I'm crazy, right? Ranting on about a Jinn?"

She shrugged. "Who's to say who is crazy and who is not? A million people have come here to a field in the middle of nowhere looking for something. Answers, peace, love, connection. Will they find it? Who knows?" She turned and looked at Jean-Paul. "But you, you are searching for something different, aren't you?"

"I don't know." He sighed. "I thought meeting the Jinn, learning what had happened, would give me peace, but I feel more confused than ever."

Clara reached over and gently stroked his cheek. "Poor, confused Jean-Paul."

He shivered. It was the first time anyone had touched him affectionately since Émilie had died.

"Sometimes, we search too hard for something," she said. "Try letting it come to you."

"You know what I'm looking for?"

"Of course. And you do too."

He gazed at her, unable to speak. He nodded mutely and gasped as the tears overtook him in a raw surge of pain, pity and sadness that tore at his heart and his throat.

He bowed his head and slowly composed himself before looking up and meeting Clara's gaze. "I need to forgive myself," he whispered.

Clara nodded. "Exactly. You've got to learn to love yourself, man."

Jean-Paul was silent as he processed her words.

Clara watched him for a moment, then pulled a small pouch out of a pocket in her skirt and skilfully rolled another joint. "First, you need to relax." She took a long drag then handed it to Jean-Paul. "Take it," she ordered, "and let go to feel your own reflection."

Jean-Paul didn't have the strength to argue. He took three long puffs and handed the joint back to her.

Clara smiled. "There you go, my beautiful Frenchman," she said. "Now you're beginning to relax."

As the marijuana worked its magic, Jean-Paul lay back and gazed at the night sky. Little by little he felt himself unwind, his throat loosen, his heartbeat slow and the knots in his shoulders loosen.

"Torturing yourself over what you might have done differently is a sure route to insanity," Clara told him. "My father said, "hindsight is always twenty-twenty." Give yourself a break. There's no way you could have known what would happen."

"But—"

"No buts. If you don't cut yourself some slack, you will never move on. It's time. Make your peace with Émilie, then let her go, let the past go, and get on with the rest of your life. It's time to forgive yourself."

Jean-Paul stared at Clara. Every word she said was a reflection of what he had been unable to confront.

He took a deep breath and a jolt of energy rushed through him. They were surrounded by people dancing, clapping and singing; people living in the moment and enjoying life. Jean-Paul jumped to his feet, grabbed Clara's hands and pulled her up.

"Thank you!" he cried.

Clara smiled and began moving to the music. Seized by a desire to be a part of life, of the joy around them, Jean-Paul allowed the music to carry him along. Tim Hardin, Melanie, Arlo Guthrie, then finally Joan Baez, one by one the icons of the age entertained the crowd, until, as the drizzle turned to rain, the music ended for the day.

As the applause washed over the massed audience, Jean-Paul turned to Clara. "Now what?"

She grabbed his hand. "Come with me." She navigated a route through the crowds and the darkness to a tiny olive-green canvas pup tent. "House rules," she told him as the rain streaked their faces. "You're still too fragile for a deep relationship, but I will hold you, help you feel cared for, comforted. Deal?"

Jean-Paul struggled to hold back the tears as he squeezed her hand. "Deal."

And so began three days of smoking weed, listening to music and talking about everything from the Vietnam War to the benefits of a vegetarian diet.

As they lay side by side on the last night, Jean-Paul broached the subject that had been bothering him since they met. "I've really enjoyed your company. What happens now?"

"Never worry about tomorrow," Clara told him. "Live for today."

"But you said you were returning to your parents" house in San Diego? What—"

Clara pressed her finger to his lips. "That's tomorrow's issue. Between now and then, we've got hours to create more beautiful memories."

Jean-Paul started to protest, but Clara moved closer and rested her head on his shoulder. "Goodnight, my beautiful Frenchman," she whispered.

***

"You look different," Budoo said, studying his face.

Jean-Paul couldn't keep the smirk from his face. "It was interesting," he told her.

"I'm sure it was," she replied, "smoking weed and pounding your little hippy girl night and day."

"We didn't have sex," Jean-Paul said.

"Right." She flopped onto the sofa. "And did you think of your beloved Émilie while you were screwing Clara?"

Jean-Paul poured a vodka and lime while he thought about his reply. "You can be very cruel sometimes," he said finally.

"And yet," said Budoo, "I somehow always get to the crux of the matter. Hit the nail on the head, as you say in English."

Jean-Paul met her fierce gaze. "No, I didn't think of Émilie while I was with Clara. I relaxed and enjoyed myself, learned how to live for today."

"Bravo!" Her voice was thick with sarcasm.

"And what about you?" challenged Jean-Paul. "You said you wanted to learn about human nature, love, what makes us capable of such devotion, and yet you have spent most of the last few months having affairs with men and women alike, seducing them and taking great pride in destroying their relationships. Do you love the manipulation? Have these people satisfied your need for human contact, or are you afraid of falling in love?"

"I do as I please," retorted the Jinn.

"Easy to say," argued Jean-Paul, "but if you really want to learn about humans, the nature of true love, you have to do more than simply gratify yourself with the same superficial sex over and over again."

"You know nothing of what I have learned about your kind," snapped the Jinn.

Jean-Paul stood staring out the window at Central Park, the lights beginning to sparkle as evening advanced. He sighed. "This arrangement isn't working."

"What do you suggest?" she said, narrowing her eyes.

"You can do what you want," Jean-Paul replied. "I need to go back to Yemen. I never had the chance to thank the old woman who helped me recover." He looked at Budoo. "If you want, you can join me. The people I met there are not as they are here. Maybe you'll learn something new, maybe you won't," he finished, knowing that her ego would never refuse a challenge.

Budoo gave a dismissive shrug. "Yemen would not be my first choice, but New York is beginning to bore me." She exhaled. "Maybe their pitiful lives will provide some amusement for me."

***

Jean-Paul stood outside Maryam's house holding a food basket and rapped on the door.

No reply.

A second knock was met with the sound of hurrying feet. The door opened, and there stood Yasmine. But rather than the hesitant young woman he had met previously, she was tall and radiant with the same intense, sincere eyes, her belly swollen in the late stages of pregnancy. "Yasmine?" he croaked in surprise.

She smiled in recognition and lifted her right hand to reveal the watch he had given her.

For a moment they both stood in silence before Jean-Paul lifted the basket. "Is your grandmother here? I never had the chance to thank her for helping me back to health."

"She passed away this summer," replied Yasmine. "Don't look shocked; it was her time. She had an amazing life and helped transform the lives of others. Her place in Jannah is safe." She smiled. "And the beautiful lady who paid for your care? Is she here?"

"No," replied Jean-Paul quickly, "she has her own business to attend to." He nodded towards her bulging belly. "When are you due?"

"The end of October."

"And your studies?"

"I passed my exams this summer," she said. "I will begin an intern at the hospital sometime next year."

"So many changes," said Jean-Paul.

Yasmine shrugged. "That is the nature of life, no?"

"I guess so..."

"My grandmother taught me the future is not for us to define, it is for us to submit to," she said, peering at Jean-Paul. "I sense you have no idea what your future might hold."

Jean-Paul simply shrugged, lowering his gaze.

After exchanging a few platitudes and handing Yasmine the basket, Jean-Paul took his leave and began to make his way towards the central market.

The Jinn appeared from a narrow alleyway and fell in step beside him. "That wasn't what you were expecting, was it?"

Jean-Paul gave her an irritated look. "Your ability to intrude knows no bounds, does it? Have you never heard of privacy?"

Budoo shrugged. "I am Jinn." She studied his face. "You had half a mind to ask her for a date, didn't you?" She gave a harsh laugh. "Your face when you saw her belly! Someone got there before you."

"Don't be so crude!" snapped Jean-Paul.

"You humans love to pretend to be so morally correct," Budoo said, "yet you spend half your lives thinking about sex and jump at it at every opportunity, no matter the consequences."

Jean-Paul stopped and stared at her. "What do you want from me? When we entered into this agreement, I thought it was for you to learn more about humans, love, devotion — the qualities that Jinns struggle to understand. Any learning must have ended months ago."

Budoo studied his face. "You are right. We have learned as much from each other as we ever will. I think it is time for us to part ways."

tank top and the slip of paper bearing a San Diego phone number nestling in his wallet.

The old man smiled. "There is hope for you yet. Perhaps you are not so foolish after all."

Jean-Paul accepted the offered glass of tea and took a sip, looking into the fire. "Perhaps …'

EPILOGUE

That is my story. You may wonder why I felt the need to share it with you?

Because, despite the Jinn's almost eternal lifespans, we too must die one day. I find myself at my end of days, recalling more memories than any human could imagine, each tainted with pain, anger, disappointment and disillusionment. I am dying, dear reader, and if you are human, I ask this of you. Please pray for my soul …

The need to ask a human for help burns in my chest; my pride is torched by the humility it demands. For over a thousand years, I have been convinced of my superiority over mankind, yet now I understand why you are indeed the chosen species. Your faith in love and your inherent desire to forgive and be forgiven — these demonstrate compassion, a divine quality we will never possess. We have always been elemental creatures who live through instinct, feeding on the energy it creates. Only now, as my tears flow in self-pity, am I able to acknowledge how much of my life has been wasted loathing your kind and justifying my hostility to act without conscience.

And so, as I lay here, the life force leaving my body, I am afraid, truly afraid, for the first time. Afraid because I have lived for over a thousand years and never prepared for the inevitable, so great was my opinion of myself. Afraid because I sat with a thousand wise elders but heard nothing, intent only on proving my superior knowledge. Afraid because I read a thousand books about love, yet when love came, I threw it away, not once, but twice, out of foolish pride and selfishness.

I do not wish to die. My soul is so wretched that not even Shaitan will bargain for it. So here I am, dying alone, without even the desert scorpions for company. And so, at the end, I am reduced to begging.

My Beloved Creator of all that exists, I bow to your creation and understand the beauty of mankind. You have blessed them in ways denied to us and given them qualities we were blind to.

Ya Allah, Lord of the universes, You are the best of forgivers and You love to forgive, so please forgive me. You love to forgive, so please forgive me... You love to forgive...

124

The Killer
(the reflective Soul)

This is Love:

To fly toward a secret sky,

to cause a hundred veils to fall each moment.

First to let go of life.

Finally, to take a step without feet.

Jalāl ad-Din Muhammad Rūmī

CHAPTER 1

Le Sentier, Switzerland

2009

Anaïse sat in her father's study, listening to the heavy tick of the grandfather clock. When she was younger, this dark room with its creaking, crammed bookshelves had driven her crazy. She had wanted to be outside, running and playing, while her father preferred her inside, reading and studying.

Her father cleared his throat and looked at her. "It's a big day for you tomorrow, leaving for university. I know you want to say goodbye to your friends, but I would appreciate your patience for a moment. I have a story for you."

Anaïse glanced at the clock and sighed. "Papa, everything you do requires my patience." Coming from anyone else, this might have sounded impertinent, but she was careful to utter it with the disarming smile she had inherited from her mother. She had also inherited her mother's dark eyes, lustrous auburn hair and finely chiselled features. However, beneath these lurked an inner strength, tinged with darkness.

She looked around the study. It was a place of quiet contemplation and reflection, a mirror image of her father. Her mother had died in childbirth and her father had never remarried, so it was just the two of them. Having such different ideas of how Anaïse should spend her time, they had reached a compromise, setting time aside for play and study. As she grew up, she came to love this room, with the smell of leather-bound books and the feel of timelessness marked by the ticking clock.

"I shall try and be brief," he replied. He glanced at Anaïse again, then moved his gaze to the window. "Once upon a time, there was a magnificent Phoenix who soared through the skies each morning before sunrise, then returned each evening at sunset. The townsfolk admired him as he streamed through the sky, leaving a trail of flames in his wake, but their admiration didn't satisfy the Phoenix's lust for adoration. He wanted to be worshipped like the sun so decided he would consume the sun and take her place."

Anaïse glanced at the clock again then smiled politely as her father continued.

"Although legend has it the Phoenix is immortal and eternally reborn, as he flew closer to the sun and felt his flaming feathers burn away, he realised the sun's intensity could destroy him. But his need for adoration rampaged in his veins as he screamed through the pain, flying closer and closer in an attempt to become the sun. It was no good. Little by little, the sun tore away his feathers, skin and flesh. It burned away his physical existence, purifying every imperfection as he gasped out his dying breaths."

Anaïse felt the pull of the clock but kept her gaze on her father.

"In those final moments, as the sun stripped him of all that the townsfolk admired and he valued, he saw how his need to be worshipped had kept him trapped in his physical form. Realising his ego had kept him in a golden cage, he finally acknowledged his true worth, his true beauty. As the last physical vestiges of the Phoenix were carried away by the wind, he relinquished his pride and thanked the sun for releasing him from his prison, allowing him to feel the beauty of Love."

Her impatience ebbing away, Anaïse leaned forward.

"In the end, all that was left of the Phoenix was the most perfect, purified, incorruptible part of him — his heart. It cooled as it fell to earth and landed in a garden, embraced by the soft, damp ground. For a long time it lay dormant, but eventually the rain fell, and a small shoot appeared. It grew and grew until, over time, the most beautiful and alluring Blue Rose emerged from the charred remains of the Phoenix's heart."

Anaïse squirmed in her seat.

"Unlike the Phoenix," continued her father, "the Rose spent her days in gratitude rather than self-adoration. She gave daily thanks to the sun for releasing her and continuing to kiss her leaves with light and to the earth for nourishing her without asking for reward. The love of the earth and the sun was reciprocated by the love of the Rose, happy to live as part of their existence rather than her own, content in reciprocity, as a mere drop in their ocean."

Once her father had finished, Anaïse smiled. "I think Mike Tyson said it more succinctly. "We are not born to be humble. We are born to be humbled."

"You think the story was about you?"

She shrugged. "I think success breeds success. You think success leads to hubris and, ultimately, downfall." She started to stand, but her father gestured for her to remained seated.

"That was not my intent," he said. "It was meant to be a prelude to this." He rummaged on his desk, retrieved something and held it out to Anaïse.

She smiled. A watch case. What else would her father give her? A master watchmaker living in Le Sentier, the heart of Swiss watchmaking. She held the box for a moment, admiring the fine leather tooling.

"Go ahead. Open it."

Anaïse slowly opened the box. Inside was an elegant Reverso, its timeless curved case redolent of art deco design, the signature horizontal lines framing the dial. "It's lovely, thank you." She looked at it more closely. "I see the dial's proportions and layout use the golden ratio?"

"So you do listen to me?"

She smiled. "Sometimes."

A cryptic expression passed over her father's face. "Turn it over."

Anaïse slowly flipped it to reveal, in delicately detailed lacquer, a blue rose beneath a clear sky and a blazing sun.

"It's beautiful," said Anaïse.

Her father's eyes were shining. "Let me help you put it on."

Anaïse watched her father secure the watch to her toned wrist. She had developed an early interest in sharpshooting and archery, quickly becoming an expert. She won not only the local archery contests back-to-back but also the Knabenschiessen, a national contest in Zurich which had hitherto been open only to boys. The photographs still held pride of place on the study shelves — Anaïse holding a rifle; Anaïse being presented with a trophy; Anaïse beaming widely as she was presented with her judo black belt; Anaïse doing her best to be a boy to please the most important man in her life.

She turned her wrist back and forth to admire the watch.

"You're sure you like it?"

Anaïse smiled and nodded. "It's perfect."

She stood, leaned over and gave her father a kiss on the cheek. "Now, if you'll excuse me, I have something I need to do today."

"I'll see you for dinner?"

"Definitely."

She hurried from the room, leaving her father alone with his clock, his books and his eternity of time.

***

Anaïse drove through the narrow streets of Le Sentier, then beside the lake, calm and blue beneath the summer sky. It was a local tourist attraction and a place where families played, yet looking at it made Anaïse shiver. Memories rushed back from another sunny day. She had been no more than six years old, playing happily in the water, when her legs got tangled in some weeds. She flailed and floundered, and suddenly she was sinking, the cold water rushing in above her, the light dimming. Just as she was about to gulp in a lungful of water, her father's strong hand grabbed her wrist and hauled her onto the grass, where she lay gasping and sobbing.

"Goodness, child," he had said. "What were you thinking, swimming among those weeds?"

Shutting out those unwelcome thoughts, Anaïse sped through the small town and out towards her uncle's house. She had been planning this encounter for years. It was a necessity she was not looking forward to but had to do before she left for university and moved on with her life.

Uncle Ralph was wealthy. He owned a large house on the outskirts of the town with a view across the lake. Growing up in Le Sentier, Anaïse had heard rumours about him — he was a crook who had made his money by exploiting others; he was a bon viveur who treated women as property, acquisitions, trophies to be snared, used, then tossed aside.

Anaïse could deal with those rumours, but there was one she could not ignore; the one she felt she could not leave town without addressing. She had heard Ralph was her biological father, that he had seduced or raped her mother, who had subsequently died in childbirth, and that Anaïse was their illegitimate offspring. She had attempted to address this with her father on a number of occasions, but he had always dismissed the topic out of hand. Rumours were spiteful gossip, to be ignored, he'd said. Paying them any heed only strengthened those who would hurt her. Despite her father's calm dismissal of the matter, Anaïse could not ignore it. She had to confront her uncle and discover the truth.

***

Anaïse parked her car on the expansive driveway and climbed out. Her nerves were jangling, her heart pounding. As at crucial moments in shooting competitions, she stretched and forced herself to focus on her breathing, following the air in and out as she slowly brought her heartbeat under control.

You don't have to do this. You can leave town, go to university, never see Uncle Ralph again.

But, deep down, she knew she could never rest until she knew.

Anaïse took one more deep breath, walked up to the front door with a jaunty step that belied her nervousness and pressed firmly on the doorbell.

If Ralph was surprised to see her at his door, he didn't show it. "Anaïse, look at you!" he boomed. He was a big man, with a year-round tan and carefully coiffed hair. He hugged her tightly — a little too tightly for Anaïse's liking — then led her through the open-plan house to the terrace. "A glorious day, isn't it? Can I fix you a drink?"

The terrace looked out over the lake. Anaïse felt an icy chill as her eyes were drawn to it. She turned to find her uncle's eyes fixed on her. "And look at you. The little girl all grown up. You've got some real curves now, haven't you?"

Anaïse said nothing. Now she was there, she had no idea how to proceed, what to say.

Growing up, she had always been aware of the tension between the two brothers. Her father — smaller, quieter, more studious — had stayed at home to become a master watchmaker and a local counsellor. Her uncle, bigger and stronger, was filled with an arrogance that came from being the best at everything. He had left town as soon as he could, made his money in shady ventures like a telecommunications company in Nigeria, then returned home to an early retirement, flaunting his wealth, living like a lord in a huge modern house by the lake, with a reputation for drinking too much and seducing other men's wives. It was almost eleven years since the brothers had last spoken to one another.

On the terrace was a marble side table, a bottle of Scotch and a large glass, half full. Typical. Not yet midday, and already he was drinking.

Her uncle followed her gaze. "It's a little early," he admitted, "but it's too beautiful a day for anything as mundane as work, don't you think?"

Anaïse took another deep breath and clasped her hands together to stop them from shaking. What was she doing here? Her uncle was virtually a stranger; she could barely recall the last time she had seen him.

Ralph picked up the glass, took a big sip, leaned on the balcony rail and gazed across the lake, seemingly oblivious to her nervousness. "What brings you out here today? It's been years since you last deigned to pay me a visit."

"I'm leaving tomorrow," she told him.

"I heard. The little scholar off to university."

Fighting back the urge to turn and run, she forced the words out. "There's something I wanted to talk to you about," she began. "Something I wanted to ask you."

Ralph sipped his Scotch and studied her with an arrogant expression. "You want some money? Is that it? You only have to ask."

Something about the way he said it irked Anaïse. "I don't want your damned money!" she snapped.

Ralph grinned and raised an eyebrow in mock surprise. "What, then?" he said. "What could possibly bring little Anaïse out here after so many years?"

A lump grew in her throat; a tightness gripped her chest. She'd experienced this sensation many times at the start of a competition, and she knew how to fight it. Breathe calmly, focus on the task, shut out everything else. "I want to talk about my mother," she said calmly. It sounded like someone else speaking.

The water lapped at the side of the lake.

"What about her?" replied Ralph coldly.

"There are rumours …" began Anaïse. "What I mean is, people say …"

"Spit it out, girl." He was revelling in her discomfort.

"Did you and my mother—"

"Did I sleep with her? Is that what you want to know?"

Anaïse nodded mutely.

"That's the question everyone in the village has been asking for years," he said, smiling with a self-important air.

Anaïse was stunned. She had always thought of it as something taboo to be whispered about, but he talked about it so casually, as though it were nothing.

"That's not your real question though, is it?" he continued. "What you really want to know is if I'm your father, right?" He moved closer and looked down at her. "What if I am?" He reached out, stroked her cheek and tucked her hair behind her ear. "You'd like that, wouldn't you? Knowing a real man was your father, not that weak watchmaker, sitting in his study, pretending he knows so much."

Anaïse smelt the whisky on his breath.

He erupted with a laugh, a sharp braying sound that sent shivers up Anaïse's spine. "Who knows?" he said. "But one thing I'll tell you for free. I had her right here on this balcony, looking out over the lake. She shouted and squawked a bit, but I knew she wanted it. She was virtually begging for it after five years married to your father."

Anaïse looked up at him in horror. "You raped her?"

Ralph shrugged. "Rape is a harsh word. She wanted a real man, anyone could see that, and I was happy to oblige." He smiled at the memory. "She might have resisted at first, but that was her Catholic morals getting in the way. She was loving it by the end."

Anaïse glared at him. "You bastard!"

Ralph smiled and brushed Anaïse's hair from her face. "You remind me of her."

She knocked his hand aside.

"Feisty, too." He drained his glass and set it on the marble table. Without warning, he grabbed her arm and pulled her close.

Anaïse struggled, but he had a firm grip. His lips brushed her cheek as he pressed his body against her.

"You know why you really came," he murmured, his fingers groping her, his eyes fixed on her. "You want it too."

"Let me go!" screamed Anaïse, but her protests seemed to excite him more and he began to tear at her clothing. In a flash, her fighting brain engaged; years of judo training in the dojo took over her body without a conscious thought.

She yielded briefly to change her balance point, then hooked one foot behind Ralph's leg and twisted slightly. Caught off balance, he stumbled, and they crashed into the marble table, sending the bottle of Scotch tumbling to the terrace. Anaïse staggered backwards to the balcony rail.

"You little bitch!" growled Ralph as he pressed his weight against her, one hand tight around her throat.

Anaïse gasped, fighting back the panic. *Focus.*

She jammed her knee into his groin and scrabbled to poke her thumb in his eye.

It was enough to distract him, and she was able to half squirm out of his grasp. The blood raced in her head, but she stayed calm to focus on escaping. She tried to pull away from him, but he caught her wrist in his strong fingers, spun her around and raised his fist.

Anaïse half ducked, half twisted, and the blow, intended for her head, glanced off her shoulder.

As his momentum carried him past her, Anaïse wrenched her wrist free, reached for the whisky bottle still rolling around on the floor and wrapped her hand around the neck. It was comforting to be holding something — anything — as a weapon.

Ralph stared at her, gasping. "You little bitch!"

Anaïse turned to face him, gripping the bottle in her right hand. "I'm not scared of you."

"Then you're stupid, because you should be!" He lunged and grabbed her.

Anaïse half stumbled backwards and swung the bottle hard at his head. His weight carried them backwards, and, still locked together, they crashed to the ground, her uncle on top of her. Anaïse's head slammed against the marble floor, and everything went black.

***

When Anaïse came to, she was pinned beneath her uncle, and something warm was running down her face. She opened her eyes and was met by Ralph's dead-fish gaze. There was a deep gash on his forehead where she had hit him with the bottle, his blood slowly dripping onto Anaïse's cheek.

Resisting the urge to scream, Anaïse pushed his body away and squirmed out from beneath him. She sat up, pawing frantically at her face to wipe away the blood.

Her eyes were drawn towards Ralph. He lay still, his cold, sightless eyes staring upwards.

She slowly leaned over and pressed her fingers to his neck. His skin was soft, his flesh warm, but there was no trace of a pulse.

A rising tide of panic threatened to engulf her. She'd killed him.

What should she do now? Her sensible side said to call the police, call her father, let them sort it out. Surely they would see it was an accident? But what if they didn't? What if they asked why she was there in the first place? How would she explain that?

Breathe.

Focus.

Stay calm.

There was an alternative. No one knew she was there. No one knew she was planning on visiting Ralph, not even her father. She hadn't touched anything, so there would be no fingerprints. As long as she didn't panic, she could leave with no trace she had been there. The only issue was the blood that had run down her face and into her hair.

Anaïse climbed to her feet and looked around, avoiding Ralph's face, the deep cut on his head and the growing pool of blood. Her panic threatened to return, but she fought it back. He was a pig who deserved what had happened. She needed to ignore him and protect herself.

Anaïse stepped onto the grass that led down to the lake. It was dry, and her feet left no imprint as she stepped lightly to the water's edge. Other houses overlooked the lake, but the chances of anyone seeing her were remote. She stood for a long time staring at the dark water, memories of her near-drowning crowding her mind, gasping for air. She had avoided the lake ever since, but now there was no alternative. Either give up and call the police, or face her fears head on.

Giving herself no time to think it through, Anaïse knelt on the rocks and plunged her hands and face in the cold water. A short, sharp wave of panic rushed over her, but within seconds it had passed, and she methodically washed her hands and face and rinsed the blood from her hair.

When she was satisfied she was clean, she stood. After ensuring she had left no traces of blood on the rocks, she walked back to the house and forced herself to look at her uncle's body. The pool of blood was bigger, spreading slowly across the smooth marble.

Think. What else do I need to do?

The bottle! Her fingerprints would be on the neck.

She cast around and spotted the remains of the bottle lying against the balcony rail. It had shattered when she had hit her uncle, but the neck was intact. She bent down and carefully wiped the neck of the bottle on her T-shirt, then set it back down.

She was done.

Without another glance, Anaïse walked past her uncle's body and out the front door, being sure to touch nothing on the way.

She was almost in her car when she remembered something else she had touched — the doorbell. She hurried back to the door and wiped the bell with the cuff of her shirt. The bell echoed through the empty house, as if chiding her that no one could answer. As she hurried back to her car, a thought flashed into her mind. *I just killed a man, and I don't feel guilty.*

She paused, the car keys in her hand. It was not too late. She could still make the call, admit to what she had done.

But even as the thought crossed her mind, she rejected it. She had made her decision; she had to live with it.

She climbed into her car, turned the key in the ignition and pulled smoothly off the driveway.

Ralph was her first kill, but far from her last...

CHAPTER 2

2019

Milan, Italy

Anaïse reached the top of the stairs, pushed open the door and stepped onto the roof. It was a crisp spring morning, the rooftops still damp from the overnight rain as she gazed out over the urban landscape. Cities always looked different from above; the cars, motorcycles and people were smaller, their individual actions merging into a coherent pattern, as though they were part of some elaborate dance, starting and stopping and starting again to the rhythm of an inaudible drum.

Anaïse made her way to the edge of the flat roof, set her black suitcase against the low perimeter wall and began to unpack. She laid out everything methodically, following a pattern honed through years of practice.

First out was the tarpaulin — black, immaculately folded — which she spread out on the damp ground. Then, one at a time, came the stock, the barrel, the firing mechanism, the sight, and the stand — the bipod Anaïse would use to steady the rifle. Next, she set her binoculars and flask of coffee beside the equipment.

After a quick look through the binoculars, Anaïse opened the flask and observed the steam as it rose and drifted away to her right. "Wind from the east, around seven miles an hour," she muttered to herself as she poured a lidful of coffee and took a sip. "Perfect."

Drinking her coffee, Anaïse scanned the adjacent rooftops and top-floor windows, making sure no one was watching her. All her movements were slow, deliberate, precise. The human eye is attracted to movement, so the less she moved and the slower her actions, the less likely it was someone would notice her.

Satisfied she was not being observed, Anaïse drained her coffee, replaced the cup on the top of the flask and carefully assembled her rifle, a classic 7.62 mm she had used for over seven years and which was as familiar as her own face. She was ready.

Once again, Anaïse lifted the binoculars and scanned a nearby window of a penthouse apartment about a hundred and twenty yards away. The open blinds revealed a large room containing a bland palette of shiny black and chrome surfaces.

Anaïse scanned the room. It was empty, but she knew her target's schedule. Last night's whore would appear first, tottering out on her stilettos, a fur over one arm and a thousand dollars tucked away safely in her purse. The target would follow five minutes later, wearing a fluffy bathrobe and towelling his thinning hair.

Once he was satisfied his hair was dry enough, he would toss the towel on the floor, then make a cup of coffee on his bespoke La Cimbali coffee machine. While waiting for his coffee, he would lean on the black marble countertop and check his phone, answer a few messages and choose his entertainment for the night. And that was the moment Anaïse was waiting for. Five minutes of a stationary target: an assassin's dream.

Who was he? What was his name? Who had he double-crossed or pissed off to wind up in Anaïse's crosshairs? She didn't know, didn't care. He was simply a mark, a job that needed doing, a human cockroach to be disposed of with as little emotion as she would expend on killing an insect.

Right on cue the whore appeared, a willowy blonde in a micro-mini skirt who looked like she couldn't get out of there quickly enough. Anaïse checked the wind one more time — holding steady — then switched from the binoculars to the scope, lining up the rifle to aim at the spot where the mark always stopped to look at his phone while his coffee machine did its work.

Anaïse lay still, unblinking, unthinking, every part of her body and mind focused on the task. *Breathe deeply. Relax.* This was her time to shut off all extraneous thoughts and focus on one thing — getting her target in the crosshairs and gently caressing the trigger...

And here he came.

He dried his hair, tossed the towel aside and set the La Cimbali in motion. Then he picked up his phone, propped his elbows on the countertop and began scrolling, positioned dead centre in Anaïse's crosshairs.

It's almost as though he wants me to kill him, thought Anaïse as she made a tiny adjustment to her aim.

Perfect. His receding forehead was at the centre of her crosshairs. This was the moment. Another deep breath, exhale and...

A single "crack" rang out across the rooftops, and a nearby flock of pigeons took flight at the disturbance.

Anaïse barely noticed them. Her target had slumped to the floor, twitched once, then moved no more. As his life blood drained from his head, she was packing everything back into its place in her bag. After a last glance around to make sure she had left nothing behind, she was gone.

They say your life flashes before your eyes when you are on the brink of death, but for Anaïse, it came after she had taken a life. She dreaded the long, restless, nightmare-filled night that followed each kill and tried in vain to drown it out with drugs, alcohol and meaningless sex. In the dark hours just before the dawn, her demons always caught up with her, showing her the faces of all the men she had killed, parading before her one by one. The final face was always that of her father, staring dumbly at Anaïse as she turned her back on him and walked away.

She would wake up, shaking and sweating. The solution was always the same — attempt to recover her humanity with one of her favourite volumes of Sufi poetry, allowing the melodic words and profound insights to massage her soul and restore her equilibrium.

*****

Anaïse stepped out of her hotel into a beautiful spring day. The trees were replete with fresh green leaves and blossom, and the birds' calls were loud enough to be heard above the buzz of the mopeds. She strolled down the Via Brera past the elegant Palazzo Citterio and turned onto Via del Carmine towards the bookstore.

There are times in our lives when everything comes together, and for Anaïse that time was now. She was financially independent, courtesy of her profession, lived a lifestyle of her choosing, and felt physically and mentally strong. People who met her commented on her radiant skin, energy and confidence.

With her business in Milan concluded, she was free to do what she wanted, and today she was on a mission, something she had been anticipating for several months. She was visiting a specialist bookstore that carried a fabulous collection of Sufi poetry.

The short walk to the bookstore was enough to get her blood flowing and allow the anticipation to build, but not so far as to be tiresome. Anaïse slowed as she approached the shop, wanting to savour the anticipation and fulfilment as she peered in the window. The morning sun threw her reflection back at her, but she barely saw it, being captivated by her first glimpse of the beautifully weathered, leather-bound editions stacked on tables, the shelves full of history and knowledge waiting to be discovered, the lounge chairs and coffee tables scattered throughout the shop. It was exactly as she had imagined it, an Aladdin's cave of ancient treasures, like a chest of time-worn pearls, their lustre enhanced by years of respectful handling and love.

As Anaïse stepped inside, the smell of worn leather and fresh coffee washed over her. Barely hiding her smile of childlike delight, she wandered aimlessly, browsing the shelves and allowing her eyes to alight on random titles with no plan or purpose, while the clerk finished helping another customer. Her eyes assessed him in her usual predatory way. Compared to the men she usually enjoyed, he looked unimpressive — mid-thirties, medium height, with a tangle of curly strawberry-blond hair, an unathletic build, and small, gold-framed glasses. Anaïse hoped he was smarter than he looked.

As the other customer left, Anaïse considered approaching him but decided to pretend to read the book in her hand, but not because he had impressed her. She liked feeling in control by making men approach her.

Instead of immediately coming over, he disappeared into the back of the bookstore. Anaïse quelled her surprise by telling herself he was probably making himself presentable for a good impression. She was happy to bury herself in the shop's extensive collection of Sufi poetry, a passion she rarely found the opportunity to indulge in.

He returned a few moments later, looking exactly the same as before — slightly dishevelled, as though his appearance was unimportant. As he approached, Anaïse glanced up from her book, ready for him to engage her in conversation. Instead, he flashed a glance at her, mumbled, "Please let me know if you need help," then scurried away.

Anaïse watched him for a moment then strolled to the desk. He looked up from writing on a sheet of paper.

"You have an impressive catalogue of original Sufi literature," she said.

"Thank you." He gave a brief smile. "Is there a particular writer or title you're interested in?"

Anaïse smiled in return. "Not really, but I just saw a leather-bound Rumi and thought it would be a good conversation starter."

Rather than take the opportunity to engage her in conversation, he smiled politely and returned to his notetaking.

Anaïse hid her irritation behind a confident smile. "Actually, I've reserved a volume of poetry by Rabia al-Adawiyya."

He looked up with more interest. "And your name?"

Anaïse gave her name and watched him scuttle into the back of the shop.

He soon returned and gently set the book on the desk. She picked it up and began to leaf through it.

"You have good taste," he said. "This is an incredible work. It's rare we find original copies, let alone one in such good condition."

"It's beautiful," said Anaïse, revelling in the look, feel and smell of the book. It brought back memories of her father's study, doing her homework under his watchful eye, desperate to get an A, desperate for his approval.

"Can I ask why you came all the way to Milano to purchase this book?" he said, with the first hint of interest.

Anaïse looked up from her investigation of the book. "What makes you think I came here just for the book?"

He shrugged. "You're not Italian. Although we deliver worldwide, this is a special title, so I thought maybe it means a lot to you and you might want to pick it up in person." He stumbled to a halt. "I mean, if it were me, I would want to collect a book like this in person …"

Impressed with his assessment, Anaïse was drawn to his perceptiveness and his calm demeanour, bordering on coolness. Behind his glasses were warm, intelligent eyes. She tried to return the compliment by displaying her powers of deduction. "You don't seem typically Italian either."

"My mother is Austrian," he said. "I grew up in the Tirol before moving to Milano to take over the family business." He smiled and nodded towards the book. "And your interest in the book? It's rather specialised, esoteric even."

"Life is a journey," Anaïse replied. "We can either stumble through it in the dark, oblivious to what is happening around us, or we can take a more thoughtful, conscious approach. I prefer the latter." She picked up the book. "Rabia freed herself from slavery through Love. She completely surrendered herself to it despite the hardships of ninth-century Iraq."

"All lives are a mixture of dark and light," he replied. "We can either embrace both sides or spend our entire lives fighting one or the other."

She nodded. "I guess we are all looking for the inspiration and courage to somehow escape our own slavery."

Anaïse felt she had laid a part of her soul bare, but he merely nodded in acknowledgement. She looked at him until he averted his gaze. "You don't talk much, do you?"

"If you have nothing to say, say nothing," he replied quickly.

Anaïse thought for a moment. "Mark Twain?"

"Mark Twain," he confirmed.

"Yes!" Anaïse punched the air playfully, a complete contrast to her usual calm demeanour. "It's a game I used to play with my father — guess the quote."

He laughed a big, childlike laugh that invited her into his world, his eyes shining as he looked at her with real warmth. "And a splendid game it is." He held out his hand. "Amato."

Anaïse shook his hand firmly. "Anaïse."

She felt him briefly permit her to see past the veils of his mind, then he quickly lowered his head and began wrapping her book. "Of course, it could just as easily be Rumi," he joked.

Anaïse slid her credit card across the counter. "Thanks for making my purchase such a pleasure, Amato."

"Do stop by when next you're in Milano."

Anaïse picked up the beautifully wrapped book. "I might just do that."

CHAPTER 3

Anaïse stood on the balcony of her hotel room, gazing at the traffic below. It was a warm spring evening, full of possibilities. Usually she would be in a bar at this time, flirting, looking, considering, but not tonight. After she had finished her dinner, she found herself wandering back to her hotel room. Now she was staring at the traffic, which was reduced to rows of red and white lights performing a dance.

But she wasn't really looking. Her mind was back in the bookshop, amid the musty old pages and the soft leather covers. She was back with Amato, the man with the warm eyes and the infectious laugh.

Why was she fixated on someone so 'average'? He wasn't her type. But, despite lacking most things she would normally consider essential in a man, he had somehow wormed his way into her head, his contagious laugh echoing in the emptiness of her life.

There was only one thing to do. She would visit the bookstore again tomorrow and ask him out for a coffee. That was the solution, the way to give herself some peace. So why did she lie awake tossing and turning in the vast ocean of her bed before she finally drifted off to sleep?

***

In the morning, Anaïse looked at the three outfits she had laid out on the bed. She wanted to make the right impression. "Which woman do I want to be today?" she muttered. "Which woman would he find interesting? Which woman do I want him to see when I walk in?"

She chose a pale-yellow pleated skirt, a simple white blouse, a cardigan buttoned at the neck and open-heeled mules. Fresh, spring-like, and a touch demure. Not her usual look, but then again, Amato was not her usual sort of man.

Anaïse had a serene smile on her face as she pushed open the bookshop door, the expectation of the chase mingling with her calm confidence. There was no sign of Amato at the desk, so she browsed the shelves aimlessly, confident he would spot her and come over.

"Hi. Are you looking for anything in particular?"

Anaïse jumped and turned to find a dark-haired woman in her thirties standing next to her, looking at her inquisitively.

"Oh, hi," Anaïse stuttered. "I was in yesterday; a young man was helping me with some questions."

"Amato," the woman said. "It's his day off. He's back in tomorrow. Is there anything I can help you with?"

"No, no, I'm fine, thanks," said Anaïse. She gave a polite smile, masking her disappointment. "Maybe I'll come back tomorrow."

She stepped onto the pavement, considering what to do. She should make the most of the day. Even though she had been thwarted in her plans, she was still in Milan. She wound her way to the courtyard of the Basilica San Lorenzo Maggiore, the sun reflecting brightly off the pure white façade, the pigeons flapping and swirling overhead. She found a table at a small café, ordered a coffee and pulled out her new volume of poetry. As disappointed as she was at not meeting Amato, she was determined not to let it spoil her day. She gently opened her book, admiring the feel of the cover and the pages. What could be better than sitting at a pavement café in Milan, reading a new book? So what if Amato wasn't with her?

As the waiter brought her coffee, Anaïse put down her book and looked up. Her stomach jolted as she saw Amato through the Roman arches leading into the courtyard. He turned and kissed a woman on the forehead, laughed, then walked away arm in arm with her, oblivious to Anaïse sitting a few metres away.

Anaïse frowned. She had gone to the bookshop to invite him for a coffee, and there he was with another woman. She shook her head. It didn't matter. She picked up her book and started to read. There were plenty more interesting fish in the sea. But she couldn't concentrate — her eyes were drawn to the far side of the courtyard where she had seen him.

It didn't matter? Really? For reasons she didn't understand, this one did matter. She had even pursued him, something she never did, and it turned out he was taken.

She knew she should just forget him and move on. There were enough good-looking men in Milan to keep her happy for months on end, yet that was not what she wanted. Deep down, she wanted someone to call her own, someone to share secret smiles and jokes, someone who would kiss her with the same tenderness that he had kissed the other woman. Amato had got under her skin.

Anaïse finished her coffee and snapped her book shut. "Don't be stupid," she muttered as she stood and tucked a five-euro note under the saucer. But even as she walked away from the café, she knew she would be at the bookstore the following morning.

***

"Hello, Rabia, nice to see you again." Amato greeted Anaïse politely, but his face lit up with a smile that creased his cheeks and made the corners of his eyes sparkle as they pushed the world away.

151

He seemed not to notice her carefully selected outfit, which had received numerous compliments in the past, but rather saw through her to a place she was not prepared to share with anyone, not even herself.

"Did you find yourself in your book?" he asked.

"Not yet," replied Anaïse quickly. "Maybe we should have coffee and discuss it." As soon as the words were out of her mouth, she regretted them; she had lost control and composure, appearing needy. She was dealing with a man she could not decipher and had immediately given him the upper hand. Before he could reply, Anaïse jumped in, not wanting to give him time to refuse her. "I'm sorry. I didn't mean to sound aggressive. I'm in town for a few days and would love to learn a little about the city from a local who knows about Mark Twain and Rumi. But if you don't have time, I quite understand." Cheeks flushing, she turned towards the door.

"Wait."

That one word was enough to stop her, to give her hope.

"A coffee sounds nice," he said.

Anaïse smiled with a mix of relief and delight.

"I'm closing for lunch in about an hour," he said. "Would it be possible for you to return then?"

She grinned. "Of course. See you at twelve."

***

To Anaïse's amusement, after carefully locking the shop, Amato led her to the Basilica San Lorenzo Maggiore. As the waiter brought their coffees, Anaïse smiled at Amato. "Do you bring all your girlfriends here?"

Amato frowned. "All my...?"

"I was here yesterday. I saw you over there kissing someone."

Amato followed her gaze towards the archway. "Ah."

"Who was the lucky woman?" pressed Anaïse.

"My first love," replied Amato with a cheeky grin. "She has all the qualities of our mother," he added quickly. "I pray she finds a man who sees all that I see in her."

It took Anaïse a moment to process what he had said. "She's your sister?"

Amato gave his soft smile. "Of course. Do we not look alike?"

Anaïse hadn't even noticed what the other woman looked like. She was too pre-occupied with the thought of him already in a relationship. "Yes, yes, of course." A wave of relief washed over her as she sipped her coffee. "Tell me about the bookshop," she said, leaning forward. "It must be a wonderful place to work."

"You clearly have a deep love of books."

Anaïse nodded. "When I was growing up, my father had a wonderful study; the walls were lined with bookcases. Once he had taught me how to handle a book properly, not bend the spine or crease the pages, I was allowed to read anything I wanted."

"Your father must have loved having someone to share his books with."

Anaïse shook her head. "Not really. He desperately wanted a son, so I think I was something of a disappointment to him."

Amato gently stirred his coffee. "What makes you think that?"

"If you met my father, you would understand immediately. He taught me how to fix the engine on his vintage Porsche, took me out hunting, made me join martial arts classes. In short, he made it clear every day in every way I should have been a boy."

Amato gave a look of mock surprise. "You can shoot, you can fight, you can fix a car? That's three things I would be hopeless at."

"And none of which you need." She caught the waiter's eye. "Two cappuccini please."

Amato smiled. "Said like a true Milanese."

"Is there any other way?"

"You'd be surprised. Most tourists pronounce it capp-a-ccino and want it served with caramel or chocolate powder. It's enough to make my grandmother turn in her grave!" He laughed.

"I'll remember that," she said. "The bookstore seems like a dream job."

"It is most of the time." Amato leaned forward, his eyes alight with enthusiasm. "You know what I love most?"

"The smell?" said Anaïse, raising an eyebrow.

"That's right up there," he replied. "But most of all, it's the possibilities. The bookstore has been there for centuries, and when I'm there alone, especially late at night, I can feel the wonderful weight of all those books. All those stories I haven't read, the authors I have yet to discover, and the possibility that, on any given day, I might discover a lost treasure that has lain hidden for decades."

The hour passed quickly, and they had to hurry back to the shop. An impatient customer was standing outside, tutting and looking at his watch.

Amato fiddled with the keys and opened the door with a flourish. The customer stomped in, leaving Anaïse and Amato standing, a little breathless, on the threshold.

"That was delightful," said Amato.

Anaïse held her breath, waiting and hoping for what might come next.

"Can I see you again?"

Anaïse tried to play it cool but couldn't help herself and blurted out, "How about tonight?"

They dissolved into gales of laughter. "Tonight sounds wonderful," said Amato.

CHAPTER 4

Anaïse had never been in love; she had never allowed herself to fall for someone so completely. She had always regarded it as a weakness, something that happened to others who lacked her inner strength and control. But within a few days of meeting Amato, she found herself questioning everything she had told herself about staying aloof and maintaining the emotion-free state her work required. His transparency and self-acceptance engulfed her, leaving her wanting to surrender despite her need for composure.

At first, he too, was hesitant, not wanting to become involved with someone who may leave town any day. Once Anaïse explained she was between jobs and had decided to stay in Milan for the foreseeable future, he expressed himself without reservation. Nonetheless, it wasn't until their fifth date that he even so much as held her hand. At first, Anaïse felt a little insulted when he didn't try to kiss her. With her looks and style, she was used to men pursuing her — but the more she thought about it, the more she liked it. Rather than seeing her as an object to possess, Amato valued her company, her conversation, her sense of humour.

When he first took her hand, as they hurried through the rain to a small restaurant around the corner from the bookshop, a tingle ran up Anaïse's arm and down her spine. It felt so natural, intimate, and yet unfamiliar, his spontaneity and warmth melting any resistance she might have had.

***

As the weeks unfolded, Amato played tour guide as they explored Milan together. From the breathtaking views atop the Duomo di

Milano to the Leonardo da Vinci Museum, from the winding streets of the historic Brera district to an evening of opera at La Scala, they enjoyed the best Milan had to offer.

With every new destination and experience, they learned more about each other, both probing and questioning how two people with such different beliefs and philosophies could find the other so fascinating. Politics, religion, history — no subject was off-limits in a flowing conversation that began anew each time they met, and only ended when they said goodnight. Amato introduced her to all his favourite cafés and restaurants — small family-run places tucked away in side streets and alleyways off the main thoroughfares, away from the tourists and the crowds. The cafés were welcoming and unpretentious, a thousand miles away from the high-end restaurants and glamorous clubs Anaïse usually frequented.

One evening, they sat at a corner table in a local rooftop bar, watching the sun set over the city. Amid the quiet buzz of conversation filling the air, Anaïse asked a question that had been occupying her mind. "How do you have such a soft heart when the world can be so hard?" she asked him.

"What alternative is there?" he responded.

"Most people I meet seem scarred by life, hardened. Yet, you remain open, loving, undamaged."

Amato ran his hands through his thick hair, looking pensive. "I understand what you are saying. But for me, it is too much work to believe that we can be in control of every aspect of our lives. When that happens, we calculate everything, suspect everything and everyone. And then, as you say, our hearts become hard, and we build a thick wall against light, love and truth, against everything that allows us to be part of something greater than ourselves."

"But you have not succumbed to that. How?"

"I believed."

He said it so simply, in such a matter-of-fact way, Anaïse was taken aback. "That's all? You believed?" She couldn't keep the surprise, disappointment even, out of her voice.

Amato smiled and repeated, "I believed."

"Believed in what?" probed Anaïse, impatience rising in her chest.

"I believed I was where I needed to be, rather than worrying if I was where I wanted to be," he said. "By accepting that, I learned to let go. And in letting go, I found that every ending led me to the next place I need to be."

His answer startled Anaïse. "And where would you like to be?"

Amato shrugged. "I can only answer from my ego. And what my ego desires is not what I need, but what it craves."

"And what does the ego crave?"

Amato paused as the waiter set their dinner on the table. Once the waiter had left, Amato carefully topped up their wine glasses.

Anaïse laughed. "OK, you've stalled long enough. What does the ego crave?"

He took a small bite of his salad, then gave her a smile that melted her. "It desires adoration, fame, fortune, material trinkets to support weak values. But if I achieve all that, I will have wasted my life."

"Why?" Anaïse pushed.

Amato smiled at her again. "You haven't tasted your dinner. I won't answer until you have given appropriate attention to your food."

Now it was Anaïse's turn to smile. "Very well."

Once she had taken several bites and made the appropriate complimentary noises, Amato answered her question. "It will be a waste because none of those things will help me find my peace with myself, or help me find my place in the world."

Anaïse couldn't decide if she was calmed or irritated by his responses. They were so different from what she had expected, the way she had always thought, the things she had always believed. "And do you know your purpose in the world?"

Amato sipped his wine. "Of course. It is to be where I need to be, and to know that this is the best for me. Tomorrow, I may need to be somewhere else, and then that will be the best for me. But tonight, it is right here, right now, with you."

Anaïse shook her head, trying to come to terms with what he was saying. "It's that simple?"

Amato reached across the table and squeezed her hand, his eyes absorbing every detail of her face. "It's that simple."

As she lay in bed that night, her mind was whirling. When do we fall in love? Is it the moment we meet someone, even though it takes us time to notice it? Or is it a more gradual process that creeps up on us, building little by little until, one day, we realise this person is 'the one', the only soul in the universe with whom we would be happy to spend eternity?

The latter was more probable — a gradual accumulation of trust and affection that built over time. She wasn't ready to call it love, but she couldn't deny she was developing strong feelings for Amato. She vowed to keep her heart and mind open and see how things developed.

It didn't take long. Day by day the feeling grew, through their walks and talks, their dinners and coffees, to the first meeting with, and instant acceptance by, his sister. One day Anaïse awoke in her rented apartment and realised she wanted to spend each and every day with Amato. For the first time ever, she was prepared to fully trust someone with her heart.

"How would you feel about having dinner with my family tonight?"

The question had come out of the blue, taking Anaïse by surprise. They had progressed to the point where they were seeing each other almost every night, but it had not occurred to Anaïse that Amato might have other responsibilities, others who might want to spend time with him.

"I want to see you again tonight," explained Amato, "and my Mamma is nagging me that she hasn't seen me for weeks."

"I'd love to," said Anaïse quickly, surprised by her answer. Was it that type of relationship already? She had always associated dinner with the parents with a stodgy, formal type of relationship, not the carefree joy she experienced with Amato.

Amato's mother lived in a crowded fourth-floor apartment, overflowing with love and children and the smell of freshly baked bread. After two quick pecks on the cheek from Amato's mother, Anaïse was treated like the other family members present — Amato's sister, Diana, and an assortment of uncles, aunties and cousins. Dinner was a raucous affair with at least three conversations going back and forth at any one time, the jokes and friendly jibes blending with the homemade dishes.

Anaïse ate and laughed more than she could ever remember, and by the time she walked out of the door, she knew this was something she wanted. For the first time in her life, she felt part of something bigger than herself — the feeling she had always hoped for with her own family but had never experienced.

As dinner wound to a close, Anaïse found herself alone in the kitchen with Diana, drying the big pots as Diana washed them.

"You're good for him," said Diana. She had Amato's mop of hair and intense eyes.

"How's that?"

"You challenge him," Diana told her. "You're unlike any girl he has ever dated. More polished, yes, but tough as nails beneath the skin."

"And he, in turn, challenges me," replied Anaïse.

"Maybe," said Diana. "Or maybe that's just life?"

Anaïse set the dry saucepan on the counter and grabbed another wet one from the stack on the draining board. "How do you mean?"

"I have always thought of life as a series of challenges," said Diana. "Life throws things at us, tries to knock us off course and defeat us, and we must find a way to make the best of the situation."

"Even when something really bad happens? Like death?"

Diana nodded. "Especially when something terrible happens. That's when we show our true colours."

Two of the aunties bustled into the kitchen. "Mio Dio!" exclaimed one. "We can't have our guest doing the dishes!" She took the cloth from Anaïse's hands, and shooed the two younger women out of the kitchen.

As they entered the living room, Diana gave Anaïse a quick peck on the cheek. "I'm glad he found you," she whispered.

The streets were quiet as the pair walked hand in hand back to her apartment block. Anaïse's mind was replaying the events of the evening and the family's easy acceptance of her.

Amato squeezed her hand.

She smiled. "Sorry, I'm miles away."

Amato's face was serious. "How can you be so alone in this world when you are so complete, so beautiful, a part of something so incredibly infinite?" he asked.

With anyone else, Anaïse would have been taken aback by such a deep question, but Anaïse had learned this was Amato's way. Deep currents ran through his mind and often emerged without notice.

"If I'm alone, I don't have to justify myself to anyone," Anaïse replied, "even to me. It's easier that way."

Amato considered her reply. "But I know who you are, who you really are, and anyone who knows the true you will never ask you to justify your thoughts and feelings." He scrunched up his face in thought. "I have always known who you are, and each moment I share with you, the universe confirms it. There is something so beautiful inside you, but you keep it locked from the world and yourself through fear."

Anaïse was lost for words. It was the most insightful thing anyone had ever said to her. It hit her so hard, she didn't know how to respond.

Amato gave a wistful smile. "There is something incredible in you, Anaïse, and I'm only sad because you choose not to see it, embrace it, celebrate it. Why are you so afraid to see the reflection of the most divine, gorgeous part of you? You read all these incredible books about spiritual journeys of others, but you're unable to find peace with your own journey. Why?"

Something was bubbling up from deep inside her. She didn't know whether to laugh or cry at his words and his sad, serious eyes. "Maybe it's because I'm looking for someone to help me find it and unlock it, and give me the strength to process it," she said.

Amato shook his head. "I can't do that. It's a journey you need to take yourself. You can't 'process' it. You can't overthink it. You have to believe in it and let it guide you."

Anaïse raised her eyebrows. "You want me to leap with both feet into the unknown and embrace it without knowing what it is?" she demanded. "Who would be stupid enough to do that without preparing or evaluating it first?'

"Rabia of Basra did. And you know all about her journey, no?"

"Yes, but ...'

They had reached the door to her apartment building. Amato leaned in close and kissed her lightly on the check. "You'll figure it out. See you tomorrow?"

In stunned silence, Anaïse watched him walk away. As he reached the corner, he turned back, saw her still watching him and gave a little wave. Then he was gone.

As Anaïse made her way to her room, her head was spinning. Not only had he kissed her for the first time — albeit a very chaste kiss — but he had also challenged her in a way she was not used to, and she didn't have a response.

Anaïse threw her coat on the bed and stepped out onto the balcony. She needed some fresh air. Gradually, she collected her thoughts. She knew in her heart he was right — this was exactly what drew her to such books — but she had made such a mess of her previous relationships, it would require a lifetime to trust herself to undertake such a journey. As she gazed down at the traffic rushing past, she knew exactly what she wanted to do. She grabbed her phone and quickly dialled.

"Anaïse, my love, what a lovely surprise. How is Milan?"

"Milan is wonderful, Papa," she replied with a grin.

"Wonderful? That's not a word I hear you use very often."

"You know me too well."

Her father said nothing. It felt as if he was giving her space to talk.

"I've met someone," she blurted out.

"Someone wonderful, I'm guessing?"

Anaïse's laugh conveyed more than she could with words. "Of course."

"Are you wearing your watch?"

She looked at her wrist. The watch's elegant design and precision mechanism, the result of years of careful refinement, were reminiscent of her father. "Always."

"Have you finally fallen to earth like the seed of the Blue Rose and received the garden's warm embrace? My wish for you is that the rain helps create something truly beautiful."

Anaïse gently reversed the watch face and ran her thumb over the picture. "Thank you, Papa."

"But never forget, into each life some rain must fall; some days must be dark and dreary."

"Longfellow?"

"That's my daughter."

"Goodnight, Papa."

"Goodnight, my dear Anaïse."

CHAPTER 5

"Where are we going?"

"Somewhere special," teased Amato as he led her down a narrow tree-lined street, its pavements cluttered with motorbikes and scooters. "Here we are."

They descended a short flight of worn stone steps. "Welcome to the Naviglio Grande," Amato announced.

A wide canal sparkled before them, hundreds of lights from each side reflecting on the water and shimmering on the surrounding buildings.

"Beautiful, no?" Amato started to lead her along the canal, but Anaïse hesitated, squeezing his hand. He turned to her with a concerned look. "Are you all right?"

She gave a nervous smile. "I'm scared of water," she said. "I almost drowned in Lac de Joux when I was a kid. I've avoided open water ever since."

"I didn't imagine you to be afraid of something like that?"

Anaïse laughed. "Maybe not. But deep water makes me nervous."

"We can go somewhere else if you'd prefer?" he said with knitted brows.

Anaïse gave his hand another squeeze. "It's all right. As long as you're with me, I'll be fine."

"You're sure?"

Anaïse smiled and nodded. "Certain."

It was a short walk to the restaurant. As long as Amato walked closest to the water, and provided she didn't look into its murky depths and focused on the lights and the people, she was fine.

When they reached the restaurant, Amato secured them a table set back from the water's edge. Anaïse sat gazing at the water.

"You're unusually quiet tonight," Amato said. "Are you sure you wouldn't rather go somewhere else? It's not too late to cancel our order."

Anaïse stared at the dark water a moment longer, then looked at Amato with a piercing gaze. "There's something I have to tell you."

Amato watched her as she bit her lip, her mind flipflopping between her need for total honesty and the desire to avoid endangering their relationship. But she knew which side of her would win. The outcome was already decided. It was just a case of how to begin.

She reached across the table and took Amato's hand. "Before you fall in love with me," she said, "there's something you should know." Was she really about to reveal her deepest, darkest secret, the one she had kept hidden for so long? She gave a deep sigh. If she and Amato were to have a chance of a long-term relationship, she would have to tell him.

"Around ten years ago," she began, "on the day I left home for university, I visited my Uncle Ralph, my father's brother. I had never had any kind of relationship with him. He and my father never spoke, and as I grew up, I discovered why. The local rumour was that Ralph had raped my mother, and I was the result."

"And you went to confront him and discover the truth?"

Anaïse nodded. "It didn't go as planned. When I asked him, he laughed in my face then tried to grab me. I fought back, we both fell, and I remembered no more. But when I came to, he was dead; whether from me hitting him or from the fall, I have no idea."

Amato stared at her, his mouth open. "What did the police say?" he said finally.

"I guess they thought it was an accident — which it was. If they suspected foul play, they would have contacted me," she added hurriedly. "But it still haunts me. Did I kill him? I'll never know." She shrugged. "Was he my father? Again, I'll never know." Anaïse sighed. Something about the deep water flowing relentlessly past them had unlocked a door deep inside her. "I'd been living a double life for so long, then I met you," she told him. "You're a wonderful man who lives in a world parallel to mine. I want so much to jump into your world, but I can't allow myself to do so with this secret lurking in my heart."

She paused as the waiter arrived with their food.

They exchanged a conspiratorial look as the waiter set two plates of saltimbocca on the table, wished them "buon appetito" and made his exit.

As soon as he was out of earshot, Anaïse resumed. "I need you know who I really am," she said, "and for the first time, I want someone to want me, the real me, not the polished image I project." She sighed. "There has always been a darkness hiding inside me, a darkness that ruined everything before it had a chance to be born." She sipped her wine and glanced up at Amato. "Then I met you. You make me feel safe. You give me space. You take me to places in my heart I never knew existed. You see in me the things I didn't want to see, that I've been hiding, and that makes me want to look behind the doors I locked tight all those years ago." Anaïse paused. "Does that make sense? You're a mystery to me; I don't understand you, but I want so much for you to understand how I feel, and the only way is for you to understand my past."

Amato nodded slowly. "It's a terrible burden to carry through life alone," he said.

"I was afraid you would run away when I told you," admitted Anaïse.

"It did cross my mind," Amato teased, "but I've already entrusted you with my heart, so I think I can trust you a little further." He fixed Anaïse with an intense look. "I suspect there is far more to this story than you have told me. Why don't you take a bite of your dinner, then tell me a little more about what it was like growing up with those rumours swirling around you?"

Anaïse smiled, intense relief washing over her. Something she had been dreading, that had tied her stomach into knots for the past few days, had been turned into something comfortable, almost every day, by Amato, with his smile and his understanding. As they ate their dinner, she told him of growing up in Le Sentier, the constant whispers, taunts and rumours, and finally of the fatal confrontation with her uncle.

Anaïse pushed away her empty plate and dabbed at the corners of her mouth with her napkin.

"How did you feel after your uncle's death?" asked Amato as she finished her story.

How typical of Amato, not asking for the gory details but wondering instead how she felt. "Scared and empty," she said. "Of all the men I wished could have been my biological father, he was the last one I would have ever wanted."

"And you've been scared and empty ever since?"

"I guess …"

Amato's eyes bored into her with passion and intensity. "He was not your father. A father's love for his family defines his existence. He puts their needs first and always strives to become a better man so that, one day, his children become better than him. Was the man who raised you like this?"

Anaïse stared at Amato, overcome with emotion. As his words washed over her, everything her father did with her, everything he did for her, everything he said to her was bathed in a different light.

She glanced at her watch. The emotive image on the back appeared in her mind. It was a message from her father she had not previously understood. *Was the man who raised you like this?*

"Yes," she croaked, the word burning in her throat and landing heavily in her heart.

Amato smiled. "Then this man was your father."

"And my uncle's death?"

"An unfortunate accident, self-defence, a life ending in the same manner it was lived. You need to find your peace with that."

A tear escaped and ran down her cheek. Amato finally understood her darkness.

"You said before I fall in love with you, I should know something," he said. "Well, now I now know it, and it's too late … I'm already there. I'm deeply in love with you."

They stared at each other for a long time, each in shock at their revelations. Amato smiled compassionately, and a wave of safety washed over Anaïse. It was going to be all right.

As Anaïse lay in bed that night, she felt a calm that had previously eluded her. Amato knew the secret that led her on the dark path of her vocation, and he still loved her. For the first time in her life, she felt accepted, albeit still living two parallel lives: the one she had carefully crafted and embellished for the world, and the one she had kept in the dark, in the closet — her inner dark wolf.

***

That same night, Amato also struggled to sleep. All his life he had had a relationship with the dark and the light. He understood his journey on earth was finite, and that sooner rather than later, he would be called. As he started to drift to sleep, in that moment of lucid dreaming before sleep overpowered him, Amato felt cold. He shivered and tried to sit up, but there was a crushing weight on his chest.

He blinked his eyes open to see a figure of beauty and terror hovering over him — the Angel of Death. Its cold, soulless eyes bored into him, and its icy breath caressed his face like a chilling frost. "It's time for you to put your affairs in order," it said.

Bile rose in Amato's throat, and he tossed his head from side to side. "No, no, not yet," he gasped as the cold air enveloped him.

"It is not for you to decide," said the Angel.

Amato tried to sit up again but was frozen in place. He forced open his clenched jaw. "But Anaïse. She needs me," he protested, his voice no more than a whisper.

The Angel's eyes bored into him, like chips of blue ice. "The longer you stay, the greater her pain will be when you have to leave," it said.

The cold was increasing, flowing through Amato's veins and creeping up his spine towards his brain. "But I love her!" he protested.

The Angel leaned forward with a look of deep disdain. "You say that..."

"I do! Truly, deeply!" argued Amato.

"If you truly love her," the Angel said, "you will know there is a time to hold someone tight, and a time to let someone go." The Angel loomed over him, a long icy spear in its hand. "Your time to let go has come." It drove the spear into his heart.

Amato screamed as the spear pierced his chest and the cold overcame him. This was it; he was going to die. But even as the thought ran through his mind, as the cold trickled through his veins, the Angel of Death began to fade. Within seconds, all that remained was the memory of its icy breath lingering in the air and an aching in Amato's chest.

Amato sat up with a start and looked around the darkened room. He was alone but still chilled to the bone, the deathly presence hanging in the air.

He shivered. The dream felt as real as life itself.

Amato reached for the glass of water on his bedside cabinet, his hand shaking and the Angel's words haunting him. He wanted to ignore them, or at least fight back, or rail against them. Was the Angel right? If he remained in Anaïse's life, would he prevent her from completing her journey?

Part of him wanted to dismiss the whole thing, write it off as a nightmare — a horrifically realistic one, for sure. He should simply dismiss it as his brain freewheeling while he slept.

But the other part of him found the message harder to dismiss. Was it true? Could Amato only take Anaïse so far? Would he have to let her go so she could follow her path? If that were true, then only once that happened would she be able to live one life, not two; only then would she have the opportunity to understand the journey of those whom she read about, the mystics and poets such as Rabia of Basra whose works she was irresistibly drawn to.

Amato searched deep within his soul, which had always guided him. The Angel was right. It had delivered a message that Amato already knew. If he remained in her life, Anaïse would never need to search within herself, never be tested, never fail, never grow. What the Angel of Death was offering was not just an ending for Amato but a beginning for Anaïse.

Amato lay back and closed his eyes. He choked back a raw wail of emotion as the tears began to flow, running down his cheeks and soaking into his pillow.

CHAPTER 6

Anaïse perched on a stool in the bookshop, leafing through a volume of poetry as Amato catalogued a new shipment of books. "It seems like a long time ago when I first walked in here to pick up my book," she said.

"Can I tell you something?" he asked. "When I received the order to reserve the book, I was immediately intrigued by the buyer. Only someone on a journey of self-discovery would be interested in such a profound work. That day you walked into the bookstore, I knew with every fibre of my being it was you."

Anaïse smiled at him.

His face turned serious. "I don't know what I'm supposed to be in your life, but I do know that, whatever is asked of me, I will do it, knowing in my heart it is right. I know one day you will find peace in accepting yourself, and you'll trust in love to support you when you let go of all that holds you back and allow yourself to fall."

"I felt something special between us the day we first met," she said quietly, "but you were so cool and aloof, I thought you hadn't even noticed me. You played it very cool. I thought Italian men were supposed to be—"

"More impulsive?"

"Exactly."

Amato laughed. "I could blame the Austrian in me, but the truth is I trust in the journey and know the journey will be my guide. If you had not come back, you would not have been the one. But you did, and love has subsequently confirmed what every pore of my body felt that day."

He stood up, stepped behind Anaïse and wrapped his arms around her. "I have no idea why I'm in your life, but I know it will change us both in a beautiful way."

***

As day turned to evening, Amato was still sorting through the new batch of books. He told Anaïse he found it a meditative process. Not only did he have to check their condition and catalogue them, he also loved to see how they were bound, how they felt, even how they smelt.

Anaïse stood, stretched and wandered to the window. Outside, people were scuttling past under their umbrellas. The street was slick with rain, and the car lights reflected on the oily tarmac, creating rainbows in the puddles. "Are you almost finished?"

Amato was studying a vintage volume, his mind lost in the book. "Hmm?"

She wandered over and perched on the edge of his desk. "Are you almost done?"

Amato looked at the box next to him. "A couple more hours, at least."

She pecked him on the cheek. "Then I shall see you tomorrow."

"Tomorrow, my love."

***

It was dark and the street was quiet by the time Amato had finished his task. He yawned as he locked the shop, his mind still on the book delivery, and turned to cross the street without waiting for the lights to change.

As he stepped into the road, he was distracted by a voice, as though someone were calling out to him. He turned towards the voice, and there was a screech of tyres. Rather than looking towards the oncoming car, Amato turned his gaze skyward as the car sent his body sprawling across the wet road.

CHAPTER 7

The soft bleep of the monitors soothed Anaïse, tempting her to sleep, but she forced her eyes open and looked at Amato's gentle face, his head still swathed in bandages a week after the accident.

He lay very still. He hadn't moved since he was brought in, lying in a deep coma from which he may never awaken, according to the doctors. There was damage to the diffuse bilateral cerebral hemisphere cortex, apparently, rendering his future unpredictable. Sometimes people wake up, they had added, but often they don't.

So, Anaïse sat and waited. Amato's family were a constant presence during the day, reassuring and loving. Anaïse had offered to take the night shift, enjoying the quiet that settled over the hospital, and welcoming the chance to continue her conversation with Amato, to keep talking to him. Could he hear her? Would it help his recovery? Even the doctors couldn't say, but there was certainly no harm in it, they'd said with a shrug.

Anaïse passed the nights telling Amato of her hopes and dreams, recalling the places they had been together, those they had yet to visit, tales of her childhood. She mused about whatever was in the news, things she had heard and seen, filling the quiet night with the same conversations they had shared before his accident.

Anaïse found she had little need of sleep. Each night she would stay awake up to four or five o'clock, then sleep briefly in a chair by Amato's bed until the nurses began their rounds at seven and Amato's family appeared for the day.

Around eleven she would head back to her apartment for a shower, a change of clothes and a quick nap, but would always be back at one for the doctor's rounds. She was desperate for any update, any news, anything that signalled a change for the better.

Amato's sister, Diana, was the one who kept them all going. Full of boundless energy, she always had a story to tell, a smile to share, a favourite song of Amato's to sing to him. Diana had a way of hiding her pain by turning what would have been a sombre, depressing affair into a joyful vigil that celebrated Amato's life, even as his days seemed to be ticking away.

Anaïse recalled the conversation they'd had in Amato's mother's kitchen.

"I have always thought of life as a series of challenges," Diana had said. "Life throws things at us, tries to knock us off course and defeat us, and we must find a way to make the best of the situation."

"Even when something really bad happens? Like death?" Anaïse had asked.

"Especially when something terrible happens," Diana had replied. "That's when we show our true colours."

There were times when Anaïse caught a glimpse of her pain when Diana glanced at her brother. Then she could see how much it took for her to remain positive and not give in to grief, but she never wavered, never allowed the façade to crack. Inspired by Diana's example, Anaïse did her best to be positive to ease the family's burden, rather than add to it.

***

Less than a ten per cent chance of waking up, that's what the doctor had said at the end of the first week. With each day that passed, the chances of a revival grew less and less, and the darkness in Anaïse's soul grew and grew, like a tumour insidiously working its way into her brain. The doctor's words were still echoing in Anaïse's brain one morning as Diana bustled into the room and began distributing coffees to everyone. How could she remain so positive? Anaïse longed to hide beneath the covers and surrender to grief, but Diana's example kept her showing up each day, a smile masking the cracks.

"Mamma, you remember when I first introduced Amato to coffee?" Diana said as she handed a coffee to Anaïse.

Her mother smiled. "You told him that to be a real Italian, he had to drink coffee."

"It's true," laughed Diana.

"But you didn't have to give him an espresso for his first time!" teased Mamma. "He tried so hard to like it, screwing up his face with each tiny sip. It took him half an hour to finish it."

Diana smiled. "I guess that's why he still drinks cappuccinos."

Anaïse sipped her coffee. She was desperate to remain positive for Amato, for Diana, for the family. "What was he like as a little boy?"

"He was very serious about everything," Diana said.

"Which is why you teased him so much," Mamma retorted.

Diana gave a guilty smile. "It was just too easy." She leaned forward. "You won't be surprised to hear he always had his nose in a book. When school ended, he would race home, ignore all the other boys playing football and head straight for whichever book he was in the middle of. As soon as he set foot in the house, there would be a trail of things abandoned on his way to his room — his school bag, his blazer, his shoes, which I would have to pick up.

"One day, I decided to play a trick on him. He was terrified of insects, so I caught a giant stag beetle in the park and put it in a matchbox on top of his book. When he saw the matchbox, he was curious and opened it. I heard his scream from the living room. He came racing out and jumped onto the couch!"

Anaïse joined in the laughter, despite her pain. If Diana could work so hard to keep everyone's spirits up, Anaïse was not going to let her down. "What happened then?"

"He demanded I catch it and put it outside. I said I would, as long as he promised to never leave his stuff lying around. If he ever did it again, I'd let loose a hundred beetles in his room."

"And did he promise?" asked Anaïse.

"He did. And he was as good as his word."

Anaïse smiled as she looked at Amato. He was lying peacefully, surrounded by his family, kept alive by the tubes and wires that snaked back and forth across him. Did he know they were there? Could he feel the love, the sheer willpower of everyone there, willing him to wake up, rejoin them? Amato had told Anaïse that love was the strongest force in the universe; it bound everything together, made life worth living. Did he feel it now, that ineffable, all-powerful force washing over him, day and night?

***

By the end of the second week, Anaïse could see that the early optimism was beginning to fade. The doctors were no longer talking about when Amato might wake up. Their visits were no more than a perfunctory check on his vital signs, while the family talked less, laughed less and more often sat in silence, each alone with their thoughts.

Yet through it all, Anaïse never lost hope, never ceased her night-time vigils. As she learned more about Amato from his family, she felt she knew him better since he had slipped into a coma than she had before. And as her knowledge of him grew, so did her trust in him, her love for him. For the first time in her life, she felt safe enough release the mechanisms that kept her sane but captive, and to reveal details about her life that she had never disclosed to anyone. And yet, as close and trusting as she felt, there was one subject she was not able to share, one area of her life she did not reveal to Amato. Her profession was a secret she feared she could never confess.

***

As the weeks passed, Anaïse began to change her schedule. She still spent her nights with Amato, but her days were spent retracing their steps, revisiting places they had shared, in an attempt to sharpen fading memories. This was partly driven by a desire to still be with him but she also recognised that she was preparing herself for life without him. Restaurants, cafés, galleries, parks, were all retraced during her restless days. At night, she sat by his bed, telling him about what she had done that day and recalling their visit to each location.

One night, Anaïse sank back into the chair with a deep sigh. What was she doing? Was she fooling herself? Was she helping him? It was past three in the morning, and her eyelids were growing heavy. A wave of panic washed over her. She scanned his face for any sign of change, any sign he was still alive inside his motionless body, but nothing ever changed. He always had the same calm, serene expression, the same steady heart rate and blood pressure. As she looked at him, a well of suppressed emotion rose within her, and the tears she had held back for so long started to flow uncontrollably. She stood up and leaned over him.

"Wake up, damn you!" she shouted. "This has gone on too long! Wake up!"

She wrapped her arms around his neck and held him tight, her tears flowing across his face. "Please, Amato, wake up. I can't do this much longer …"

CHAPTER 8

Anaïse stood at the top of the short flight of steps and stared at the dark waters of the canal. This was the one place they had visited that she had not yet returned to. She had only been able to go there at all thanks to Amato's steady, loving presence. He made her feel safe, but right now he wasn't there, and she felt anything but safe as her faltering footsteps took her to the canal's edge.

Her gaze was drawn irresistibly to the slow-moving water. How deep was it? Certainly deep enough to drown, especially for as poor a swimmer as Anaïse.

The sight of it brought back memories of Lac de Joux, her foot cramping up, and the waters drawing her into their cold embrace. She had managed to fight it then and had struggled back to the shore to flop on the rocks like a dying fish, but she wasn't sure she could fight it now if it came to it.

The sharp ringing of her phone startled her. Her legs felt weak and she stepped back from the edge. She tottered away from the water as she pulled her phone out of her pocket. It was Diana.

Anaïse immediately feared the worst. "Diana?"

"Hurry! Amato is awake, and he's asking for you!"

***

Anaïse couldn't remember getting to the hospital, only flying down the corridor to Amato's room, her running feet echoing down the hallway. Diana was waiting in the doorway to his room and ushered her in.

As Anaïse hurried in, the family cleared a path for her.

Amato was sitting up in bed, sipping a glass of water. As soon as he saw her, he set the glass on the nightstand and held out his arms. His warm embrace immediately soothed her, a feeling of utter peace enveloping her as the tears began to flow.

***

After four more weeks of intensive care and monitored recovery at his mother's house, Amato was finally deemed strong enough to be released to his own home. His whole family was crammed into his apartment to welcome him home. Anaïse felt as though she were at the centre of a whirling storm as cousins and uncles and aunties popped in and out, all bringing food. They all wanted to see and kiss Amato, and embrace Anaïse, without whose constant presence, they assured her, this miracle would not have occurred.

"You're like a celebrity," Diana teased during a quiet moment. "Saint Anaïse!"

Anaïse laughed as she felt Amato's eyes on her from across the room. She turned and caught him gazing at her before another new arrival descended on him with kisses and good wishes. She knew what he wanted.

Anaïse glanced at her watch. It was just past nine o'clock. She thought, not for the first time, about the Phoenix and the Blue Rose.

Diana noticed her time check and clapped her hands. "We're all delighted to have our beloved Amato home safe and well," she announced. "But we mustn't wear him out on his first day home."

With expressions of love and a few grumbles, Amato's friends and family gathered their things and made their way out. Within twenty minutes, Amato, Anaïse and Diana were the only ones left.

Diana emerged from the tiny kitchen, a dishcloth in her hands. "All tidy," she announced.

Anaïse was sitting by Amato's chair, holding his hand and talking softy.

Diana smiled. "I'll leave you two alone. See you tomorrow for dinner?"

Amato nodded. "That sounds wonderful."

"Buona notte." Diana kissed them both, gave Anaïse an extra hug and a whispered "thank you" and skipped out.

As the door closed, Amato let out a deep sigh. "Finally, some peace and quiet."

Anaïse gazed at him. How was it possible she had fallen even more deeply in love with him while he was in a coma? Day after day, she had sat by his bed, trying in vain to come to terms with a life without him, only to realise how little prepared she was to be alone again. It almost felt as though she brought him back to life by sheer force of will.

"I knew you were there the whole time," he said.

Anaïse bit back a sob. "I thought I'd lost you."

Amato's soft smile embraced her. "Not yet."

Amato stood slowly, took her hand and led her into the bedroom. The intensity of the moment burst inside Anaïse, a wordless sign that let her know he wanted to spend the rest of his life with her, discovering the world together.

CHAPTER 9

Amato awoke early. The sun peeking through a crack in the curtains shone in his eyes. He kissed Anaïse on the shoulder as she slept and inhaled the warm scent of her hair, then climbed from the bed, hungry and restless to begin the new day.

He was still feeling weak, but after so long in hospital and at his mother's house, he was eager to get back to normal, everyday life. He pulled on some clothes, taking care not to wake Anaïse, then wrote her a brief note before scooping up his keys and heading out the door.

Emilio's coffee shop was busy, mostly with people grabbing pastries and coffees before dashing off to work.

"Hey, Amato, we haven't seen you in a while," Emilio said as Amato strolled in. Emilio had run the coffee shop for years and knew all his regulars.

Amato ordered some coffee and cakes. "Yeah, I've been away for a few weeks," he said.

"Then welcome back, my friend," said Emilio as he carefully lifted the cakes into a box. He set the box on the counter. "Coffees coming right up."

"Thank you." Amato turned and looked around the café. He frowned as everything shone brighter, the light reflecting off the tables and chairs, off the window, brighter and brighter and brighter...

***

Anaïse woke from a troubling dream in which she was back in the lake, struggling to stay afloat, striking frantically for the shore but not getting anywhere.

A siren had woken her. She sat up and stretched. "Sounds like an ambulance or something," she said. Her gaze drifted to the bedside. A note was propped against the light, her name written across the front in Amato's flowing handwriting.

She picked up the note and smiled as she read it.

Buongiorno, beautiful Anaïse. I've gone to get some cakes and coffee – cap-a-ccino – keep the bed warm for me.

As Anaïse set the note back on the nightstand, a frown crossed her face. The sirens seemed to be right outside their window. A surge of panic rose within her; she jumped to her feet, threw back the curtains and looked into the street below. Paramedics were rolling a gurney out of the coffee shop and into the ambulance. Amato's curly hair was clearly visible.

"No!"

Anaïse grabbed the first clothes she could find, stumbled down the stairs and reached the street just as the paramedics were closing the ambulance doors. In her broken Italian, she explained she was Amato's girlfriend, and they let her climb inside and sit beside Amato as the ambulance pulled away, sirens blaring.

The paramedics worked frantically on Amato. They spoke so fast, Anaïse couldn't understand what they were saying.

"Please, please," she asked. "Is he all right?"

Amato lay very still, with only the ventilator attached to his face showing any sign of movement.

The paramedics exchanged a glance and sat up. One of them wiped his brow on the sleeve of his orange jacket. "You say he was recently in a coma?"

"Yes. From a car accident."

"He had a brain haemorrhage?"

Anaïse nodded and bit her lip. She didn't trust herself to speak without crying.

"I think he's had another." The paramedic glanced at Amato. "We tried to resuscitate him before we left the café, but he's non-responsive."

Anaïse glanced back and forth between them. "What does that mean? Will he be all right?"

The second paramedic shook his head. "We've done everything we can." He reached across and lifted the mask from Amato's face. "I'm sorry, but he's gone."

CHAPTER 10

How do you go from everything to nothing? How does life continue when, with every breath, you wish it were you who were dead?

The weather mirrored Anaïse's dark mood. A cold wind whipped around the mourners' legs as they stood at the graveside listening to the priest, squally showers darkening the earth and soaking their heads and shoulders.

Anaïse stood silently while Amato's family hugged her and offered their condolences, but resisted speaking in case the bile and anger brewing inside her should spill out. Even Diana was unable to reach her.

***

Following the funeral, Anaïse rapidly spiralled downwards, lost in a numb miasma of pain and grief. She couldn't eat or even get out of bed for days on end. Her new life was over, ended almost as soon as it had begun, and the one person who could help her was gone forever. Anaïse felt broken, and with Amato gone, there was no one to put her back together. Unable to face her new reality, she lost herself in a torrent of drugs and alcohol, emerging from one daze only to quickly disappear into another.

Days turned into weeks as she lay on her bed with the television blaring, sipping from a bottle of vodka, oblivious to her surroundings. A gentle knock at the door failed to rouse her attention. It was only when it turned into insistent pounding that Anaïse dragged herself from the bed and opened the door. "Diana?"

"Mourning is over," Diana announced as she marched into the room. She looked at the unmade bed, the clothes on the floor, the empty bottles on the coffee table. She strode to the window and threw the curtains back. The bright sun flooded the room.

Anaïse covered her eyes, blinking rapidly. "Why are you here?"

"I miss you," said Diana. "It's bad enough losing one person you love, without losing another." She began picking up the empty bottles and putting them in the bin.

Anaïse watched her. She had tried so hard to be numb, to shut everything out, and now here was Diana, breaking through her carefully constructed carapace.

"Talk to me." Diana sat on the couch and signalled for Anaïse to join her. "Tell me what you're thinking."

Anaïse moved slowly across the room and sat beside her but couldn't meet her gaze.

"We're all hurting, Anaïse," Diana said, "but when you lock yourself away, you hurt not just yourself, but others too. Mamma misses you. I miss you."

Anaïse opened her mouth to speak, but all that came out was a raw sob, rising from deep inside her belly.

Diana wrapped a protective arm around her shoulder. "Let it out."

For several minutes, all Anaïse could do was cry. Finally she found her voice. "Nothing tastes right. I can't walk, every breath burns, everything aches. I just want things to go back to how they were before," she said pitifully.

Diana stroked her hair. "We're all broken. We're all lost in the dark looking for something to ease the pain. But never forget Amato fell in love with you just as you were. If you want to honour that love, why become a different person? Why hide yourself, your loving nature, in a bottle? Fight to remain the beautiful person he loved and cherished."

Anaïse's sobs slowed and she felt calmer, less raw.

"Whether or not you acknowledge her existence, that person is still in there," continued Diana. "Accept it, embrace it, give yourself to it and lose yourself to it."

"I can't," sobbed Anaïse. "If I face reality, I'll have nothing. I'll go mad. I need to maintain control to stay sane."

"You call this control?" challenged Diana, taking in the dishevelled apartment with a sweep of her hand. "You call this staying sane? Amato showed you your true beauty and how accepting it without fear would complete you. Do you want to throw that away and go back to who you were?"

Anaïse rubbed her eyes and tried to calm her breathing. "He completed me," she said. "Don't you understand? Now he's gone, and I'm empty. I don't have him to give myself to, to be a part of. I can't go back, and I can't move forward. I have no function, no purpose. The pain where his voice once lived is ripping me apart." As she scrubbed the tears from her face, an image of Amato sprung into her mind. "I can't even drink coffee without thinking about him. Nothing has any taste. The sun that once kissed my skin is irritating, the sound of laughter and happiness unbearable. Just as I finally found someone who embraced my darkest self and celebrated me, he is gone, leaving me numb from exhaustion and confusion."

"He was not here to replace one addiction with another," Diana said softly.

"Then why was he here?"

Diana leaned forward and took her hand. "Who really knows? Like I said, life throws challenges at us, and we have to find a way to make the best of them. Amato showed you a possible path to love, acceptance and peace. He helped you understand life's beauty is not in perfections or imperfections, but believing in the moments needed to reveal your beauty, to strengthen your connection with all that is divine in the universe."

"And now that he's gone?"

"You have to find a way to maintain that connection and not give in to the darkness."

"How can you be so positive?" asked Anaïse.

"You think it's easy?" snapped Diana. "Mamma is devastated. The whole family is in shock, but we can't simply give up. Life goes on. Good and bad, beautiful and ugly, sacred and profane. All we can do is try to learn and grow from each experience."

Anaïse's eyes were once more drawn to her watch, to the story of the Phoenix, and she gently caressed the face's outline. Diana squeezed her hand and she looked up.

"Amato is gone," Diana said gently. "There's nothing we can do to change that. All we can do is break free from the darkness and despair, step out of the prison and never look back." She gave a bitter smile. "I know it's not easy, but I would find it a lot easier if we did it together."

As Diana squeezed her hand again, Anaïse's tears returned, but this time they were tears of relief. She patted Diana's hand and nodded. "Together."

CHAPTER 11

Was Diana right? Was it time to accept what had happened and move on? Diana's words had sounded so reasonable, so logical at the time, but after she left, as day passed into evening, the warmth of her visit began to fade, and the darkness crept back in. Without Amato, she was nothing; life was nothing.

As Anaïse sat alone in the dark, she knew what she must do. But did she have the courage? She forced herself out of her chair, slipped on some shoes and a jacket, and headed into the dark streets.

She didn't need to think about where she was going; she simply let her feet carry her relentlessly onward until she stood looking into the murky depths of the canal. It was late, the restaurants and bars had closed and the walkers and lovers had gone home. The water swirled and rolled beneath her feet, calling her, tempting her. With her limited swimming skills, she would soon drown, quickly slip beneath the surface into sweet oblivion, all her pain and turmoil gone as she joined her beloved in the forever.

"Hey, baby."

Before Anaïse could turn and see who had spoken, strong arms grabbed her and a stubbled face was thrust against her neck, the smell of alcohol washing across her.

She struggled but was held tight.

His hands began to grope her, his body pressed against her as he leaned in to roughly kiss and lick her neck.

Anaïse was still struggling as the attacker began to pull up her skirt. Although shocked and exhausted, she fought to find the willpower or the energy to resist.

She could feel him getting excited as one hand gripped her throat, his breathing getting more laboured as he fumbled to force himself on her. An image of her uncle flashed across her mind — the way he had held her, the things he had said.

Were they true? Had her mother wanted her uncle to seduce her? Had Anaïse invited this on herself? Anaïse didn't believe it of her mother, wouldn't believe it of herself, and as she thought about it, a sense of rage filled her, and she struggled hard. Her attacker tightened his grip, but she knew what she had to do. She leaned her weight against him then stepped forward — one, two stumbling steps, then over into the water.

Anaïse gasped as the cold water hit her. As she sank beneath the dark surface, she knew she had to live. Live for herself and everything that mattered to her.

Spluttering and flailing, Anaïse surfaced, her attacker beside her.

"You bitch!" he snarled, reaching for her hair.

Anaïse instinctively grabbed his arm and spun him around, forcing him into an arm lock with his head beneath the water's surface.

All her training came to bear as she held him under, using his buoyancy to keep herself afloat. He wriggled and squirmed beneath her firm hold. No matter how hard he fought, she maintained her grip.

As his struggles began to weaken, Amato's voice came to her: "How can you be so alone in this world when you are so complete, so beautiful, a part of something so incredibly infinite?"

With her training and skills, she could easily kill her assailant and no one would know; it would look like a simple drowning. But she could no longer exist in that self-made cage in which Amato had a created a door for her.

She held her attacker until she felt the fight leave his exhausted body, then released him and kicked him away. He came up gasping and swam clumsily across the canal, away from Anaïse.

She splashed to the side of the canal, climbed out and flopped onto her back on the cold stone. The stars were twinkling through the city haze.

"Are you OK?" Several people had gathered round her, looking anxious. "Should we call the police? Or an ambulance?"

Anaïse sat up and brushed her wet hair from her face. "I'm fine, thank you. I was looking at the stars. I missed my step and fell in."

They looked at her dubiously as she jumped to her feet and shook the water from her clothes. "Thank you for your concern, goodnight."

***

Anaïse sat alone at the far end of a small bar, nursing a glass of sambuca. Somehow, in the midst of being attacked, falling in the water and almost drowning, she had found enlightenment.

Death wasn't the answer. She had tried to fill the emptiness in her life with books that wouldn't put her on the spiritual path, hollow sex incapable of teaching her love, and substances that didn't numb the pain. She had looked for quick answers to life's questions by looking from the outside in, instead of having faith and jumping in with both feet to experience them at first hand.

Life was the answer. Life lived to the full in the joyous spirit Amato had taught her. She glanced at her watch and flipped the face. Once she had thought the sun was her father, the earth her mother and she the rose. Now, the beautifully lacquered illustration represented Amato, her and their love.

She rolled her glass in her hands as she pictured Amato talking to her. Sometimes the truth might feel cold and gloomy, he would say, sometimes hot, other times stormy, but the soul is like a muscle, as is life. For it to develop, it needs to be tested. The journeyman on the spiritual path — and Anaïse was most certainly a journeyman right now — can expect to be tested more than most, not only to assess the strength of her conviction but also to forge the impurities in her character.

She recalled a quote from the Quran that Amato had told her: "Do people think that they will be left to say, 'We believe,' and that they will not be tested?"

Her musings were interrupted by the buzzing of her phone — her work phone. She looked around the bar to check no one was looking at her, but everyone seemed lost in their thoughts.

Anaïse pulled out her phone and looked at the screen. The message was as brief and cryptic as always:

Frankfurt

April 18–20

$35,000

Y/N?

Anaïse stared at the phone for a long time. Amidst everything else, the one thing she had not thought about was her work and how it fitted into any kind of life with Amato. Now he was gone, and work was tugging at her sleeve. Her "little jobs', as she called them, gave her a good life. If she stopped, what else would she do? Apart from a few summer gigs while she was at university, she'd never had a proper job. Explaining her lack of work experience would be tricky, to say the least, but she could hardly put "Contract Killer" on her resume.

As she stared at her phone, Amato's voice came to her again: "Do people think that they will be let go merely by saying: 'We believe,' and that they will not be tested?"

Her mind turned to her father. He had always loved her, always tried to show her his love in his own way. In her need for adoration, she hadn't loved him back, but instead had tried to impress him, which only served to push her further from him. Now she realised he had never needed to be impressed by her, he had just wanted to love and protect her from her darker self. Anaïse had been unable to see that or allow him to do that, so they had grown further and further apart since she had left Le Sentier.

A void opened up inside her as she thought about how many years she had wasted by not understanding her father, not understanding herself. But as the realisation washed over her, she felt relief, as if a great weight had been lifted. Her mind turned again to the story of the Phoenix, consumed in the fire then reborn, and, for the first time, Anaïse understood the concept of catharsis. She had been through the flames and emerged alive and intact on the other side. She knew what she should do.

Anaïse downed her drink in one gulp, set twenty euros on the bar, then stepped outside onto the quiet street, her phone still in her hand. She looked up and down the road. No one was watching. In one decisive movement, she dropped her phone onto the pavement, crushed it beneath the heel of her black leather boot and kicked the remains into a drain.

Anaïse looked at the heavens, inhaling new life. It was time to go home.

***

The familiar ticking of the grandfather clock in the hallway was comforting, as was the smell of books drifting from the study. Even her father's cologne as she hugged him tight brought a rush of memories. Anaïse was surprised how comforting his arms felt around her, how much she had missed him. So much time had passed since they had been close, and Anaïse could sense her father's longing as he held the embrace longer than usual before releasing her.

"Come, come, sit," he said, leading the way into his study. He walked a little slower, and the grey hair now covered most of his head, but other than that, he was the same man she had always loved, even if she sometimes forgot that.

"Sit tight while I make the coffee," he said, leaving her alone in the study.

Anaïse looked around the room. "Strange how time and life change not just our future but also our past, the narrative we give to the events we experience growing up," she reflected quietly.

Dull, old and fusty is how Anaïse remembered the study, but now, as she sat taking it all in once more, it felt safe, secure and comforting — the very epitome of her father's unconditional love.

Her father returned with the coffees, set one beside Anaïse and settled into his favourite chair, a battered leather wingback, his coffee resting on his leg. "Now, tell me everything. It's been too long, no?"

Anaïse nodded. "Far too long." She told him about Amato, their love, his death and how she was struggling to find meaning in her life without him.

When she had finished, he nodded slowly, tears in his eyes. "I am happy for the love you shared," he said, "devastated at your loss, and glad you chose to come home and share it all with me."

"Me too," Anaïse said. She opened her mouth to speak, then closed it.

Her father leaned forward. "Say it. Say whatever is on your mind."

Anaïse took a deep breath. "It is only now I have experienced true love that I can see what I did when I was younger," she said. "I spent years pushing you away because I felt I had to earn your love."

"And now?"

"I can finally see how stable and consistent your love has been throughout my life. I ran away from everything when I left here, thinking you were always disappointed in me. I was tired of trying to impress you and be the son you never had …"

"I never stopped loving you, but after your mother's death, I struggled to deal with my own pain and wasn't always there when you needed me."

Anaïse nodded slowly. It felt good to share, but there was one more thing she needed to tell him. Diana had said she must reject the darkness, not let it infect her soul, and the only way Anaïse knew was to bring the dark thing into the light, expose it and address it. Nonetheless, her heart beat faster at the thought. How would her father react?

The ticking of the clock was the only sound as Anaïse took a deep breath. "Papa?" she began. "There's one more thing I need to tell you."

"You can tell me anything," he replied calmly, his steady gaze on her.

Anaïse blinked. Did he somehow know what she was going to say? That was ridiculous. Pushing the thought away, she forced out the words before she lost her nerve. "The day I left town, the day Ralph died," she began. "I went to see him. I had to ask him something."

Her father nodded. "I know."

She gasped. "You know? But how?"

"Ralph's neighbour, Karl, is a good friend of mine. He saw you washing the blood from your face in the lake. He called me, and I called Otto, the local chief of police. We went to Ralph's house together and discovered the body." He gave a gentle smile. "We both agreed it was nothing more than an unfortunate accident, not a surprise for such a heavy drinker."

Anaïse stared at him as a wave of unimaginable relief washed over her. "You knew?" she said, her face flushed. "All these years you've known I was there; you knew I killed him?"

"I've always known you were there," her father said, "I saw the body, the broken bottle, and I doubted you had much to do with it. It was the fall that killed him." He sighed, his lined face looking ten years older. "I wanted to tell you a hundred times, my little one, to ease your burden, but never knew how."

"You still loved me, even though you knew?"

"You are my daughter — *my* daughter. I've always loved you. I always will. I don't know what else to do."

Anaïse hurried over to her father and hugged his neck, inhaling his cologne. "Thank you so much, Papa," she sobbed. She stood back up and wiped the tears spilling down her cheeks. "I've carried this for so long, so long..."

Her father smiled as he pulled out his immaculately pressed white cotton handkerchief from the breast pocket of his blazer. "Time heals all wounds, right?"

"Rose Fitgerald Kennedy?" sniffed Anaïse as she took the handkerchief.

"That's my daughter," he said with a laugh as she returned to her seat as he reflected on the remainder of the quote, "I do not agree. The wounds remain. In time, the mind, protecting its sanity, covers them with scar tissue and the pain lessens. But it is never gone."

"And now? What should I do now, Papa?" she asked.

"Maybe your Amato was right," he replied. "Maybe his role was to open you up to love."

Anaïse glanced at her watch and nodded slowly. "Then I must be like the rose? Thanking Amato — the sun — every day for releasing me, for continuing to kiss my leaves with light?"

Her father nodded. "And thanking the earth for nourishing you and seeking no reward."

Anaïse smiled. "So you are the earth?"

Her father shrugged. "That's not for me to say. The picture represents something different for every person. That, my love, is the beauty of the picture, and the beauty of life."

Anaïse gently rested her hand on her stomach. "And with each generation, each life, the story begins anew..."

The Boy
(the Soul that inspires)

"There are only two emotions: love and fear. All positive emotions come from love, all negative emotions from fear. From love flows happiness, contentment, peace, and joy. From fear comes anger, hate, anxiety and guilt. It's true that there are only two primary emotions, love and fear. But it's more accurate to say that there is only love or fear, for we cannot feel these two emotions together, at exactly the same time. They're opposites. If we're in fear, we are not in a place of love. When we're in a place of love, we cannot be in a place of fear."

Elisabeth Kübler-Ross

CHAPTER 1

London

1990

The Reader gazed through the window into the darkness of the tunnel as the train travelled north on the Victoria line from Green Park. Sometimes he saw a string of lights, sometimes nothing. He smiled as he remembered all the years he had spent travelling the London Tube and marvelled that he was so certain today was different.

As the train rushed through the tunnel, he returned to his book, marking words and phrases that caught his attention with his metal-tipped clutch pencil. A buzz of expectation rose from the pit of his belly and his nerves tingled as the moment approached. "Soon, soon, soon," rattled the train, over and over.

The doors opened at Euston, and five young men boarded, full of the anger and confusion of youth, yet empty of the manners that maturity brings. The Reader looked up momentarily, casually checking out each one. He'd seen the type many times before. It was always the same. Strength when travelling as a pack, with fake, insecure bravado hiding layers of fear, insecurity and resignation.

The group had a typical dynamic:

The Alpha, with the biggest ego, led the pack, chest out, gaze challenging anyone who dared to look at him. The others following willingly, drawing energy from the tension created by their presence.

Then there was the Muscle, easy to control by the Alpha, explosive in a hostile situation. Destructive yet inconsequential.

The Yes Man was clearly marked by his trailing position in the pack, feeble in every way. Every pack needed yes men. This pack had two. They knew they were nothing without the pack and clung to it for dear life. The Alpha often taunted them for it, partly to assert his position, partly to feed his ego, but mainly to ensure they understood they were safe as long as they were under his protection.

Finally, there was the Adviser. The Boy. It wasn't his shaggy hair or slim frame that stood out to the Reader, it was the way he looked at the crowd, taking in every detail. The Reader watched as the Boy's eyes scanned every face; he could virtually hear the thoughts organising themselves within the Boy's mind. Quick-witted and smarter than the rest, he knew the volatility of the group and used it for his own protection. He also saw through the machismo of the Alpha and knew it was only a question of time before the distrust he had for the others would be turned on him. He was the only member the Alpha sought council from, the one the Reader had been waiting for. All he needed to do now was find the time and means to separate him from the group.

The Reader went back to his book, but he could sense the group's voracious energy, their need to make their presence felt. They strutted through the carriage, staring at passengers, searching for signs of nervousness.

The Reader smiled to himself. They were looking for someone to intimidate. It was never about mugging someone; it was all about the power game. They loved power, revelling in the knowledge that the mental torment they could inflict would leave an indelible mark.

The Alpha was well versed in the game of torment. He drew energy from it and used it as a mechanism to reinforce his position within the group, but that was all it was for him — a game. His slave mindset had no interest in understanding the consequences of his actions, either for himself or his victims. Realising consequences required an understanding of what would happen tomorrow, but the slave mindset is not interested in planning for the future; it only thinks of now, of satisfying immediate needs and wants.

Resignation, self-pity, envy and resentment were how the slave mindset strived to justify its enslavement, caring neither for its spiritual evolution nor thinking about a future. And why would it? It was convinced that the future, to the extent it could imagine it, would be choked by the system that separated the 'haves', the others, from them, the 'have nots'.

The Reader felt the Alpha's eyes running across him. Tall, slim, neatly dressed, groomed hair, his nose buried in a book — nothing intimidating about him. He no doubt looked like the perfect soft target.

The Alpha was probably looking forward to some fun. The Reader's watch would make a nice trinket for the afternoon's high jinks. The make and type would be inconsequential to him. It wasn't about the spoils, it was about the game, it was about taking what you own and making it his. And if the victim's shoes were nice, the Alpha would gun for those too, for the sheer pleasure of humiliating the person and watching him walk off the train barefoot.

There was no doubt he thought his victims deserved it. The Reader would look like he had a good life, like he had everything the Alpha knew he would never have. And if the Alpha couldn't have it, neither could he. The pack advanced on the Reader, filling the empty seats opposite and the two behind, hovering over him in a deliberate move to induce fear. The Alpha smirked. The theatre that was his life could now unfold another sad, pointless chapter, with him as director.

As the gang closed in around him, the Reader smiled, knowing what was about to unfold. He continued to look at his book, pretending to read, and focused on maintaining his heart rate so as not to give the impression he was intimidated. He knew the signs they were looking for, but they had no idea which ones he was looking for. The Alpha sat next to him. It was deliberately close, the Reader knew, to invade his personal space and unsettle him. Even though he kept his eyes down, he could see the Alpha turn towards him, shoulders rolled back, chest puffed out.

" 'ey!" the Alpha rasped.

The Reader ignored him. He would play the game, but not by the Alpha's rules.

" 'ey!" the Alpha repeated, visibly agitated that the Reader hadn't responded.

The Reader continued to mark words in his book with his clutch pencil.

"Oy!" the Alpha shouted with a sense of urgency.

The Reader knew the Alpha could feel his control waning. His credibility was at stake. Taking his time, the Reader slowly and purposefully closed his book, turned his body so his shoulders were square on with the Alpha and met his demanding gaze.

The Alpha blinked.

The Reader knew the calm in his eyes would unnerve the Alpha, which would make the rest of the group uneasy.

The Alpha's shoulders were ever present in the Reader's peripheral vision, which was vital. Any sign of attack would come from the shoulders first. If you kept your eyes on the shoulders, you could pre-empt any sudden physical movement — the Gardener had taught him that. He could see the Alpha's chest tighten in his fitted T-shirt, heart rate increasing.

"I like your watch," said the Alpha in a hushed, raspy tone, knowing the pack was enjoying his masterclass in intimidation. Other passengers helplessly looked on, feeding his ego to the point of intoxication.

"I like your face," replied the Reader with cold calmness. "You're pretty," he added, never breaking eye contact with the Alpha as he slowly chipped away at his power.

"What?" came the Alpha's irritated reply. His head tilted slightly. Did the man really just say that? He glanced at the pack, who were looking to the Alpha for a suitable response, demanding that control be restored fast.

"Look in my eyes, boy!" snapped the Reader. "What do you see? Do you see fear? Pain? Helplessness? Do I look like someone who's afraid to die?" He wrinkled his nose. "I've seen so many wars, so much pain, so many young men with their limbs blown away for a cause they never understood." Sadness rose in his chest. "Their souls ripped from them before they had a chance to live." His sadness hardened. "You have a chance to live but instead invite death. And for what? A watch? Is that all your life is worth?"

The Alpha looked confused. He clearly wasn't expecting to confront a man who wasn't intimidated by death. He had to think fast to restore control and credibility, but the Reader wasn't going to give him time to think.

"Answer me, boy!" the Reader demanded.

One of the Yes Men, seeing the opportunity to earn his stripes and gain credibility by supporting the Alpha, leaned forward and hissed, "Eh, teacher man. He wants ya watch. Give it 'im."

"Eh!" nodded the second Yes Man, while the Muscle wound up mentally for an explosive escalation. "Hand it over."

The Reader took a second to reflect on the available permutations. Should he break eye contact with the Alpha and destroy the Yes Man? Not a good idea; the Muscle would probably step in, and he would lose his advantage. Better to keep the focus on the Alpha, who wouldn't allow the Muscle to step in and steal his thunder because that would undermine his position. The Alpha was trapped by his ego, and the Reader knew it.

The Reader remembered the lesson the Gardener had taught him: to ensure the message is received, it has to be communicated in a way the recipient can understand.

Maintaining eye contact with the Alpha, he spoke to the Yes Man, while subliminally addressing the pack. "If I hear one more word out of your stinkin' bitch mouth," he said softly, "I'll pull you over this seat and make you my girlfriend. Now get your rank breath out of my face, boy."

The choice of words was deliberately misogynistic, partly to ensure the Yes Man understood his intent, but mainly to provoke the other passengers as they helplessly watched it unfold. The Yes Man withdrew, slack-jawed, while the whole pack went silent. The Muscle started laughing loudly. "You got cussed by teacher man!" he taunted.

The rest of the pack joined in, pointing at Yes Man with a hand over their mouths to emphasise his embarrassment — all except the

Alpha, who clearly felt his control slipping through his fingers. His slave-mindset ego kicked in again, demanding an immediate, short-term solution, the same slave mindset that prevented him from strategising and coming up with an alternative game plan that would allow him to regain control.

The Reader wasn't intimidated, which left two options. Beat him into the ground, taking what spoils they could, or walk away to find an easier victim and thereby restore his position as Alpha.

The Reader never broke eye contact, reading the Alpha's mind. He could tell the young thug was assessing his own quickly diminishing chances of survival if a fight broke out.

Before the Alpha could react, the Reader was back at him. "Your girlfriend's got a big mouth." He nodded in the direction of the chastened Yes Man. "Looks like you can't control your ladies."

"What!" roared the Alpha, leaning forward in a futile attempt to assert himself.

"That's all you got? 'What'!" teased the Reader. He looked at the Alpha's shoulders for any hint of an attack. Seeing nothing, he took the initiative.

The Reader lunged at the Alpha and grabbed his neck with his left hand, while his right hand pierced the side of his neck with the metal-tipped clutch pencil, just above the jugular. Time was running out. The Reader needed to isolate the Boy from the pack, and quickly.

The Alpha screamed, partly from the pain of the metal tip working into the side of his neck, and partly in a desperate plea for someone to get this psycho off his back.

The Reader jammed the Alpha's head against the metal pole behind the seat, forced his knee on the Alpha's crotch and quickly turned to the Muscle. "The pencil is in his jugular vein," he lied. "You jump me, I'll pull the pencil out, and the blood will gush out so fast, he'll be dead in minutes."

If any other passengers had been ignoring events up to this point, the Alpha's scream would have pierced their apathetic sleep.

The pack, meanwhile, were frozen, stunned by the turn of events, bereft without the Alpha's control.

The Reader's eyes settled on the Muscle. "What do you want to do? Kill me? Or save him? You don't have time for both."

He returned his focus to the Alpha. "Everything in life has a consequence," he said calmly. "Do you think you can just walk away without paying the tax? Do you?"

"Fuck you," croaked the Alpha.

His eyes gave away his panic, as a trickle of blood worked its way down his neck, stealing what was left of his composure.

"Wet 'im!" screamed Yes Man Two to the Muscle.

The Reader reacted by working the pencil's metal tip in a circular motion against the Alpha's neck, inflicting the greatest imaginable pain without deepening the wound. The trickle of blood increased, causing the Alpha to scream even louder.

"I wouldn't …" the Reader said, raising an eyebrow.

"You're a dead man," stuttered the Muscle.

The Reader nodded. "Yep."

He looked deep into the Muscle's angry, confused eyes while maintaining pressure on the Alpha's throat. "How you gonna kill something that's already dead?"

He glanced at the other passengers, who were now fully engaged in the sudden escalation, the unexpected turning of the tables.

Some wore expressions of glee, no doubt vicariously exacting revenge on their school or workplace bullies through this man who had the courage to make a stand. Others looked concerned, probably wondering if the Reader was willing to kill the Alpha or if he was bluffing. Did he truly have nothing to live for?

There were two passengers in particular who caught his eye, one of whom leaned forward. "You've made your point," he said softly. "Let him go."

The Reader examined the speaker. He was stocky and had a clean-shaven, ebony complexion. His calm strength was reflected in his attire, complemented by a sliver of the timeless elegance of a Patek 2526 peering from his sleeve. Could he be a mentor? The Architect, maybe? In which case, the other was probably the Poet.

The train slowed, prefacing its arrival at the next station. Perfect. The pieces were in place, leading to the moment he was waiting for.

"Looks like this is your stop," he told the Alpha. "Keep your finger over the wound and get to A&E before you lose too much blood. Understood?"

The brakes screeched, and the train rocked from side to side as the Reader took the pencil out of the Alpha's neck and released his grip. As he did so, he whispered in his ear, "What's the value of knowing a thousand ways to kill a man if you don't know one way to save him? As long as there is breath in you, it's never too late to come back and answer the call."

The train juddered to a halt and the doors opened with a loud hiss, matching the sighs of relief from the transfixed passengers.

The pack, visibly relieved to be alive and not butchered by the psycho army teacher man, circled around their vanquished leader and headed for the doors.

The passengers slowly slipped back into their apathetic, comatose state, returning to their music, their books, their newspapers, their emails.

As the pack started to exit the carriage, the Reader jumped to his feet, grabbed the Boy and pulled him back in. "Spoils of war," he told the pack. "You can pick him up later."

"What the fuck?" croaked the Alpha.

The doors closed, and, with a jolt, the train started its remorseless journey toward the next stop, the Boy trapped on the train with the Reader.

CHAPTER 2

The Reader dragged the Boy back to where the drama had unfolded and shoved him unceremoniously onto the seat. The Boy didn't resist; he was traumatised by what he had been party to and accepted for now that the Reader was the new Alpha. To say the Boy resigned himself to his fate would suggest he once had a chance at a balanced life. He hadn't. His environment had taught him that. School had taught him that. Society had taught him that. Even his parents had taught him that.

The system had trapped him, designed to make him dependent on a cocktail of benefits and limited opportunities, drip-feeding this toxic diet until he either died or fell into a life of crime.

Moving up socially was not an option, but that didn't stop the dream being dangled by the media, only to be snatched away by real life. It provided a cold, unrelenting reminder of the difference between those who served and those who were served, between slave and master.

"What do you want?" he said in a nervous, shaky voice.

The Reader studiously cleaned the bloody tip of his pencil on a used tissue and dropped it into his shoulder bag. "What do *you* want?" he replied.

"Right now, I want to get the fuck away from you," the Boy snapped back.

The Reader smiled. "And then what, Donkey? Rejoin your girlfriends and continue living day to day, walking around with your chests puffed out, acting like men when you're still little boys?

Trying to prove to everyone you're better than them when you know you're at the bottom of the ladder and no one cares whether you live or die?" His eyes bored into the Boy. "You're not one of them. Why do you hang with them?"

"What do you want with me?" repeated the Boy.

"I want you to see that you don't have to become what the system wants you to be — but be the person *you* want to be. You don't know it, but you have the strength to let go of everything holding you back, including those losers. All they do is feed on you, and when you have no more to give, they'll throw you aside for fresh meat."

The Boy sneered. "You don't understand, man. You have a nice life, you wear nice clothes, you have skills, you have money. You movin' forward."

The Reader smiled. If only the Boy knew how close their lives were, how closely their destinies intertwined. But he couldn't tell him. Not yet. The Boy would have to find out for himself. "How do you expect to get anywhere in life if you hang with guys who can't help you become what you want?" asked the Reader.

"They're ma brethren, ma clan, ma crew," protested the Boy.

"And, in return, you allow yourself to be a slave to them. Their bitch. Is that it?"

"Fuck you, man. They're all I got. This is who I am. Do I look like some rich white boy whose parents are gonna pay for everything? This is my life, and I let it take me where it wants. When you don't give a fuck, you got nothin' to lose, you feel me? That's how it works."

"And your parents?"

The Boy shrugged. "Too busy to give a fuck, working double jobs to put food on the table, too worn down to be present. They don't live. They survive."

***

The train slowed as it entered the next station. The Reader needed to get the Boy to the Gardener before he bolted. "Do you know why I pulled you back?" he asked quickly.

"Coz you a fag?"

The Reader ignored his answer. "I'm going to ask you to make a decision. It's a simple one, but it will determine how you live your life. Quite simply, you need to decide if you want to find out what you can become, what you're capable of becoming, or if you're going to leave now and never see me again."

The Boy was confused. The passengers were hanging on every word, waiting for the Boy's answer as the brakes screeched and everyone rocked forward. The Boy wanted to run, back to his safe haven, back to the rhythm and routine that had been his prison and his comfort for as long as he could remember.

But as he started to rise in his seat, the same voice that had pleaded with him to hear what the Reader wanted spoke again. No matter how great the desire was to run, he needed to stay and listen. With a deep sigh, he settled back in his seat. "How do you know so much about my life and what I'm gonna be?" he demanded.

"Let's just say I've been where you are," said the Reader.

When the carriage doors opened, several passengers shuffled off the train and joined the herd moving slowly along the platform. The memory of the attempted mugging and the stranger who tried to save

217

the Boy already began to fade. Those who remained returned to their phones and newspapers. The drama was over.

As the doors closed, the Reader turned to the Boy. "What did you want to become when you were a kid?"

The Boy hadn't expected this question. What did this guy want with him? Why did he keep badgering him with these questions? Why did he care what the Boy thought? Not for the first time, the Boy felt opposite forces pulling him —his ego urging him to tell the Reader to fuck off and run, his inner voice warning that this life path led only to a life of regret. And the worst? In prison, or dead from some pointless street fight. So, despite his fear and confusion, he stayed.

"A pilot," the Boy whispered. "I wanted to learn to fly so I could get the fuck away from here." He immediately regretted sharing details of his life with a total stranger, but at the same time, it felt good that he was not being written off because of who he was or where he came from.

"What happened?"

"What d'ya mean?"

"I don't know many pilots who waste their afternoons trawling the London Underground for people to intimidate."

The Boy stared at his feet. "Life happened."

"Maybe you're simply not good enough to be a pilot?" teased the Reader, smiling as the Boy looked up.

Almost despite himself, he started to relax. "Oh yeah? Why not?"

"Why not, indeed."

The answer was comforting, and the Boy squinted. How was this the same man who, only two stops ago, had sent the Alpha to hospital?

"Do you know what's stopping you from becoming what you would love to be?" continued the Reader.

"Easy," said the Boy. "They'd never hire someone like me."

The Reader shook his head. "Nope. It's fear, one of the tools the ego uses to keep us in our place. People are so afraid of failure, most of them never start the journey. This keeps them enslaved. As long as you remain a slave, all your actions are controlled by your fear."

"How can I stop being a slave?" the Boy asked.

"Excellent question, Donkey!"

The Boy scowled at the name.

"There are three stages," said the Reader. "The first is to decide whether you want to commit to the life you want or whether you prefer to remain a slave."

"And then?"

"Figure out a path that will help you overcome your slavery and reach your goal."

The Boy nodded. "And the third?"

"Look for people who have taken the journey, who can guide you through the tangled weeds of the ego, to provide a light in dark times and help you stay on the path."

The dark tides of doubt that ruled the Boy's life began to rise once more. "Let me guess — that's you? My Jedi master, my personal Obi-Wan Kanobi. Is that what you're selling?"

The Reader laughed as he remembered his own love for the *Star Wars* movies. "Me? No, no. I'm just here to help you understand what it means to be a master of your own life."

"Let's say I wanna take this journey," said the Boy sceptically. "Then what?"

"Then your intent will decide which journey you take and the people who will accompany you."

The Boy sighed. "How is this Zen ego bullshit gonna help me make a living? Real life is all about cheddar. Get cheddar, you can eat in all the nice places. Get cheddar, you fuck all the bitches you want. Get cheddar, and you can sleep in a big crib. But if you got no cheddar, you got no food, no bitches, no crib."

"Good point," said the Reader, smiling. "And what happens once you've eaten until you're fit to burst, fucked until you're exhausted and slept until you've got bed sores?"

"Simple. Eat new food, fuck new bitches, sleep in new beds," said the Boy, beaming.

The Reader laughed too. "What would you say if I told you that you could be rich *and* happy?"

"If you make me rich, I will be happy!" answered the Boy quickly.

The Reader glanced at the other passengers. It was time to provoke them, see who would stand out. There were two in particular he had his eye on. "Look around," he told the Boy. "How many of these people are "getting cheddar', as you put it?"

"They all look like they're doing all right."

"Check out the ones who look particularly pleased with themselves," pressed the Reader. "What do you see? What makes them look so smug? Is it what they're wearing, carrying, reading?"

The Boy scanned the passengers. "Most of 'em are tossers," he began, deliberately loudly to unsettle those who defined themselves by consumable trinkets. The weaker ones shuffled their feet, scratched their necks, or tried to hide their trappings of success in their bags or under their shirt cuffs as the Boy continued to deliver his verdicts. He pointed at the man who had spoken up before. "Except him."

The Reader nodded. It was the Architect; he was sure of it.

The man leaned forward. "And what do you think of me? Am I a slave?"

"Nah. You look pretty uptown to me," replied the Boy, scanning his elegant attire.

The Architect glanced at the other passengers, then back at the Boy. "You have a God-given talent for reading people. Imagine what you could achieve with the right education, the right guidance, the right support."

"Oh, let me guess. You want to help me too?" the sarcasm returning to the Boy's voice. He had spent years yearning for a male role model willing to help him but knew better than to expect anyone to front up and help him. His father had been emotionally absent, resentment constantly simmering below the surface of his obligations and perceived failures in fatherhood. His older brother had moved out as soon as he could and was now doing five to ten in prison for armed robbery. And his teachers? They had taken one look at his hand-me-down clothes and written him off. Only the Alpha had ever given him any time, made him feel a part of something.

"If you want to make something of yourself, follow this man's advice. You can trust him." The Architect stood and handed his business card to the Reader. "He needs to let go of everything that holds him back. If he wants to learn a trade after that, call me." He turned back to the Boy. "Learn from him. In those moments when you feel your vision or your heart are clouded by darkness, think of this day and all that has happened." He tapped the Boy's chest with two immaculately manicured fingers. "Your heart is your greatest force against the darkness in your life. Protect it at all costs from the bitterness, envy and hatred surrounding you." He tapped the Boy's temple. "And this is your greatest asset, your biggest weapon. Nurture it. Let it absorb the world around you." He straightened his tie and adjusted his cuffs. "And when you're ready, if you want to learn how to make a living, I'll show you."

The Boy was silent, unable to find any words with which to respond. For the first time since he had boarded the train, his heart wasn't racing, he wasn't angry, he wasn't scared. A calmness flowed through his body as he slowly processed all that had happened. How had he gone from hanging out with his gang to being attacked by a passenger, to being offered the chance to be a part of a world that would otherwise be denied him?

Another passenger had been listening intently to the dialogue. He leaned forward. "A man's soul cannot be still until he has faced the pain he carries, the fears he hides, and the questions that pursue him," he declared.

The Reader smiled softly to himself. The Poet.

The Boy gave a harsh laugh. "That sounds gay, man. You a poet or something?"

"Yes," replied the Poet. "Guilty on both counts."

"Yeah...?".

The Boy scanned The Poet up and down, eyebrow raised.

The Poet shrugged. "It's OK. I've found my peace with my world, and you should too. Today a man saved your life for no reason other than to wake you up to all you could become. Grasp the chance with both hands, nurture it and make a new life."

"How?" asked the Boy, a whirlwind of emotions contending for his attention.

"Find a way to ride the donkey without the donkey throwing you," the Poet said cryptically. Like the Architect, he handed his card to the Reader for safekeeping then turned back to the Boy. "To learn a trade is important for your material existence, but to be able to understand and express the pain in your heart is important for your salvation. Call whenever you want to talk, and if I can help, I will." He smiled and added, "As long as you don't have a problem sharing your thoughts and feelings with an old gay man."

The train slowed, and the Poet and Architect took their places by the doors, ready to disembark. The Reader also climbed to his feet. "This is my stop," he told the Boy. "Meet me tomorrow morning at ten by the rose garden in Green Park if you want to change your life." He moved towards the doors.

"Wait! I got questions!"

The doors opened, and the Reader glanced back at the Boy. "Do you believe in coincidences?"

The Boy shook his head.

"Me neither. Which means all this was meant to happen. Grab it, believe in it, give yourself to it, and let it show you what you can become." He stepped off the train. "Tomorrow morning at ten. Green Park, the rose garden," he repeated.

The Boy leaped up and ran to the door. "Why you doin' this?"

"I had a debt to repay," replied the Reader as he strode down the platform, placing his Walkman headset on. "Today I was blessed with the opportunity to repay it."

The Boy stared after him, but the Reader was already lost in the crowd. "Why you keep calling me Donkey?" he muttered as the doors hissed shut.

CHAPTER 3

The Boy woke early the next morning, the previous day's events still fresh in his mind. He was thankful to still be alive, despite the psycho teacher jumping him, but confused about why he had been offered a lifeline to become something more.

His bedroom window was still open from the night before. The sun's warmth and the smell of diesel fumes rose from the street. What would have happened if he had died yesterday? Would the papers have even reported it? Would his parents have coped? Would any of the pack have missed him, or would they have simply replaced him? And what about people from the neighbourhood? What stories would have done the rounds?

He sat up and rubbed the sleep from his eyes. Who cared? He was alive, and that was all that mattered. Teacher man was clearly a psycho; he'd probably stood too close to a couple of landmines and lost all perspective on reality. The Boy would have to be stupid to go back into the lion's den, especially voluntarily.

He climbed out of bed and pulled on his jeans and a T-shirt. It was his yard, his patch, his hood. He needed to forget the psycho and stick with what he knew.

After grabbing a bowl of cereal, he slumped on the faded couch in front of the TV. The flat was quiet. His mum would be at her crappy job stacking shelves at the corner shop, and his dad? Who knew? Struggling to be a positive role model but always emotionally absent or exhausted.

He glanced at the TV and sucked down another bite of sweet cereal. The news was on. "Two teenagers died last night," announced the newsreader, "in what police suspect was a postcode-related gang shootout."

"Fuck." The Boy shovelled in a spoonful of cereal. Is that how cheap life had become? Kids dying because they strayed into the wrong neighbourhood.

The news quickly moved on.

"The latest unemployment figures show an increase for the third month in a row — grim reading for a government that campaigned on lowering unemployment and adding further pressure on the need to devise reforms to help a generation that critics argue are in danger of becoming structurally unemployable."

The words "structurally unemployable" rang in the Boy's head. He knew exactly what that meant. A lifetime of handouts, being dumbed down, working menial jobs for cash, cheating the system and, ultimately, spending time in prison, all the while blaming someone else.

The teacher man's last words jumped into his head: "You're the debt I need to repay." What did that mean? He wanted to put the man out of his mind, but there was something about him that wouldn't allow the Boy to drop the idea of meeting him.

He had told the Boy exactly what he was going through and what he was feeling, and the Boy's curiosity wouldn't let him forget the guy.

The Boy was tired from thinking, tired of watching depressing news, exhausted from yesterday's madness. He just wanted to get high and let it all pass by him.

He turned off the TV in favour of the best pirate station, Radio Invicta, serving the community with sounds and news from the streets. As Omar's "There's Nothing Like This" came on, he lit a joint and closed his eyes, keen to push the world away. But he couldn't. The Reader's words wouldn't allow him to forget the emptiness of his life or dismiss the thought that someone had offered him a lifeline. Perhaps it was the only chance he'd ever get to escape his miserable existence.

"Fuck it. I'm goin'. The Boy stood, a surge of energy flowing through him. There were too many questions in his head, and the only way he could get answers was by meeting the Reader.

What did he have to lose? He could always join the pack later to swarm around the West End. They were probably all still asleep, and even if they weren't, there was no way they'd understand why he'd want to meet the very man who had attacked them. He'd have to keep this under wraps, but that didn't mean he'd go unprepared.

He went to the chest of drawers in his room, removed the cheap chipboard panel under the bottom drawer and pulled out a telescopic baton. It was small enough to tuck into his jeans but destructive enough to inflict a serious injury and allow him to make his escape if need be.

He stepped out into the pale winter sunshine. He was missing the bravado he had left with yesterday, but in its place was a determination to take control of his life, and not, as the Reader had told him, be ruled by fear.

He walked up the stairs at Green Park tube station, his heart quickening as he wondered whether he had made the right decision to come. His ego was trying desperately to cloud his thoughts with doubts, distractions and 'obligations' he should attend to. But the harder the ego tried, the more the Boy wanted to find the crazy teacher. To his surprise, this conviction gave him a strength he had rarely felt, a strength that didn't come from the confirmation of others but from some place deep within. It felt like the right thing to do, and this newfound confidence pushed all other thoughts away, giving him a feeling of clarity and calm. As he marched into Green Park, London's smallest Royal Park, he was confident he would quickly find the Reader. However, after several loops, all he'd seen were tourists, pensioners reading on the rows of benches alongside the tree-lined walkways, and a gardener, head down as he tended to a small vegetable patch. He was beginning to have doubts about the whole thing. Had he dreamed it? Or got the time wrong? Or was the Reader playing him?

As he walked towards the Gardener for the third time, the old man stood up, looked at him and smiled. "Ah, there you are, Donkey!"

That donkey again.

The Boy cautiously looked around. "You know me? I'm supposed to meet someone."

The Gardener set down his trowel, wiped his sweaty forehead on his sleeve and eased down onto the grass. "Tell me something about him. You know, I work here most days. If he's supposed to be here, I might know him."

The Boy hesitated then sat next to the old man. "The teacher man?"

"If that is what you call him, yes."

"We met on the Tube yesterday. Me and the crew were fuckin" around, and the teacher —" The Boy paused. "Well, he told me there was a different way to live —" When he said it out loud, it sounded pretty lame. He looked around. "He told me to meet him here … what did he tell you?"

"What makes you think he told me anything?"

"He called me Donkey. You called me Donkey. I fuckin' hate donkeys!" As he heard the words coming out of his mouth, the Boy started to laugh at how stupid it all sounded.

"It seems," laughed the Gardener, "that the Donkey sees through the vanity of it all."

The Gardener sat Japanese-style on the grass, hands on knees, and looked into the Boy's eyes. "It seems a lot happened during that Tube journey. How many stops?"

"Four. Why?"

"All that happened in four stops?" asked the Gardener.

"You calling me a liar?" snapped the Boy defensively. This could be a scam. Maybe he should get out while he could.

The Gardener smiled. "Do you think it could have been a dream?"

"Nah, man, it was real," the Boy assured him. "Teacher man stuck a pencil in my brother's neck. There was blood and everything."

The Gardener nodded. "Did you call your friend to check how he is? I'm sure he'd appreciate the call."

It dawned on the Boy that the gang had left him at the mercy of teacher man; they didn't even call him last night to see how he was. A sense of betrayal welled up as he thought of walking to the nearest phone box to call the Alpha. What would he say? The last thing the Alpha would want was a reminder of his humiliation.

The Boy was aware of the Gardener's steady gaze. "Is that what you'd do?"

"Do what you think is right."

"Thanks, Obi-Wan," snapped the Boy. "I knew this was a waste of time," he murmured to himself.

"Ultimately," added the Gardener, "our actions determine the outcome of our lives. Deep inside, you know what is right for you. You have to decide. Do you move forward or backward?"

To call or not to call. He had always known running with the gang meant he'd either wind up in prison or in an alley with a blade in his guts and his blood spilling out, but he'd never felt he had any alternative.

The Boy put the thought out of his head and turned back to the Gardener. "It happened. I know it. I saw blood, and there was an architect and a poet; they offered to help me. They even gave their business cards to the teacher man for me."

"Did they now?" said the Gardener quietly.

"Yes!" insisted the Boy.

"And those business cards you're referring to, are they the ones in your back pocket?"

"Nah, man, I told you, they gave them to teacher man," replied the Boy, frustrated at the old man not grasping the situation.

The Gardener nodded slowly. "It sounds like a fantastic story, but I find it hard to believe. After all, you can't find the man you claim told you to come here today, and you declined to call the friend you claim was assaulted. And I guess these men's business cards have apparently disappeared with the man you were supposed to meet?" He smiled benignly, which triggered the Boy even more.

"Fuck off!" he snarled. "It's all true, just like I told you."

"And you are sure the cards are not in your back pocket?"

"I told you, old man, you deaf or somethin'? Look, nuthin' here!" He stood and turned around so the Gardener could see his hands go into his jeans. He froze as his fingers pulled out two business cards, one belonging to the Architect, the other to the Poet. He gazed at them, disbelieving. "Fuck!"

The Gardener smiled. "Not quite the word I would have chosen, but your surprise is understandable."

The Boy glared at the Gardener. "What kind of mind trick is this? You fuckin' with my head?"

"No trick. Just your calling," said the Gardener. He gently probed the soil.

"What callin'? What the fuck you talkin'' about, old man?"

The Gardener unscrewed the cup from his Thermos flask, filled it and offered it to the Boy. "Would you like some water?"

"No! I want some fucking answers!"

"You mentioned the teacher stabbed your friend in the jugular," said the Gardener.

"And?"

"Interesting choice, the jugular," said the Gardener. "In the holy book of the Muslims, God says he is closer to you than your own jugular."

"Are you trying to tell me I met God yesterday?"

The Gardener's laugh vibrated through the Boy. "You and I are going to get along well!" He wiped the tears from his eyes and sat up straight. "Let's start. What would you like to know?"

The Boy frowned. "Why is teacher man not here? He was supposed to teach me stuff. You know, mind stuff to make my life better."

"Really?"

"Yeah." The Boy looked around. "Where is he? And come to think of it, who is he?"

The Gardener gave a soft smile. "Your first good question. The 'teacher man' is you, Donkey."

"What?"

"Strictly speaking, he's you in another time and place," continued the Gardener, "but he's still you. Who else could have read you as well as yourself?"

"And we exist at the same time?"

"Not exactly. He is who you could become. You needed to send a message to yourself that would make you want to come to me. What could be more compelling than sending your future self — or at least a version of it?"

"So everything that happened yesterday was a dream?" the Boy asked, his brow creased.

"Not really a dream, but not quite reality either. More like a request for you to take a journey."

"Could have saved yourself a lot of trouble if you'd just belled me," snapped the Boy, his eyes still narrowed.

The old man smiled. "True, but where would have been the fun in that? And to be honest, something had to happen that would wake you up from your normal life and make you look at the world anew. I don't think a phone call would have done the trick."

The Boy thought for a moment. "Who were the Architect and the Poet? Why did they want to help me?"

"They are what you have always wanted to be but were too afraid to become. They were once slaves, much as you are now, but they found the way out, the way to become masters. They now understand the language of love, humanity, the Divine, and they use this teaching to help others who wish to free themselves from their slavery."

"Why me? Why not one of the others?"

"Most people are content being slaves. They enjoy and accept being bound by their egos, staying trapped in a world of material success. They allow themselves to believe the deception that they will find happiness and fulfilment in these things. They have been living the lie for so long, they're too afraid to look in the mirror to see what they've become, let alone want to find the truth or a way out."

"And what is the truth?"

The Gardener's eyes shone. "I like your focus. Straight to the point. The truth is that we need to focus on very few things in life to find the truth, be it the truth about ourselves, love, life, or the universe. Everything else is a goal-driven distraction that diverts our energy away from the very thing we search for our whole lives."

As the Gardener explained further, the Boy listened, but his attention soon wandered. If there was one thing he had learned, it was that he needed to find out things for himself. "Is it too late for them, the others?" he interrupted.

"Never too late. But the longer you deny the existence of the truth or stray from the path, the stronger the transition is."

"But it's never too late?"

"It's never too late."

"And what if I don't want your help?"

"Then you'll run the risk of being a slave your entire life, no matter how successful and rich you become."

"Sounds all right. Being rich and successful and all, you know, like Architect man."

"But you will still be a slave, and your master will feed on you until you are consumed. Why do you think so many of your peers are unable to free themselves from the life they lead? Do you think it's the system holding them down? Lack of opportunities? No, it's their masters. But if you became aware of your master, you could be free of it; its chains, its whip."

The Boy's mind was jumping around, trying to make sense of it all, as a barrage of questions threatened to overwhelm him. "Who are you?" he said. "Why did you call me here?"

"I am the Gardener, of course!" The old man picked up his trowel and waved it at the Boy. "Isn't that obvious?"

"Funny. But why did you call me here?"

"I didn't."

"Huh?"

"OK, I did, but only because you asked me to."

"But I've never met you."

"That's all you need to know for now. The rest will become clear as we progress."

The Boy's mind flooded with more questions. Part of him wanted to roll his eyes at the old man and walk away, but every time he started to do so, another part of him urged him to press on. "Fair enough," he said. "One last question. Why do you keep calling me Donkey?"

He had expected the old man to laugh, but his face turned serious. "The Donkey is a representation of the unruly ego, intent on doing what it wants irrespective of its owner's wishes. You are a slave to your ego, your donkey. Therefore, until you start to progress, you are Donkey."

The Boy processed this, his brain bouncing between "This is a crock of shit" and "Maybe this is important'. "How do I become less donkey?" he said.

"We must help the slave understand his slavery, so the master can understand his mastery," the Gardener replied. He rummaged in a tatty canvas shoulder bag on the grass beside him, extracted two books and held them out to the Boy.

Rather than take the books, the Boy gave the Gardener a flat stare. "Really? After all your fancy words, all you've got for me is a couple of crappy books? I thought you were gonna show me how to live a better life, you know, like the Reader and those other fancy players on the train."

"It's often the simple things that initiate the greatest changes," said the Gardener. He thrust the books towards the Boy. "Trust me."

The Boy snatched the books and scowled at them. "I thought with all this Zen Jedi shit you've been spouting, you'd send me on some quest or something. You know, kill a monster, save a princess, wash your car."

"Let's start with the books and save the quests for another day," said the Gardener.

The Boy turned the books over in his hands. The first was Nietzsche's *Beyond Good and Evil*. The second was Joseph Conrad's *Heart of Darkness*. "Never heard of them," he snorted.

"They're both very 'gangsta'." The Gardener laughed. "I think you'll like them."

The Boy looked at them again. "They don't look gangsta. They look boring." He gave a deep sigh. "When do you want them back?"

"Tomorrow."

"What? I can't—"

The old man cut him off. "Relax. Bring them tomorrow and read them to me."

"That's it?"

The Gardener nodded. "Every journey starts with the heart. All great change for the better starts with doing small things with the right intent."

The Boy laughed. "Sounds like it's gonna take a loooong time, old man."

"Where are you in a rush to get to, Donkey?" said the Gardener. He held out his hand. "Help me up, will you?"

The Boy held the books in one hand and helped the old man up with the other.

"Thank you," said the Gardener warmly. He gently tapped the Boy's heart with two fingers as they looked into each other's eyes.

The Boy inhaled sharply as everything around him slowed down.

"And with that simple gesture," the Gardener said, "you created good for no other reason than good itself. The pureness of your action was blessed by the Divine. Small things!"

"I just helped you up, old man," said the Boy.

"What you did was give of yourself without expecting anything back." The Gardener smiled. "Congratulations. You're waking up."

The Boy nodded. It was an alien feeling. For a moment, he forgot the chaos of his life. He didn't want to lose this sensation — this high.

"You have to let it go and return to your daily life," the old man said, reading his mind, "but it will come back. It's a part of you that was always there. You just couldn't see it." He hoisted his bag over his shoulder. "See you tomorrow?"

The Boy nodded. "Tomorrow."

"And you won't need that weapon anymore," said the Gardener.

"Weapon?"

The old man nodded towards the Boy's ankle, where the baton was tucked inside his sock.

With a little wave, the Gardener headed down the path towards Buckingham Palace.

The Boy watched the old man walk away, then headed back towards the underground station. As he passed a rubbish bin, he stopped, pulled the baton from his sock and tossed it into the bin. A weight lifted from his shoulders, and he couldn't help but smile.

His mind was swirling as he descended the stairs and boarded the train. The Gardener had said he was the same person as the man on the train. How was that possible?

He settled in his seat as the train picked up speed, the lights of the station flashing past before they were swallowed up by the tunnel.

For better or worse he had started the journey. All he could do now was see where it took him.

A feeling of peace washed across the Boy as he rested his head against the cold window and let the darkness and rhythmic rocking lull him into a state of contentment.

CHAPTER 4

Some years later ...

"My schoolteacher's driving me crazy," laughed the Boy as he sat in the shade of a spreading oak, the vibrant green leaves providing shade from an unseasonably warm spring day. The Architect was in a suit, as usual, complemented with a crisp white shirt. "She's so uptight; she seems to have forgotten about the beauty and pleasure of good literature. All she focuses on is the exam and what we need to know to get a good grade."

"Of course. That's her job." He nodded towards a large mound of newly turned soil at the far end of the garden. "Would you shift that pile over here so we can get the new season's seeds in the ground?"

The Boy frowned. "If I have to." He stood and grabbed the handles of the wheelbarrow.

"You can't use that."

"What?" He turned and stared at the Architect.

"Humour me."

The Boy sighed. "Fine, no wheelbarrow." He marched to the mound, grabbed a spade and dug it into the soil.

"You can't use the shovel either."

"What?" came the Boy's irritated reply. "It'll take me all day by hand."

"Why?"

"Because I've got nothing to put it in."

"Now you know how your teacher feels," the Architect said.

The Boy gave him a puzzled look. "I still don't get it."

"Come. Sit." The Architect patted the seat beside him.

"I don't have to move the soil?"

"No, you don't have to move the soil."

The Boy sat down.

"That's what it's like for young people," explained the Architect. "They don't have a vessel, a container, so their thoughts go everywhere, blown by the wind, carried away by the rain. Left to your own devices, you would read anything that took your fancy and would never pass your exams, never go to university."

The Boy squinted in thought. "And how do we get that vessel?"

"Time. Life. Experience." He turned to the Boy. "Your teacher is not just teaching you about literature, she is also teaching you about life. If you want to achieve anything, you must first learn to focus. Remember when you met the Gardener, and he started giving you books to read? You went off in a hundred different directions, reading anything and everything you could get your hands on, with no plan or structure."

"Don't remind me."

"Gradually, over time, you began to shape your love of literature. At first, it was towards your GCSE, then your A Level. These are providing vessels of sorts, the need to focus your efforts, but they are imposed by other people. In time, you will form your own vessel, your own way of containing your learning. You'll do it because being a butterfly will leave you unsatisfied. You'll want to focus and will learn how to develop your own vessels, your own style."

The Boy nodded slowly. "Can I apply this to other areas of my life?"

"Can and should. Whether it's work, love, friends or travel, you have to decide on the scope of your desires. That is what focus is about, and if you want to achieve something in your life, you must develop that focus, refine that vessel, then decide how you will fill it."

"You think I'm unfocused?" the Boy said with a scowl.

The Architect shrugged noncommittally. "I was too." He glanced at his watch and climbed to his feet. "Speaking of focus, I have a meeting with a new client this afternoon. I need to get my game face on." He held out his hand. "Until next time."

***

The Boy was thinking about his conversation with the Architect as he made his way home through the estate. He didn't see his old crew lurking in the shadows until it was too late.

"Well, look who it isn't."

"The little student."

"Still butt-fucking your teacher man?"

The Boy stopped. He had no choice. The gang — his gang — had surrounded him.

"Wa'gwan?" he said.

The Alpha looked him up and down like a horse trader inspecting an old nag. "You don't have time for us no more?"

"I'm just trying to move forward. Keep my old man off my back."

"I heard you were going to college now?"

"Sometimes." The Boy tried to sound as disinterested as possible. He was glad he didn't have his book bag with him but was conscious of *The Catcher in The Rye* crammed in the back pocket of his jeans. "But it's full of fags."

The Alpha's hard eyes bored into him. "And what about the teacher man? I heard you were seeing him?"

"Not for ages. He came onto me, so I butted him and broke the fucker's nose." The lie came easily to him, but as soon as he said it, betrayal washed over him.

His words broke the tension. The Alpha laughed and turned to leave. "I told you, bro. Stick with what you know, you feel me?"

The others turned to follow him.

"See you around."

"Yeah, see ya'," replied the Boy, relieved at their departure.

He watched them until they disappeared around the corner then turned and bolted for the sanctuary of his parents" flat.

***

As he made his way to the Poet's apartment the next day, the Boy felt guilty about the betrayal. He toyed with the idea of saying nothing, but the moment he saw the Poet's face, he knew he couldn't keep it to himself.

As the Poet opened the door, the rich aroma of turmeric and garlic wafted out. The Boy stepped in, took off his shoes and hung up his coat.

The Poet glanced back at him as they walked into the kitchen. "Oh dear! Who died? Please tell me someone didn't actually die?"

"Nah." The Boy described his encounter with his old gang.

The Poet looked at him intently. "You shouldn't beat yourself up. We've all done something similar at one time or another."

"I feel like I've failed," said the Boy, dropping his head in his hands and flopping onto a stool. "I failed you, failed the Gardener, ignored everything you've all been trying to teach me." He didn't flinch as the Poet put a consoling hand on his shoulder. "Living in two different worlds can be hard. For a long time, I was scared of who I was — what I was. A gay man hiding in a straight world."

"Must have been rough."

"Rough? It was horrendous. I kept it secret from my friends and family, juggling my two lives. In one, I was the bon vivant, witty, erudite — I even dated a few beautiful women, enough to keep my cover. And in the other, I was gay, embraced the gay lifestyle, had gay friends and gay lovers. But deep down, I knew it couldn't last. I was tearing myself apart."

"What happened?" the Boy asked, sitting up straight.

The Poet bustled around the kitchen. "Hand me those tomatoes." He put the ripe fruit and a bunch of other ingredients in the blender and watched as it blitzed everything into a fine paste.

"The worst thing," he said when the machine had finished. "I fell in love with the most inappropriate person possible."

"A bloke?"

"Of course," laughed the Poet. He tasted the mix. "Perfect. But not just a man," he added. "I'm Christian, and I fell in love with a Hindu."

The Boy shook his head. "Even I know that's a big problem. What did you do?"

The Poet poured the sauce into a large pan. "The scariest, most stupid, most liberating thing possible. I came out. And not only did I come out, I introduced my lover to my friends and family."

"Christ. I bet the shit hit the fan."

The Poet nodded sadly as he stirred the pasta sauce. "One might say that." He looked away for a moment, then turned back. "Pick up that bottle."

"The olive oil with the herbs?"

"That's the one."

The Boy picked it up and examined it. "It's kind of beautiful."

"It is, isn't it? Take a moment to really examine it, fix it in your mind, what it looks like, where everything is."

The Boy did as instructed. "Got it."

"Now shake it, vigorously."

"You sure?"

The Poet nodded.

The Boy gave the bottle a good hard shake.

"Let it settle."

The Boy watched the bottle as the ingredients gradually settled back into place.

"Does it look the same?"

"The same, but different."

"And that's what happens when the shit hits the fan, as you so delicately put it. We are each of us vessels, full of emotions, hopes, dreams. From time to time, life will shake the vessel — just like today — but if it's strong, it won't crack."

"And let me guess. Once everything settles again, it will find its new form, which may be better than before?"

The Poet smiled, stirring his pasta sauce. "Exactly."

"Did everyone eventually come around?" asked the Boy. "Your family and friends?"

The Poet shook his head. "I lost a lot of so-called friends, and I haven't spoken to my father in seven years. He reached for two bowls, filled each with a scoop of pasta and topped it with a serving of sauce. "When the time comes, you'll know what to do."

***

It was almost inevitable that the next time the Boy ran into the Alpha, he was on his way to sit his English Literature A Level. If there was ever a time he wanted his mind to be clear, this was it. However, as he rounded the corner of the estate and saw the Alpha ahead, he found himself eager for the confrontation.

The Alpha blocked his path. "Wassup?" He gave the Boy a searching look.

"Going to my exam."

"Exam? What kind of exam?" The Alpha's voice was too full of surprise to contain its usual venom.

"A Level. English."

The Alpha looked puzzled. "What you wanna do that for?"

"Dad's on the dole and moonlights on crappy construction jobs," said the Boy, "and mum works the night shift for minimum wage at McDonald's. I can't live my life like that. Look around, bro. This estate, it's sucking the life out of us. We all know our future coz it's written in the stories of our families."

The Alpha scanned his face. "You think you can do better?"

The Boy shrugged. "Don't know, man, but I can't live and die like this. I need to find a way to be the master of my destiny, and not just another slave to theirs."

The Alpha glowered at him. "Yeah? Think you're better than us? That you're gonna improve your future?" He snorted. "Me? I love this place. It's our hood, our patch, our peoples. And you want to leave it all for what? To show you a better man? And when reality kicks in, where you gonna be then? Right back in this shithole with the rest of us."

"Maybe," said the Boy. "But I got nothin' to lose, and you don't either."

"Nah, man. I'm good here. But you're prepared to gamble it all on 'the maybe'?"

"Yeah, I'll take the maybe."

For the time since they'd known each other, the Alpha allowed his guard to fall. "Then you take that fuckin' maybe and you run with it." Just as quickly, his ego reasserted itself. "Teacher's pet, are ya?" he sneered.

"Nah. She thinks I'm a waste of space and I'll fail my exam, so I'm gonna prove her wrong."

The Alpha was intrigued. "Bitch said that to you?"

The Boy shrugged. "I see it in her face."

"Fuck 'er!" The Alpha stood aside. "You go show that bitch Crowstone Estate boys can do anything them posh boys can." He clapped him on the back, "Yeah, you show 'em, you show 'em all."

"Yeah."

As the Boy marched away, the Alpha shouted after him. "Crowstone Boys!"

"Crowstone Boys!" he shouted back, punching the air with his fist.

***

As he sat with the Gardener later that day, the old man's eyes were on him. "Something bothering you?"

The Boy nodded. "I ran into the gang leader again today."

"And?"

"Sometimes I feel as though I'll carry that shit with me forever."

The old man thought for a moment. "I want you to try something. When you feel like you're done with something — an emotion, a fear, a memory you struggled with — I want you to imagine putting it in a small metal box, locking it and burying it in the garden."

The Boy frowned. "What? Dig a hole right here in the garden?"

"Why not?"

The Boy looked around. "Where?"

"Anywhere," the Gardener replied with a shrug. "Under that tree. Or right there. Or over there with the tomatoes."

The Boy nodded slowly. "OK..." He did as instructed, making peace with an unpleasant childhood memory and banishing it to the ground.

The old man watched him carefully. "Done?"

"Yeah."

"And how do you feel?"

The Boy gave a shy grin. "Yeah — not bad."

The old man turned his beaming smile on him. "Little by little, the donkey is leaving us..."

248

CHAPTER 5

"Yo, rent boy!"

The harsh voice stopped the Boy in his tracks. He saw the Alpha strutting towards him, his usual cocky expression fixed firmly in place. The rest of the gang trailed behind him.

"Well, well, look who it ain't," he said, his eyes scanning the Boy. "Still putting out for your rich boyfriend?"

"I haven't seen him since, you know …"

"And we haven't seen much of you, either."

A bus rumbled past, engine growling and diesel spewing from the exhaust pipe.

"Been busy," said the Boy evasively.

The Alpha glared at him. "Yeah? Well, whatever the fuck you're doing, you're not doing it tonight."

The Boy looked around uneasily. He had been trying to avoid getting dragged back into the gang and their affairs.

"Remember that video game you and me played back in the day?" said the Alpha.

"*Zombie Crusher*?"

The Alpha grinned. "Yeah. They got *Zombie Crusher 2* at the arcade, and you and me, we got unfinished business."

"Na, you're good," replied the Boy. "I've got shitloads of homework."

The Alpha's smile vanished. "Homework?" He turned to the rest of the gang. "You buying that, boys? Or maybe man's a scared little pussy who's gonna get whooped?"

"Here, pussy, pussy," teased the Muscle.

Their words hit the Boy like a slap in the face, a reminder of the bullying he'd endured at school before he'd joined the gang. "Fine," he told the Alpha. "I'll be there. But be ready, coz ya gonna get licked down!"

The Alpha gave his face a playful slap. "Keep telling yourself that, boy!"

***

As the Boy stalked down rain-slicked Severn Sisters Road towards Finsbury Park, he berated himself for being so weak, for not rejecting the Alpha. He knew a night at the video arcade would be followed by roaming the streets, looking for some hapless mark to roll, or hanging out in the pedestrian tunnel across from the estate.

He had been tempted to run to the Gardener, to draw from his strength and wisdom, but this was something he had to deal with on his own. One night. One night, then no more.

It was easy to find the gang in the arcade. They occupied the whole far end of the room, surrounded by the digital cacophony of video games and speakers blaring out Afrika Bambaataa, intimidating other players with their noise and aggression. As the Boy made his way towards them, he noticed the Muscle's face — a black eye, a swollen lip, cuts and abrasions on both cheeks. "What the fuck happened to you?" asked the Boy.

The Alpha clapped the Muscle on the back. "Blood got jumped by three of the Archway Gang, but he took care of business, didn't you?"

The Muscle nodded. "Had a shank, wet one, the other two split."

"Ma man! They'll think twice before trying to fuck with the Crowstone Boys again," said the Alpha.

The Muscle nodded. "Yeah."

The Alpha turned to the machine, a two-player game. "Ready for that beatin'?"

"In your dreams," laughed the Boy.

"Let's do this." The Alpha fed a handful of coins into the machine and grabbed a control stick. "Game on!"

The Boy grabbed the other controller as the screen dumped them into a nightmarish post-apocalyptic world of zombies and shotgun-toting vigilantes, backed by a thumping soundtrack and a barrage of gruesome zombie noises.

It was clear the Alpha had been practising, but the Boy was a natural games player and kept in striking distance the whole way through.

****

The gang crowded round them, engrossed as the Alpha and the Boy battled it out. None of them saw the leader of the Archway Gang moving stealthily through the crowd; none of them saw the long blade in his hand; none of them saw as he slid it into the Muscle's liver.

251

All the Muscle felt was a sharp pain, then a wave of cold that permeated his entire torso as he collapsed in a heap on the grimy carpet.

"Fuck! Who bumped me?" growled the Alpha as the Muscle fell against him.

The Boy looked around and saw the Muscle on the floor, the blood soaking his white T-shirt, then jerked his head to the door as the enemy slipped out the arcade.

The Alpha read the situation in a single glance. "Get that fucker!" he snarled.

His order snapped the other gang members out of their trance, and they set off, shoving the shocked punters out of their way.

The Boy, the Alpha and the Muscle remained.

The Alpha dropped to his knees and cradled the Muscle's head in his lap in a surprisingly nurturing gesture. "It's all right, man. You're gonna be all right." He looked up at the Boy. "Call an ambulance!"

The Muscle groaned softly. For an instant, his eyes met the Boy's.

The Alpha looked at his blood-soaked jeans and bloody hands then jumped to his feet. "We need to split, quick, before the Old Bill get here." He dashed out of the arcade.

The Boy looked at the Muscle's lifeless body, then he rushed to the door.

***

"I can't get that image out of my head," the Boy told the Gardener. "The way he looked up at me, he knew he was dying, and in that moment, when he was scared and alone, I ran away and left him."

"Self-preservation is a strong instinct," said the Gardener.

"That's how we rewarded his loyalty."

The Gardener watched the Boy's restless pacing. "Sit down."

The Boy considered arguing with him but stopped and flopped heavily onto the soft ground.

"Close your eyes and picture the garden," the Gardener said.

The Boy scowled at him. "Why would I do that when I'm sitting in the garden right now?"

"Because I want you to clear your mind of the image of the dying boy, but you can't 'not think' about something, so you must replace it with something else."

"Right." The Boy closed his eyes. "OK, I can see the garden."

"Now picture the geraniums."

"The pink ones with the crinkly flowers?"

"That's them."

The torment slowly started to abate. He felt calmer, and his breathing had slowed down. "Good. Keeping that image in mind, tell me what's really bothering you."

The Boy opened his eyes in a moment of realisation. "What was I doing there in the first place?"

The Gardener smiled. "And there we have it."

The Boy sighed. "I should have said no."

"You cannot serve God and mammon at the same time."

"Mammon?"

"An ancient Greek word for money. It means you cannot serve two masters simultaneously." He pointed at the garden. "Where are the tomatoes?"

The Boy pointed to his left.

"And the cabbages?"

"On the far side."

"Do you know why?"

The Boy shrugged. "Coz that's where you put them?"

The old man shook his head. "They can't flourish together. One will dominate, and the other will wither away. Life is like that. You either commit to this path or go back to your old life, back to the gang. You can't do both."

"But it's so hard," said the Boy. "They're my peoples."

"Of course it's hard. Remember when you met the Reader?"

The Boy smiled. "How could I ever forget?"

"He said you had to make a second decision. It's time to choose. Which path will you take?"

***

The estate looked bleaker than usual as the Boy made his way between the tower blocks, the heavy sky threatening more rain. His footsteps echoed through a trash-filled passage between the monolithic buildings, his firm stride suggesting a confidence he didn't feel. After sending the Alpha a text to arrange a meeting at their old hangout, the Boy had spent the afternoon psyching himself up for their meeting in a weed-infested empty lot at the back of the estate.

As the Boy approached, he could see the red glow of the Alpha's cigarette shining in the gloom, like a beacon to bring him home.

The closer he got, the more the Boy's confidence ebbed away. He pushed through a gap in the fence and moved hesitantly forwards.

The Alpha exuded confidence and certainty, dressed in his signature tight white T-shirt that showed off his powerful physique. "What's so important?" he demanded as the Boy approached. "Dragging me out here on a shitty night."

"I wanna talk," replied the Boy.

"You always wanna talk," snapped the Alpha. "It's all you've ever been good for."

"I keep thinking about, you know…"

"He's dead. Can't change it." He took a drag on his cigarette. "I got better things to do than hang around here all evening."

"I've been thinking," began the Boy. "Last night was fucked up. It's only a matter of time before it's me, or you."

The Alpha peered at him. "You goin' soft?"

"Nah," the Boy said. "Comin' to my senses." He waved his arms to encompass the whole area. "There's more to life than this shitty estate, and I'm not dying here."

"You're quitting the Crowstone Boys?" The Alpha glared at him, the blood vessels on his temple throbbing. "I should break your arms for even thinkin' it!"

"But you won't!" the Boy snapped back, "because you know I'm right. All this shit with local gangs, it used to just be someone getting beaten up from time to time, but now, with everyone carrying blades and guns, it's next level." He shook his head. "If we keep doing this shit, there are only two outcomes, prison or death, and I'm not feelin' either." He took a deep breath. "I'm out, and if you have any sense, you'll quit too while you still can."

Without waiting for a reply, the Boy turned on his heel and stalked away. He was expecting the Alpha to call him back, or chase after him and grab him by the scruff of the neck, but nothing happened. No angry shout, no rushing footsteps. When the Boy finally looked back, all he could see was the red glow of the Alpha's cigarette in the darkness.

***

The Boy carefully weeded around the base of the tomato plants under the Gardener's watchful stare. He glanced up and nodded towards the far side of the plot. "I was thinking of moving the chives over here with the tomatoes."

"And why would you do that?"

"I was reading last night about growing tomatoes," explained the Boy. "It said chives repel aphids and stuff, so if you plant them near tomatoes, they'll keep the insects away."

"A sound plan," replied the Gardener.

The Boy made his way across the plot and began easing a bunch of chives out of the soil.

The Gardener began, "So it appears that—"

"Don't even say it," said the Boy, looking back.

The Gardener smiled. "You think you know what I was going to say?"

"Sure. Something like, "It appears the company we keep can improve our ability to flourish." Right?"

The Gardener's smile widened, illuminating his whole face. "The student is becoming the teacher, and the teacher is becoming predictable."

"And long may it continue!" grinned the Boy.

"Indeed," smiled the old man back. "At this rate, the day will soon come when you no longer need me."

The Boy's face turned serious. "That's a day I can't imagine."

CHAPTER 6

It was a beautiful late-spring morning as the Boy strolled through Green Park, the flowers pushing their heads up to greet the sun, birds calling from tree to tree. He was wondering what book the Gardener might have for him today, what lesson he might learn.

As he approached the garden, he frowned. There was no sign of the Gardener. The Boy's step slowed. Where was the old man? The park was full of tourists and locals enjoying the sunshine, but no Gardener. As he looked around, he knew the truth.

The Gardener was gone.

A sudden emptiness filled his heart followed by numb panic. He sat heavily on the bench. How could he continue without his teacher and closest friend? Who would be there for him now? What was the point of all this knowledge without having his guide, mentor and role model there to assess his progress?

"Mister Jameson?"

The Boy forced himself to look up. A middle-aged man in a baggy suit was looking at him.

"My name's Simpkins, from the local council. He said you would be here." Simpkins pointed to the bench. "May I?"

"Of course." The Boy felt overwhelmed; things were happening too fast for him to process.

Simpkins sat beside him and ran a hand through his thinning hair. He plopped a battered leather briefcase on his lap and slid out some papers. "He prepared these a while ago," he said as he handed the

Boy a sheaf of papers. "I've marked the places you need to sign with sticky notes."

The Boy looked at the papers. Half a dozen yellow Post-its poked out from the stack. He frowned. "What is this all about?"

Simpkins smiled. "The garden. He has bequeathed it to you. There are the usual covenants regarding use. Essentially, you can only use it as a garden, can't build anything on it." He smiled. "I've never been here before. It's a lovely place, isn't it?"

The Boy stared at the papers.

The Gardener was gone.

The garden was his.

He was the Gardener.

His mind jumped to their conversation a few weeks ago.

"At this rate, the day will soon come when you no longer need me," the Gardener had told him. Did he already know he was dying?

And what had the Boy said? "That's a day I can't imagine."

"And yet, like all progress," he recalled the Gardener saying, "it will happen whether we imagine it or not."

"Ready to sign?" Simpkins held out a pen.

The Boy let out a deep sigh and signed without reading a word.

As soon as he had completed the last signature, Simpkins scooped up the papers. He handed one set to the Boy, slid the rest back into his briefcase and snapped it shut. Then he stood and offered his hand. "Congratulations. You are now the official custodian of this beautiful space."

***

As he looked around the garden — his garden — the Boy recalled the conversation he'd had in the train carriage with his future self. There were two decisions he had to make; the first was to decide whether to recognise the blessings of the day and start the journey in faith, not knowing where it would lead.

And the second? The one his future self couldn't tell him? It was recognising that even the most profound teachers can walk with us only so far; only in their absence can the roots of their wisdom break into new leaf and branch.

As he gradually absorbed the Gardener's loss, the Boy realised the fear of letting go was what had always prevented him from moving forward in life. It was the mechanism his ego had tried to use to contain him — his donkey.

The Boy slowly allowed himself to watch the passers-by as he adjusted to the reality of life without the Gardener, learning to use the lessons the old man had taught him.

More than anything, the Boy had learned about faith and belief. As long as he remained true to the essence of his heart, anything approached with sincere intent would succeed.

He wouldn't need months, weeks, or even days to complete each journey. Every action of every day had the potential to either reinforce his faith and belief, or question it.

In recalling that, he found the strength to let go, to continue the journey. The most important part of the Gardener was still with him — his smile. A smile imprinted on everything he had ever imparted to the Boy, embedded in everything the Boy did. That smile represented a love the Boy never previously knew could exist; a love he would never have fully understood had it not been for his mentor.

The Boy settled back in his seat, closed his eyes and allowed the sun to wash over him. He felt peaceful, enlightened, more at ease than before. The face of the Gardener floated past, mingling and merging with those of the Architect and the Poet, and various other mentors who had helped him on his journey.

The Boy surveyed the garden. He pictured dozens of small boxes, each containing something of value, buried under tree after tree. They looked so real to him that, for a moment, he half-imagined they *were* real rather than figments of his imagination.

The Boy settled back on the bench, closed his eyes and pictured himself as the student, the donkey, then took those images, put them in another little box and buried them deep beneath the old apple tree. Bye bye, Donkey...

The Gardener would be proud of him.

CHAPTER 7

"So, this is where you hang out?"

The Boy reined in his amazement as he turned and saw the Alpha scanning the garden. He finished tamping the soil round a new plant and stood up. "Hey," the Boy replied, embracing him. "Never thought I'd see you here."

"Yeah, things change, ya know?" The Alpha lifted his T-shirt and revealed a long pink scar across his ribs. "I thought I'd, well, check it out."

He looked like a fish out of water. The Boy wondered if he had looked so out of place the first time he had visited the garden. "Why don't you give me a hand?" he suggested.

"I don't know nothin' about gardens."

"That's how we all start. Here, give me a hand with this pruning." He handed the Alpha a small pair of hand pruners. "You cut right here, just above the new branch, like that. Got it?"

The Alpha nodded. "I can do that."

"Cool. All six need doing. Give me a shout when you're done."

The Alpha looked back and forth between the Boy and the bushes. "And you do this for fun? Voluntarily, like?"

The Boy nodded. "Give it a go."

"Seems like a waste of time. You do all this work to make something grow, then you cut it down."

The Boy recalled having the same conversation with the old man. "Uncontrolled growth has no form or purpose," he told the Alpha, "But when we prune it, it grows back stronger."

To his surprise, the Alpha nodded. "Makes sense."

They worked in silence for a few minutes. Every so often, the Boy glanced over at the Alpha, who seemed engrossed in the pruning.

"All done," he announced. "Wanna see?"

The Boy wandered over. "It looks great."

"It's not as hard as I thought," said the Alpha. He stood up, stretched his back and looked around. The traffic hum carried faintly from the road, but other than that, the only sound was the flutter of birds from tree to tree. "Peaceful here, innit?"

"Always."

The Alpha nodded. "Nice. So, what's next?"

***

The second time the Alpha came, he brought another gang member who looked disapprovingly around the garden.

The Boy recognised him as one of the Yes Men and realised he didn't know his real name.

"That's it?" The Yes Man looked at the Alpha. "When you said a garden, I was picturing something fancy, like on the telly. This is just a garden!"

"Stop moanin' and listen," ordered the Alpha. "When you're here, our boy's the boss. You do what he says. Got it?"

"It's just a fucking garden," the Yes Man muttered.

The Alpha shoved him. He turned to the Boy. "What do you need him to do?"

"The vegetable patch needs weeding."

"You heard the man. Chop chop."

The Boy gave the Yes Man a hand trowel and showed him the difference between the crops and the weeds, and how to get the weeds out with their roots attached. Once he was sure the Yes Man was doing it right, he returned to the Alpha, who was wandering around, taking everything in. "I wasn't sure you'd be back."

"Yeah, well, it shows you don't know everything, don't it?"

The Boy nodded, trying to keep the grin from his face. "Yeah, but why did you come again?"

"I fuckin' knew you'd ask me that!" protested the Alpha.

The Boy stayed silent to let him think for a bit, a trick he'd learned from the Gardener.

The Alpha squinted at the sun trying to break through a bank of thick cloud. "Dunno. It's quiet here, innit? I found when I was doing that pruning, all the other shit faded away." He looked back at the Boy. "Got any more of that pruning for me?"

***

The local council offices were dreary, with cheap furniture, magnolia walls, and harsh fluorescent lights. The Boy was getting tense just sitting there. He had invested so much in this, but now the moment had come, he was afraid it would all fall apart.

He heard footsteps and saw Simpkins approaching. The man's baggy suit and thinning hair looked at home in the council offices. The two men shook hands.

"Do we have an answer?" asked the Boy.

"We do."

The Boy held his breath.

"The scheme has been approved in principle," Simpkins said. "For every verified twenty hours they spend working in the garden, your volunteers will get one adult education course free of charge."

"Yes!" The Boy couldn't keep the smile from his face.

"We still need to work out the details, of course," said Simpkins, "but I have to say, these young people are lucky to have someone like you to guide them."

As he followed Simpkins down the corridor, the Boy could almost see the Gardener's smiling face. "I can no longer call you Donkey," he was saying. "You have truly become the Gardener."

CHAPTER 8

"Focus on your breathing and allow yourself to gradually return to this space as I slowly count backwards from ten," said a soothing voice.

The Reader breathed deeply and slowly opened his eyes.

He was in a well-appointed office, reclining on a comfortable chaise longue.

A smiling face welcomed him back. "How was it?"

"Amazing," gasped the Reader as he tried to contain the sense of discovery and excitement threatening to overwhelm him. "How long was I out for?"

"Oh, about a lifetime or so. Did you find what you were looking for?"

The Reader nodded. "I found my donkey and made my peace with it."

"That's good."

"But why did you have to die?"

"The only way one knows one has truly learned to ride the bicycle is when the stabilisers are removed. I needed you to know that, even without me, your journey would continue."

The Reader nodded slowly. "How did you know I'd find you?"

"I didn't. I had to trust you would, and you did." She offered the Reader a glass of water. "Now you have found your peace, where would you like your journey to take you next?"

"Good question..."

EPILOGUE

The Reader stepped out of the office into a wood-panelled corridor. As he reached the top of the stairs, a young woman was labouring up, looking around nervously. "Excuse me? Is this the right place for the past-life-regression therapist?"

The Reader smiled. "Doctor Gardener? Last door on the right."

"Thank you!" The woman hurried down the corridor, clutching her handbag.

"Say hi to your donkey for me," whispered the Reader.

***

The noise of the traffic hit the Reader as he emerged from the building and hurried across the busy road towards Green Park. He needed the peace and sanctuary of the open air for a few minutes to clear his brain, but as he walked towards the park, the skies unleashed a heavy spring shower.

The entrance to Green Park tube station loomed ahead. He glanced at the park for a moment, green and lustrous in the rain, then at the pedestrians hurrying into the shelter of the Tube station.

He paused for a moment and smiled softly, as though recalling a half-forgotten memory lodged in the recesses of his brain. "Maybe another day," he muttered as he strode past the park and into the station entrance.

***

The Reader gazed through the window into the darkness of the tunnel as the train travelled north on the Victoria line from Green Park. Sometimes he saw a string of lights, sometimes nothing. He smiled as he remembered all the years he had spent travelling the London Tube and marvelled that he was so certain today was different.

As the train rushed through the tunnel, he returned to his book, marking words and phrases that caught his attention with his metal-tipped clutch pencil. A buzz of expectation rose from the pit of his belly and his nerves tingled as the moment approached. "Soon, soon, soon," rattled the train, over and over.

The doors opened at Euston, and five young men boarded, full of the anger and confusion of youth, yet empty of the manners that maturity brings. The Reader looked up momentarily, casually checking out each one. He'd seen the type many times before. It was always the same. Strength when travelling as a pack, with fake, insecure bravado hiding layers of fear, insecurity and resignation.

He smiled softly to himself.

The Shepherd
(the Soul at peace)

270

"The true shepherd knows his flock, each soul, each blade,

His heart a mirror, where Light softly plays.

He seeks no praise, no worldly recompense,

But lives for love, in pure benevolence.

For in the healing of a wounded land,

He finds the touch of the Beloved's hand."

Anonymous

CHAPTER 1

Persia, sometime in the nineteenth century

Noor surveyed the rocky hillside, watching the shadows lengthen as night approached.

His flock often visited this patch; it was a good spot to spend the night. The pasture was plentiful, there was a stream trickling through the rocks on one side, and the grass was soft for sleeping. In his early twenties, Noor was tall and slender, but what really marked him out among his people were his pale-blue eyes, like frozen dewdrops on a blade of grass in winter.

After a last scan for wolves, Noor settled down in a grassy bower and ate his dinner, gazing at the surrounding hills. He felt truly blessed. He had a wife who loved him, a father, Aasim, who was wise and beneficent, and the caress of the Beloved whose Love shone a universally connected Light on all creations.

His father had moved to the village many years ago, after Noor's mother died in childbirth. After a time, the villagers, impressed with his education and wisdom, asked him to become their elder, the leader of the village.

Aasim had taught his son to read and write, but from the first time Noor climbed into the high meadows of the Zagros Mountains with his flock of sheep, he knew his calling. It was a hard decision — not only was Noor the son of a village elder, the heir apparent, but he revered his father and would do almost anything to please him. Despite that, it was the hills that seduced Noor, not his responsibilities in the village.

The hills were where he felt free, at peace and connected to the universe as he lost himself gazing at the star-flooded heavens on a clear night. It was where he felt complete. Noor embraced the hills, and the hills embraced Noor. To an outsider, the hills might have looked bare and barren, almost devoid of life, but Noor had come to know all the animals and birds. They were his companions, and he soon became as much a part of the governing fabric of the land as the finches and the pheasants, the musk deer and the black bears, the ibex and the wolves.

As the light began to fade and the shadows of the mountains closed around him. Noor settled into the soft grass, pulled out a strip of paper and a pen, and began to write a note to his wife, Rukhshana, waiting for him in their village, four days away.

Each night he wrote her a note professing his love, and each night his falcon carried the note to her. Noor's loving father had also taught his daughter-in-law to read and write during his son's absences, and Rukhshana cherished every intimate message she received from her husband. As soon as she had finished reading Noor's note, she always immediately set about writing him a reply.

Noor dipped his pen into the small pot of ink he carried with him, but as he lifted the pen, he paused. The sheep were restless. Noor frowned. Something had spooked them. Noor wanted to write his note before darkness fell, but he had learned never to ignore the warnings from his flock. He was attuned to them, and they to him, and it was wise to listen to their messages.

He stood and peered into the gloom. The flock were edging towards him, bleating, moving away from the small ravine where the stream cascaded down the mountain.

"Let's see what all your fuss is about," muttered Noor as he pushed through the flock towards the ravine. They opened to let him through then crowded back together as soon as he had passed.

A howl rang through the still air.

Noor froze.

The flock scurried away from the shepherd, the ravine, the noise.

Noor listened to the silence of the evening then answered with a long howl of his own. After a moment, an answering call came. But Noor knew from experience it was not the sound of a wolf on the prowl, not the call of a pack closing in on its prey. It was a howl of pain.

Noor moved cautiously towards the ravine, his footsteps light on the soft ground. When he reached the grey, lichen-covered rocks, he peered down.

A pair of pale yellow eyes looked up at him.

Why did the wolf not run? While wolves can be aggressive when in a pack, a solitary wolf is a cautious creature. Then Noor saw it — the wolf's leg was caught in a hunter's trap.

Noor hesitated. A wolf was a potential threat to his flock, but he could not bear to see any animal in pain. With a deep sigh of resignation, he climbed down over the rocks towards the wolf.

As he got closer, the animal's eyes followed his every move.

Noor stood in front of the wolf and looked at it. The wolf looked at Noor. It was a distinctive creature, with a thick white blaze of fur running down its muzzle.

"Looks like something has bigger teeth than you," said Noor.

He took a step closer. The wolf drew back its lips to reveal its teeth, its yellow eyes glinting in the pale moonlight.

Noor took another step closer. He was almost close enough to touch the wolf. Slowly, carefully, he extended his hand towards it.

The wolf never took its eyes from Noor's as his hand reached out. It lifted its nose and sniffed his fingers. Noor let it sniff his entire hand before moving even closer, gently stroking the top of its head.

He saw the wolf relax. It looked at its trapped leg, then back at Noor.

"Let's have a look," said Noor softly.

The wolf's front leg was gripped tight in a rusty old trap. From what Noor could see, it was bleeding a little but did not look deformed or broken.

He sat beside the wolf. "This may hurt a bit," he warned.

The wolf sniffed his face and neck. Despite their proximity, Noor felt no fear as he carefully grasped the two sides of the trap and pried them apart.

Almost instantly the wolf snarled, pulled its paw free and jumped back.

It stood and considered Noor then turned and, without a backwards glance, limped away.

Noor threw down the trap, then stood and watched as the wolf was swallowed up by the darkness.

When he returned to the flock, the sheepy huddled around him. It would be a while before they settled down. Noor lay in the grass and picked up his paper and pen. The wolf was still out there. And yet his heart was easy; he felt no threat. He finished writing his note, touched it to his heart, kissed it, then gently tied it to the falcon's leg. He held the bird aloft and watched it streak away into the darkness.

It was a cool night, and he had lit a small fire to keep him warm. The flock stayed close to him that night; all Noor saw from where he sat was a wall of sheep, standing patiently, some wide awake, some dozing.

He reached in his bag and pulled out a book his father had given him. Aasim still hoped Noor would change his mind and travel out into the wide world, so he gave him books about other countries and other people, full of travel and adventures. Noor, however, found everything he wanted in the books. He carefully turned to the first page, settled back on his blanket, and let the words carry him to far-off lands.

CHAPTER 2

Not all villages were like Noor's — lush, verdant and productive. Others were cold, dark places, shadowed by towering peaks and carpeted with arid soil, where people clung to life with the same tenacity as the alpine primroses and saxifrage that dotted the rocky hillsides.

Halima, had suffered in silence for years, waiting for the moment when their village elder died, the moment when, by sheer force of will, she had got the villagers to choose her son, Shahzor, as their new leader. It was a poor village, with limited water and a paucity of good grazing. Halima and Shahzor had turned that to their advantage, convincing the people that the only way they would ever taste the good things in life was by snatching them from the lips of others.

For such a young man, there was much anger and resentment etched in her son's face. He had been fed a diet of bitter milk from his mother's breast, and little had changed since. With no father to raise him and no other male role model, Shahzor imbibed Halima's view of the world. It was a cruel place where you should expect no kindness from anyone, people were not to be trusted, and the only way to get what you wanted was by brute force.

As a result, the village survived mostly from the spoils of banditry, the farmers becoming thieves and bullies under Shahzor's brutal tutelage. The infamy of the village grew year by year as their rampaging raids extended further and further from their homes. Little by little, what had once been a peaceful village, trading crops of lentils, potatoes and barley with their neighbours, had become a rough and inhospitable place. The people lived hand to mouth, their fields abandoned, the men away raiding while the women waited anxiously for their return.

Halima glanced at her son as he stomped through the muddy streets his sword clanking at his side as he pushed his way into a large tent. He made his way to the head of the table and sat heavily next to her. Shahzor, her blessing and her curse, a son born of betrayal, a burden borne alone, and a mirror of the shame and the village's scorn. And despite that, he was her son, the only way she could ever have returned to power, the only way she would ever be revenged.

Shahzor poked at a chunk of meat with a long-bladed knife. "Are they back?"

"We were waiting for you before they shared their news," Halima replied.

Shahzor stabbed his knife into the tabletop, where it quivered as he chewed noisily. "Then send them in!"

She watched him lean back, shoulders pulled back as four ragged men trooped in, their clothes and sweaty faces encrusted with the dust of the road.

"Go ahead," said Shahzor.

"We travelled many miles," began the first.

"Through wind and rain," added the second.

"To bring me news of your hardship?" said Shahzor.

"No, sire," murmured the first.

"Then perhaps you might tell us what you found?"

The first man nodded. "Yes, sire. Our journey took us over three high passes to the valleys that lie beyond. Further than we have ever travelled."

Halima's son pulled his knife from the table and began picking his nails with it. "And?"

"We found a valley like the ones in the prophecies," the scout responded. "A free-flowing river runs through it. The sun is warm and plentiful. Bees fly amidst the orchards, and the hillsides are green and soft."

"The people are happy," added the second scout, "ruled by a village elder whose wisdom is matched by his education."

Shahzor leaned forward, his face giving nothing away. "Bees and green grass and a man of letters? That was what you found?"

The scout nodded, his eyes fixed on his feet.

"Were you clear on your mission?" asked Shahzor.

"Yes, sire."

"Then we are both clear," continued Shahzor. "I didn't send you out to find farmers. I sent you to find riches, correct?"

The scout nodded miserably.

Shahzor turned to his mother. "How can we expand and grow if our scouts continuously fail us?"

Halima had bided her time while the scouts gave their report, but her eyes betrayed her excitement. A valley like the one in the prophecies. Like the one in *her* prophecies... "Perhaps there is gold amidst these pastures," she told Shahzor.

"Please, mother, no more of your alchemy," he groaned. "We need gold, gems, riches, and they bring us back reports of content farmers."

Halima gently touched her son's arm. "Tell us more about this village leader," she asked the scouts.

Shahzor slumped back and resumed picking his nails with his knife.

Halima nodded to the second scout. "Continue."

"He is tall, with striking pale-blue eyes. He speaks softly, but his words carry authority."

"And does he have a name?"

"Aasim."

Halima's eyes widen as she turned her head away, staring the floor to avoid Shahzor's gaze, "That is where we should go next," she replied calmly, disguising her dark arousal.

Shahzor gave her a startled look. "Why? We don't need a farm. We need things we can steal, things we can carry, not apples and potatoes."

The hungry looks of the scouts suggested otherwise.

Halima leaned towards her son. "Think of it. We don't just raid there and steal food. We take over. Move our whole village there."

Her son frowned. "Why would we do that? What about what we have here?"

"Our ground is barren, the river runs dry, our people go hungry. There we would have all the food we needed, and the villagers would be our slaves, working the farms and orchards for us." She gave him a sly look. "And from there, we could seek out new territories to subdue."

Shahzor narrowed his eyes. "Go on."

"There is nowhere left to raid from here. We have stripped the nearby villages of everything of value. But if we move there, not only will we have all the food we need, we can also start to scout even further afield, extend our power into neighbouring territories, places we haven't raided before."

Shahzor's face broke into a smirk. "You're right." He stood, pushed away from the table and marched towards the scouts, who took a step backwards as one man. "Are these villagers well armed? Will they resist?" he demanded.

"We watched them for two days. They are but simple farmers," the first scout told him, his eyes straying to the long, curved blade in Shahzor's hand. "We will meet little resistance."

"Very good. We'll go in two waves. I will lead the attack. Mother, you follow one moon later with half the village."

"Half the village?"

"I will not lose everything we have here based on the words of these scouts."

"A good plan," his mother replied, "but I should come with you when you attack."

Shahzor gave her a dismissive look. "Really, Mother, you are many things, but you are not a warrior. Remain here and keep order in the village."

"Indeed," Halima replied smoothly, "but once you have subdued these farmers, you will need someone to organise them, keep the food supply flowing, and prepare the ground for the arrival of our people. Such things do not happen by themselves."

Shahzor turned towards the door. "Do what you think best." He nodded at an older man with a luxuriant grey beard. "Kasim can organise things here while we are gone."

"It would be my honour, sire," replied Kasim.

Shahzor turned to the scouts. "How many days" march from here for our raiding party?" he asked.

"Six, sire."

Shahzor nodded. "Very well. Tell the men we march in the morning. Be ready." He turned back to Halima. "Mother? You shall have the land of milk and honey that your prophecies foretold. And we, the warriors, will have new pastures to explore!"

He turned back to the scouts, who stood in a small knot by the door. "You still here? You have your orders."

The men needed no further invitation to leave. As one, they scrambled for the door.

Halima watched them go, but her eyes were far away. She pictured a tall man with striking pale-blue eyes and an infant boy with the same blue eyes, her first born, the one true love of her life.

Shahzor stared at his mother, uncertainty etched across his face. "Do my plans please you, Mother?"

"I'll be pleased when you bring me the village elder's head on a stake," Halima hissed.

CHAPTER 3

By the time the sun had cleared the hills, Noor and his flock were already on the move. They had awoken together, the sheep milling around him as he ate some bread and filled his water skin from the stream. He guided them towards a high, rocky ridge that led to the next high pasture.

Noor's mind was filled with images from the book he had been reading. He was daydreaming of the Alhambra in Andalusia, of lush orange groves and the sound of Sufic drums and Umayyadian lutes. Very different from the simple tunes he played on his pipe to amuse himself at night.

Thus engaged, Noor was startled when he stumbled upon an extraordinary battle: a mongoose and a cobra locked in combat.

He stood frozen, unable to look away, and the flock, sensing his mood, paused behind him. It was like something had gripped his feet, trapping him in place, as everything around him fell away. All he could focus on was the mongoose as it darted around the cobra, switching directions, looking for an opening to grab its foe while evading the cobra's deadly bite.

Their motions seemed to slow as terror gripped Noor's stomach.

Stalk.

Strike.

Counter strike.

Neither creature could gain an advantage or simply leave while their mortal enemy was this close.

The cobra darted once again towards the mongoose, who, lightning quick, swatted the cobra's head with its sharp claw and sank its teeth into the cobra's neck.

The cobra twisted and squirmed, but the mongoose held it in a tight grip, its powerful jaws clamped around the cobra's neck while its paws pinned the cobra in place.

The snake squirmed but could not escape or even turn its head to inflict a deadly bite.

Little by little, the cobra's movements weakened. With a final shudder, it went limp.

The mongoose stepped back, surveyed its inactive opponent and turned to scurry away.

But the cobra was not dead. Summoning up every ounce of remaining energy, it struck one last time, sinking its fangs into the mongoose's neck.

Exhausted, it sank to the ground. Its yellow eyes watched as the mongoose took two, three steps, then shuddered and collapsed.

Sensing that the danger had passed, the flock began to move, Noor with them. But he could not shake the battle from his mind. Growing up so closely aligned with nature, Noor had learned to trust his instincts, to listen to the signs and signals that others might miss. His gut told him this was not a random event, that he was supposed to see it. But what did it mean?

The replay of the battle in his mind was interrupted by the screech of his falcon, returning from its nocturnal journey. Noor surveyed the cooking fires of the village from the hilltop and was reassured all was well if the falcon had returned unharmed. He tore two strips of paper from a sheet as his heart told him what to write to his beloved

Rukhshana. Noor sent the falcon on its way with a message tied to each leg.

Still shaken by the fight, Noor turned towards the village. He had plenty of food and had not intended to return for another week, but he could not help feeling the battle was a premonition. He needed to return home as soon as possible.

Noor had always been conflicted by his obligation to the village and his father's assertion that he should preparing for the day he would assume his 'rightful' place as heir to the village. Although he had never questioned it, Noor had always sensed an inner rage within his father, something from his life before he arrived at the village. Nonetheless, he had always taught Noor to shun violence and encouraged him to seek his higher self in everything he did.

As so often, his mind turned to a mother he had no memory of. His father avoided the subject whenever possible, despite Noor's gentle probing, and Noor had always assumed this was because his father loved her so much, recalling her was too painful. His father had told Noor that his mother had died in childbirth, and that was that.

The more Noor thought about the fight between the mongoose and the cobra, the more certain he became that the village might be attacked. Since childhood, he had experienced premonitions that came to pass and had learned to trust his instincts.

Noor redoubled his speed, driving the flock before him, and by nightfall could see the lights of the village in the valley below. He settled the sheep down for the night but was up and moving again by the time the sun painted the hillsides with a rosy morning hue. As Noor hurried into the village, his eyes were busy searching for signs of trouble, anything that might support his premonition, but everywhere was tranquil. His friends and neighbours were going about their lives, greeting Noor with a smile and a wave.

Noor had a joyful reunion with his wife, who was surprised and delighted to see him. As she made him some tea, Rukhshana asked Noor to read his last message to her, a little ritual they had every time he returned from the hills. When Noor had once asked her why, she had said, "Noor-Jaan, listening to you carries me to a place where time does not exist. Once I hear the words from your lips, they stay with me forever."

He smiled and unrolled his last message. "The minute I heard my first love story, I started looking for you, not knowing how blind that was. Lovers don't finally meet somewhere. They're in each other all along. Rumi."

As Noor read his message, he wished he could suspend this moment forever, captured by the sincerity of love in his wife's eyes and the scent of pure rose oil on her skin.

"Something troubles you, my love," she told him once he had finished. "What is it?"

He took her hand and described what he had seen in the hills, the mongoose and the cobra, and the fear he held in his heart.

Rukhshana listened carefully. "Talk to your father," she said. "He will understand what you have seen."

He stood and kissed her. "You always know what to do."

***

Birdsong drifted on the breeze as Aasim cast a small net into the swiftly running water. He turned on hearing footsteps, and smiled warmly at Noor, noting the concern on his face. "Welcome home, my son." He drew in his net and cast it out again.

Despite his desire for his son to follow in his footsteps as village elder, he had long accepted that Noor trod a different path, one that called powerfully to him. And with Rukhshana unable to bear children, it seemed the family line would end with Noor.

His father continued fishing as Noor sat on a large smooth boulder on the riverbank. "I saw something strange yesterday," he said after a few minutes. "It unsettled me."

Aasim listened intently as Noor explained, continuing the gentle rhythm of his fishing, casting the net out, drawing it in. From time to time, a small silver fish flapped in the net, then Aasim would extract it and drop it in a bucket of water on the bank.

"I'm sure what I saw was no coincidence," Noor finished, "but I don't know what I'm supposed to take from it or how to prepare."

Aasim sighed and gathered in his net. He picked up the bucket and sat beside Noor, brow furrowed. "There's something I need to tell you. Something I should have told you a long time ago." He rubbed his forehead, wondering how much to tell Noor. Would it matter after so many years, or was he reading too much into what Noor had seen?

Noor glanced at his father. "It involves my mother?"

Aasim's eyes widened as the sound of birdsong became muffled. "How did you know?"

Noor shrugged. "You're reacting the same way to this story as you always do when I ask you about my mother."

Aasim gazed at the pond skaters skimming across the sparkling water in a dizzy dance. "She's not dead," he said finally.

A jolt went through Noor, numbing both birdsong and stream to a murmur. "Where is she?"

"In a village far from here."

"You left her?"

"Perhaps," said Aasim, "if you know the full story, you will not judge me so harshly."

And so, he told Noor the story of Aasim and Halima.

***

Halima had come from a wealthy family of money lenders in her village and was the only one who was literate. As a child, she loved reading. She devoured books as fast as her family could bring them to her, but she was not allowed to show her talent to the people of the village lest she intimidate a potential future suitor. Her strong character and curious mind were considered inappropriate for a woman, so she was forced to keep her light hidden under a bushel.

Halima's parents had betrothed her to an older man from a family of equal standing, but she refused to marry him. Her father, knowing the stubbornness of his daughter and fearing the reputation of his family would be tarnished by her potential outbursts, reluctantly succumbed when Aasim's family requested that he and Halima be married.

It was a marriage of love. Halima taught Aasim to read and write, and he dedicated his life to loving her, teaching her about the hills and the valleys, the plants and the animals. As Aasim's passion for reading grew, he became fascinated by alchemy and sought out books that described how one could change things and influence outcomes.

At first, Halima was delighted by Aasim's newfound love of learning. She followed him down his murky path, out of love as well as curiosity. However, she soon became consumed by works on dark magic, delving deeper and deeper, and Aasim realised she was out of control, her curiosity changing into a lust for power. The darkness she was exploring was pulling her own darkness to the fore.

In the end, despite his pleas for her to stop, Aasim felt the only way he could save himself and their son was by leaving the village and fleeing as far from Halima as possible. Instead of using the strength of their love to lift her out of the darkness, he left behind an embittered wife, pregnant with their second son.

***

Noor bit his lip. The man he revered and saw as his role model had lied to him his whole life, despite so many opportunities to tell the truth. "Why are you telling me this now?

Aasim exhaled deeply, and his eyes filled with shame as he looked at his son. "How can you tell something such as this to a young child? Then, once the lie becomes entrenched, it is hard to change it."

"But it is many years since I was a child."

"It is a hard thing to tell your offspring at any age," said Aasim. "How could I tell you that I ran away when my wife, the mother of my first child, needed me most?"

Noor stared at his father's profile, anger burning in his chest. When he was growing up, his father had seemed the wisest man in the world, and Noor had never questioned anything he said or did. Hearing this, Noor saw his father in a truer light for the first time. As the veil of his father's perfection fell, so did Noor's unquestionable admiration for him. For the first time, Noor saw his father clearly, from the lines on his face to the demons that haunted him.

"You raised me to be a man known by his fidelity, the integrity in his words and steadfastness in his actions," Noor said through clenched teeth. "Today I ask you to restore my belief in these values in you." Tears trickled down his cheeks as his body quivered in anticipation. "Please … tell me truthfully what happened."

***

They say every parent cries three types of tears in their lifetime: tears of happiness, tears of pain and tears of shame. Now Aasim realised how painful it was to see tears of disappointment from Noor, to watch the admiration drift from his son's eyes and dissolve with every word Aasim spoke.

Aasim beckoned Noor to climb down from the rock and sit next to him by the riverbank. As they sat in silence, Aasim knew that not even the soothing sound of the water could alleviate his son's pain. He wanted to word his response carefully. He took a deep breath and began the detailed story of Noor's mother, unwilling to deny the shameful truth any longer. As Aasim finished the story, any hope of cathartic release was replaced by the naked reality of his cowardice.

"And the mongoose and the cobra?" pressed Noor. "Mother is the cobra, who will one day strike back at you, me, the village?"

His father shook his head as though waking from a deep and troubling dream. He knew Noor was worried. So was he. But he composed his face, pushed his shoulders back and patted Noor's arm. "I think we're reading too much into something that is simply two animals doing what their instinct drives them to do."

"Then there's nothing to fear?"

"No." He forced himself to smile. "All you should concern yourself with is enjoying your time here in the village, then replenish your supplies and return to the hills. Your flock needs to be fatter if it's going to make it through winter…"

Noor nodded. "I'll leave first thing tomorrow."

CHAPTER 4

The bandits set a hard pace as they marched, their weapons over their shoulders and a small bag of provisions on each man's back. Halima kept up with them, the fires of retribution burning brightly inside her as she tramped at her son's side, matching him stride for stride. The fury that burned inside her allowed no room for weakness; her mind was blinkered on the tall man with the pale-blue eyes and their beloved child, Noor, whom he had taken from her.

By the end of the fifth day, they were in the hills above the village, looking at the warm yellow lights twinkling in the valley. Shahzor and Halima stood on a rocky outcrop looking down on the unsuspecting settlement, their men making camp around them. "We should approach in the pre-dawn darkness and attack as people are waking up," said Halima.

"The men are tired from the march," said Shahzor.

"Tomorrow they can rest in clean beds with freshly cooked food brought to them by the women of the village," his mother replied. "Believe me, their tiredness will vanish the moment we attack."

Shahzor seemed unconvinced.

"There's another reason I'm keen to attack this village," Halima took a deep breath.

"I believe this is where your father now lives. I believe he is the village elder the scouts described."

Shahzor turned to her, his face scarlet. "The betrayer?"

Halima nodded.

"And we shall finally have our revenge?"

"We shall. One more thing. You have a brother. It's likely he is still here."

Shahzor's face darkened and his eyebrows knotted in a frown. "A brother?"

"Perhaps. We shall see." She studied his face. "So, shall we wait or descend on them at the earliest opportunity?"

Shahzor gave a wicked grin. "I shall give the order."

Halima watched as he moved among the men, communicating the plan. She knew her son better than he knew himself. He was strong but impulsive. Fierce but hot-headed, courageous but thought only of the moment, never developing a plan. But, above all, she knew he would obey her. His need for her approval was stronger than anything. As long as Halima could rely on that, she could get him to do whatever she wanted. He revered her as a powerful talisman whose magical powers kept him and his men safe and gave them strength and protection when they raided villages. Halima counselled her son, whispering her thoughts and ideas in his ear, but she left the execution of her plans in his hands. Halima was the puppet master, Shahzor her puppet.

As dawn illuminated the village, Shahzor and his ruthless warriors descended like a relentless storm, leaving nothing but wreckage in their wake. Their ferocious onslaught was swift and merciless, engulfing the villagers in chaos and terror before they could comprehend the gravity of their situation. In a whirlwind of violence, homes were ravaged, lives were shattered, and the once tranquil sanctuary was devastated. The men of the village, valiant in their attempt to defend their families and homes, were mercilessly struck down, their bodies bearing the grim marks of their struggle. The remaining villagers, hearts heavy with grief and fear, were herded into the village hall, their spirits broken by the brutal assault.

Halima stood in the shadows at the back of the hall and watched Shahzor strut to the front and survey the cowering villagers.

"My name is Shahzor," he announced to fearful silence, "and I am now your leader." He preened his moustache, surveying the women. "Everything in this village belongs to me. Half of your food will be given to my men, and in return we will stay here and protect you from bandits."

Aasim stepped forward, his face bloodied and bruised. "We had no need of protection until you came," he said. "We will gladly give you all the food you need for your men. I can see they are hungry — but there is no need for you to stay here."

The villagers murmured in agreement.

Halima's heart raged as she immediately recognised Aasim's voice from her hidden position. Her son turned his eyes on Aasim. So, this was his long-departed father, the man who had abandoned him. "You are the elder?" he asked.

Aasim nodded. "It is my honour to be considered so."

"That a man such as you can be considered their leader speaks very poorly of these people," Shahzor told them. "An elder should be wise, honourable and trustworthy. You are none of these things." Halima listened intently as a murmur of surprise rippled through the village hall, her husband's cowardice confirmed in her eyes.

Despite the violence of the attack, it was common for such acts to be followed by courtesy. Shahzor was displaying nothing of the sort.

"You, however, represent all that is wrong in a man. Abandonment, cowardice, dishonour — these are your stock-in-trade."

Aasim shook his head. "Sir, I believe you have me confused with someone else."

"Did you not leave your wife with an unborn child, at the time of her greatest need?"

There was a murmur of disbelief among the villagers. "That was a long time ago," replied Aasim, his face flushed. "And I had good reason to do so."

"Good reason?" sneered Shahzor. "What could ever justify leaving your son to make his own way in the world?"

Halima's eyes were hungry with anticipation as the realisation of Shahzor's identity hit Aasim. "You … my son?" he gasped. He looked around, regaining his composure. "Then my case is proven by your presence here. I see many of your mother's qualities in you."

"And what would those be?" demanded Halima, striding into the centre of the room.

Aasim staggered back as though he had been struck. All his past demons had emerged to threaten the new life he had built. Despite his attempts to outrun his destiny, the universe had returned to exact its revenge. His mind flashed to Noor, alone in the mountains with his sheep.

Halima stood tall in front of Aasim's hunched demeanour. "Did you really think you could run away from me and hide forever? I have dedicated my life to finding you, and my son has been taught from childhood to hate you."

Halima surveyed the cowering villagers. "Where is the boy?"

"Boy?" replied Aasim. "There are plenty of boys here."

Her ferocious gaze met his wide eyes. "Don't test me!" she hissed.

"He is pure, connected to the Divine," he whispered, bringing a trembling hand to his face. "Unobtainable and incorruptible." His gaze fell on Shahzor. "Everything your son is not."

"Liar!" screamed Halima. She grabbed the knife from Shahzor's belt and sliced Aasim's jugular in one clean stroke.

Aasim's eyes widened. He clutched at his throat then dropped to the dusty ground, blood spurting from his neck.

Halima dropped to her knees beside him and whispered in his ear. "And indeed We have created man, and We know whatever thoughts his inner self develops. And We are closer to him than his jugular vein." Her cold eyes bored into him. "Where is your god now?"

A shocked silence fell on the village hall as Halima climbed to her feet and stalked out. A smile played on her lips. She had taken her revenge, and it was sweet. Now the villagers would understand who had the real power in the village. "Burn his house to the ground," she ordered as she marched out.

***

Shahzor pushed through the crowd to the end of the room and sat in the elder's chair, his bodyguards around him. "My men are hungry," he shouted. "Bring us food."

The villagers huddled together, whispering.

Shahzor frowned. "What is there to discuss?" he demanded.

A grey-haired man stepped forward. "Shahzor-Jaan. We welcome your presence and that of your men." He gave an obsequious bow. "This is a plentiful valley, with fruit trees, meadows and a fast-flowing river. Why not have your men work with us? We could all benefit from the extra help. We have more than enough fields and livestock to care for, and we can teach you all the skills you need to lead a fruitful, halal life. Become part of our community and we can all grow together." He looked from Shahzor to the villagers, many of whom nodded at the wisdom of his words.

Shahzor inhaled deeply. "This is what your people think?" he asked.

The old man nodded.

Shahzor stood and walked towards him. "Why should I work, when I can simply take what I want?" he said. "My desire is to conquer and rule over these lands, not earn a meagre living working them." He stood in front of the old man and slowly drew his sword. The light from the hall's entrance glinted on the blade. "No, I believe we shall do as I say. I rule, you serve." Slowly, almost gently, he ran his blade into the old man's belly, clean through to his spine. As he withdrew it, the old man dropped to the ground, lifeless. Shahzor's cold eyes roamed across the villagers, revelling in their paralysed fear, the sudden silence echoing their helpless, forced servitude. "Does anyone else have a suggestion about how I should run this village?"

Silence.

"Then bring us food! Now!"

The villagers turned and raced outside as one.

CHAPTER 5

Noor led his sheep along a high ridge, one side still in darkness, the other bathed in crisp early-morning light. The birds were singing before the heat of the day settled in. His conversation with his father had maimed him. To discover the story of his life was based on a lie had wounded his heart. His respect for his father was compromised; he now saw him as fallible, full of the faults and the flaws he had previously only seen in other people.

As Noor walked, he noticed a shadow on the hillside ahead. The sheep halted and clustered around Noor. As he stepped forward, the shadow detached itself from the dark hillside. It was a wolf.

Noor scanned the hill. Wolves were rarely alone, but his sharp eyes saw no more.

He stepped forward and waved his arms, but rather than scampering away, the wolf trotted towards him.

Baffled, Noor once more waved at the wolf and shouted, but it kept on loping towards him. As it emerged from the shadows, he noticed a distinctive white blaze down its muzzle. It was the wolf he had rescued.

The wolf stopped a few paces from Noor, its yellow eyes surveying him, its raised nose sampling the air.

Noor watched it for a moment, then, as before, he held out his hand.

They looked at each other, man and wolf, ancient and implacable enemies. The wolf took another pace forward and sniffed Noor's outstretched hand, then turned and trotted away. Noor smiled as it melted back into the shadows. "Nice to see you too," he thought to himself.

***

Noor ambled along with his flock. He had decided to move them to a high meadow a little further from the village. It was a day's walk, but it was rich with grass and clover, a perfect place to do as his father had said — start fattening up the flock for the bitter winter ahead. There was a rocky pass to cross, the highest point around, and Noor was looking forward to the views from the top. From there, he could see all the surrounding valleys and felt like the king of the world, surveying his domain, the brown hills stretching in every direction finally blending with the distant snow-covered peaks.

Noor scrambled up the rocky path, his flock trailing behind him. He was breathing hard from the climb and the altitude but with a feeling of perspective restoring itself in his heart. In that moment, the pain of knowing his mother was alive had subsided. Where else could a man live with such freedom and beauty? The trail passed through a cleft in the rocks, plunging Noor into the shadows, before emerging onto the high barren ridge.

As he emerged into the sunshine, the chill wind that blew on his face was welcome after the exertion of the climb. The sheep clambered up to join him. Wherever he looked, he was greeted by an expanse of rolling brown hills, dotted with patches of lush, green high pasture. Noor knew there was a whole other world out there, a place of oceans and cities, deserts and jungles, but from where he stood, the hills seemed to go on forever.

As the breeze cooled the sweat on his face, he turned and looked back to his village far below, hidden in a deep crease in the hills. What was that? A plume of smoke was drifting up from the valley, climbing high before dispersing on the breeze. Noor frowned. The cooking fires were too small to create such a column, and it was too early to harvest the grain and burn the stubble.

An image of the mongoose and cobra appeared unbidden in Noor's mind. Had the omen come true? Something was wrong, and despite his refusal to follow in his father's footsteps as leader, he could not ignore it.

Noor raced down the green hillside towards the village, the flock scurrying along behind him.

His stomach sank as he thought about how quickly his father had brushed off his question. The mongoose was his mother. The cobra was his father. Surely they were connected to the smoke that poured from the rooftops of his home? He hoped there was a chance he was wrong.

The flock was usually in tune with Noor, but his panic and haste had unsettled them. They kept stopping, forcing him to double back and drive them on ahead. Despite Noor's relentless pace, it was dark before he reached the village. At the outskirts, he left the flock to find their own way and hurried towards the village hall. There were signs of an attack everywhere — bloody bodies and burned-out huts — but no signs of life. Fear built in his throat as he breathed the acrid smoke. He couldn't tear his eyes away from the bodies of the fallen villagers, men he had lived among since he was a small boy.

As he reached the hall, two armed guards emerged from the shadows. "We've been expecting you," one said. They grabbed him and dragged him into the hall, lit with flaming torches.

The guards threw Noor onto the hard ground in front of the subjugators, sitting side-side like a king and queen.

"You are Noor," said the woman with certainty.

Noor climbed to his feet and looked around. "Where's my father? Who are you?"

"I'm Halima," she said proudly. "Your father is dead. I killed him. A fitting punishment for his betrayal."

Noor's breath caught in his lungs, and the blood rushed to his head. He forced himself to stay upright as a rush of thoughts flooded in. His father was dead. His village was overcome. His heart pounded faster at the thought he had to step up now. "Betrayal?" he gasped.

"He always said love was the most powerful force in the universe," said Halima, "but in my time of greatest need, instead of being my light, he left me alone in the darkness."

Noor's realisation of who sat in front of him stabbed him with singular clarity. As his mother spoke, dark echoes from his father's tale validated, he longed to tell Aasim how much he loved him. He knew he would grieve later, but for now he had to be calm and clear-headed for his people. "You got what you came for," he said, composing himself. "You have exacted your revenge, taken whatever you desire. Now it is time for you to leave."

***

Halima smiled at his bravery, his clarity. My son, she thought. My last true love...

Shahzor felt discarded as he saw her smile at Noor in a way she had never smiled at him. He leaped to his feet and marched over to Noor. "You do not give orders!" he snarled. "I rule this village now, brother." He stalked around Noor, like a hyena circling its prey. "You had everything: a nurturing father, a wife, and you're loved and accepted by all in the village. I am told they see you as a wise and natural successor to your father."

Noor said nothing. His eyes were still fixed on Halima. His mother. The mother he had dreamed of all his life, only to be told she had just murdered his father.

"And yet, with all these things, you chose to be a shepherd," spat Shahzor, his voice dripping with disdain. "You don't deserve to live. The world will be a better place once any reminder of my father's treachery is wiped from the earth!" He drew his dagger and pressed it to Noor's throat. "Have you anything to say before your blood joins your father's on the floor of this hall?"

Noor didn't flinch as Shahzor pressed the blade into his skin. Halima felt his eyes scan her face as blood trickled down his neck to his shirt.

Halima raised her hand. "Wait! This is not the time to act in haste."

Shahzor scowled at his mother. This was not what he had imagined from a mere shepherd. Killing Noor like this would be like slaughtering a sheep. He wanted Noor to react, beg for his life, fight back. Something, anything rather than this meek acceptance.

Halima stood up. "Patience, Shahzor," she said. "We can kill him any time it pleases us."

"It pleases me to kill him now," snapped Shahzor, pressing the blade harder into Noor's neck. "With this pathetic worm dead, there will be no one with the courage to take revenge or fight back." He glanced at his mother. "But if Noor lives, there will be villagers loyal to him who one day might try to kill us." He glared at Noor. "What say you?"

Halima moved slowly towards her two sons. "Act in haste, repent at leisure," she said. "Let us think this through."

Shahzor glowered but said nothing.

"Take him away and guard him well," she told the soldiers standing at the door.

They marched up to Shahzor, whose dagger was still pressed to Noor's throat, and looked from him to Halima.

"Fine!" With a deep sigh, Shahzor withdrew his knife from Noor's throat, stared at his brother, then struck him a vicious back hand blow across the face before marching from the hall.

As Noor staggered backwards from the blow, the guards grabbed him and dragged him from the room, leaving Halima alone.

CHAPTER 7

Noor sat in the dark tent, listening to the activity of the village through the canvas. He had failed his father, his wife, the whole village. If only he had listened to his intuition.

Footsteps and voices approached, the tent opened, and Noor was momentarily blinded by a lantern. When his eyes adjusted, he saw Halima standing before him, her dark eyes surveying his face.

Noor's features remained impassive as he regarded her. How does one react when a mother, long-thought dead, returns like this? Noor chose to feign calm acceptance, hiding the conflicting emotions swirling through his head while he tried to understand the woman who was his mother.

Halima squatted beside him and set the lantern on the floor. She touched his bruised eye and bloody cheek. "He should not have struck you," she said finally. Her eyes examined him, taking in every feature. "So much like him," she murmured.

Noor met her intense gaze, as though by looking in her eyes he could see into her very essence, understand her story without exchanging words. At the same time, he was struggling to understand why she was there, what she wanted from him.

"You knew we had invaded your village, and yet you came," she said. "Why?"

"They are my people, my family," Noor said.

Halima furrowed her brow. "Only a fool walks into the fire knowing its nature."

"I didn't wish to extinguish the fire," he replied. "To defeat it would only mean living in fear of the next spark. But if the river can meet the fire, perhaps both will learn their limits — even if one is eventually consumed by the other."

Her eyes probed his face, as if trying to understand his calm demeanour. "What did your father say about me?"

"For most of my life, I believed you had died in birthing me," said Noor. "But a few days ago, he told me the truth about how and why he left you."

"Then you understand my bitterness?"

Noor nodded.

"Revenge is a cruel mistress," sighed Halima. "I know it has corrupted me, but it was all your father left me with, all I had to cling to through the dark years."

"You had reason to hate him," said Noor, "but he was a good man and a wise leader for our village."

The tent entrance was thrown open, and Shahzor stood silhouetted in the doorway. "Mother, it is time to put an end to this dog and teach the village a lesson."

Halima jumped to her feet and wrapped an arm around Shahzor's shoulder. "I have been questioning him," she said. "He is a simple man, with little in his mind. He is no threat to us." She glanced at Noor. "If we kill him, he will soon be forgotten, and the villagers will learn nothing."

Shahzor frowned. "What would you have me do?"

"Exile him," his mother said. "If he is banished to the hills, he will be a constant reminder to the village of your strength and wisdom.

Any man with a sword can kill another. It takes a strong man to cast out his enemy, to show he is unafraid of any man."

Shahzor looked at Noor sitting quietly. "Banish him?" A cruel smile crossed his face. "Show them my strength?"

"We can use the threat of killing him whenever we want to prevent a revolt," Halima said, her chin raised as she looked Shahzor in the eye.

"Publicly humiliating him in this way will ensure the villagers fear us; no one will dare retaliate," said Shahzor slowly.

"And I will take his wife as my slave," said Halima, "as a guarantee against him ever doing anything rash."

Noor gasped. He was powerless.

Shahzor nodded. "Yes." He grabbed Noor's arm and dragged him to his feet. "Let's do it now."

CHAPTER 8

Once more Noor was in the hills with his flock and the wild animals for company. He hadn't taken the sheep with him when he had tramped off alone into the darkness, but in the morning, he had woken to their familiar noise and smell.

The villagers needed to shear the flock, so that evening after dark, he led them down to the village, while Shahzor's guards were sleeping, and penned them up, then headed back to the hills unseen. But sure enough, when he awoke, they were once more on the meadow around his resting place, waiting for him to lead them deep into the hills.

Noor gave up trying to return them after that. Despite the veneer of domesticity, ultimately the sheep were wild animals and would do as they pleased.

His days soon fell into a familiar pattern of waking and sleeping, tramping the hills by day and settling down with a small fire at night. It was only then, when normally he would have been sending messages to Rukhshana, that his thoughts turned to the village and those he had left behind. He missed her desperately. Despite living a peaceful existence, in tune with the rhythm of nature, he missed his wife terribly but could do nothing about it. Accepting his exile was the only way to keep her alive.

And so, Noor found himself turning more inwards with each passing day, becoming more a part of the hilly wilderness and less a part of man's domesticated world. The village lay far below, but he had long ago rejected the responsibility for their well-being, a decision which his exile had reinforced. His father's choices had set up a cycle of revenge that Noor refused to continue. His future was a solitary one in which he would use his loneliness to strengthen his bond with the Divine.

There was little food to be found in the hills, but Noor was slowly losing the need to eat. His mind was consumed with his inner conflict and his rejection of tradition and the leadership of the village. He had chosen a spiritual path that required the ultimate sacrifice: the surrender of his corporeal self in service of a higher calling.

***

One morning, several weeks after his banishment, Noor awoke to see a small group of people climbing the steep hillside towards him. As they drew closer, he recognised four village elders. He sat, patiently awaiting their arrival.

They exchanged greetings, and Noor invited them to sit with him and enjoy the cool morning air before the sun rose over the ridge.

Noor had not eaten for three days and gratefully accepted the fresh bread, soft cheese and crisp juicy apples they had brought. "How did you find me?"

"Noor-Jaan," one man replied, "each night we see your light burning in the hills. It is a beacon of hope for us in a cruel world, a sign you are there for us, biding your time, waiting for the moment."

Noor frowned. "The moment?"

The men nodded. "When you will return and lead us in a revolt," another said. "The people are ready. We just await your word."

"I am not your leader," Noor said. "I am not the person to lead a fight against the bandits."

"Your father was our leader," a third elder said, "and now you are." He uttered this with such simple certainty, Noor could not think of a response.

"How is my beloved Rukhshana? Is she safe?" he asked.

"She is safe, for now, under the protection of Halima. We couldn't tell them we were coming through fear that Shahzor would find out and kill us."

"And the rest of the village?"

"We are surviving," the first elder replied, "but we are afraid and hungry, giving most of what we grow to our new master. We need you, Noor-Jaan."

"Now is the time to attack," added another. "Shahzor has shown his weakness by sparing you. He is afraid of you."

"Let's attack them now, master, when they least expect it," said a third. "With you at our head, we cannot fail."

There was such fervour in everything they said, Noor felt overwhelmed. "Please, listen to me."

The men leaned closer. "Yes, master."

"I am neither your master nor your leader. I rejected that path long ago." He raised his hand to silence them as they started to argue. "I am a simple shepherd. Shahzor has banished me to the hills, and here I will remain."

The men looked at each other, clearly uncertain how to proceed.

"Please, leave me in peace," Noor said.

They tried to persuade him further, but it was clear Noor was not for turning.

Slowly, reluctantly, they climbed to their feet, bowed to Noor, then headed back down to the village.

Noor watched until they vanished from sight then pulled himself wearily to his feet and began climbing towards a high meadow. He would not be so easy to find the next time.

As he climbed, a burden began to lift. The further he got from the village, the more separated he felt. By lunchtime, he was high on a rocky ridge, the whole world spread out before him. He sat and opened the cloth from the villagers. The warm aroma from the bread washed over him as he broke it open, a perfect match for the tangy cheese and fresh fruit. After three days without eating, he should have been ravenous, but as he looked at the food, his hunger faded, the cavity in his stomach resonating in harmony with the drum beat of the universe.

Noor stood, broke the bread into small pieces and threw it into the wind. The birds that always followed him swooped down and pecked at the morsels.

Next, he took out his knife, cut the apples into chunks and threw them into the meadow. Within a few minutes, a family of rabbits appeared and feasted on the fruit.

Noor looked around. The wolf with the white blaze was standing on a rocky outcrop watching him, as it often did since Noor had freed it. Unafraid, Noor walked to the wolf and held out the cheese. The creature studied Noor, its implacable yellow eyes taking in every detail, then it carefully sniffed the cheese and gently took it from Noor's hand. It gulped it down in one, turned and trotted off.

Noor settled onto the grass, closed his eyes and breathed deeply. "If I no longer need food," he thought, "I am free to focus on healing, not revenge. I am part of the hills, and the hills are part of me."

***

Hearing of his wife in captivity had torn through him. He'd written to Rukhshana of the sacrifice he needed to make to break the cycle of destruction in his family, restore his father's honour and save his people. Her belief in his mission was a burden forced on Rukhshana not of her choosing, and Noor could not forgive himself, knowing his wife would hear about him only through stories. His love for Rukhshana was as intense as the pain of not being able to protect her, to hold her.

***

One day without food turned into two, then three, then a week. In time, the outer world no longer held any appeal. From time to time, Noor wondered how things were in the village and thought about Rukhshana, but he had long ago accepted these were things outside his control. His body was nothing but a shell, a vehicle for his thoughts and conflicts, his struggles and revelations.

Freed from everyday concerns, his mind wandered freely, roaming into the deep, dark valleys of madness, then soaring into the high mountains of ecstasy. Waking dreams merged with hellish nightmares; moments of lucidity were peppered with jolts of fantasy and imagination. He was losing his grasp on the real world, but rather than fight it, he welcomed it — this detachment from the material.

Day by day, his beard and hair grew longer and wilder, and his clothes became more stained and torn, until they were nothing more than scraps clinging to his emaciated frame.

Temptation, when it came, visited him in the cold hours before dawn. The chill of the mountains would penetrate him to the bone as he lay on the hard ground. Visions of lying beside Rukhshana in a warm bed came unbidden, calling to him, teasing him with the perfume of her skin.

Your people need you, said a voice.

You have deserted them.

It is time to take up your father's mantle, to become the man you should be. You have only to take up the cudgel and lead your people to victory over Shahzor, then everything will be yours.

He could almost taste the food as he imagined sitting at the head of the table celebrating their victory. The table was heavy with roast lamb, the hot juices dripping from his fingers as he bit into a succulent chunk of meat or downed a cup of rich nectar.

The villagers would fete you. Instead of living a life of misery alone in the hills, you would live comfortably, loved and respected by all.

But whenever his thoughts began to waver, other images would appear — pools of blood, the hacked and mangled bodies of the villagers who had trusted him as Shahzor and his men took their bloody revenge...

And then Noor would awaken, force his feeble frame upright and walk until dawn splashed the peaks with soft pinks and yellows to announce the arrival of another day. It was then, with the first rays of sun on his face and his flock around him that Noor felt most alive, most certain in the difficult path he had taken.

He would often stretch his skeletal arms wide to accept the dawn and let forth a howl of pure animal energy at having survived another day, at having taken another step towards the Divine.

Little by little, his journey took him from madness to enlightenment and back. The veils of all that bound him fell away, and the Light shone through him with increasing ferocity. He experienced emotions he couldn't explain as he sensed leaving his body with increasing frequency.

On one such occasion, he felt a peaceful, undefinable presence.

"Am I hallucinating?" asked Noor.

"No," the presence replied, "you are sensing other dimensions, transcending, unrestricted by the elements."

"Who are you?"

"I was here before the earth, wind, fire and water. Each contain the history and stories of this world. I see the past and the future. I was present at the creation of the universes and at the end of days, and I traverse between them."

"You are … Time?"

"I am Time. I have experienced every moment of every soul on every earth that exists in the universes."

"There's more than one earth?"

"Multiple earths, multiple skies, multiple dimensions, all connected through the fabric of time."

"What is Time?" asked Noor, trying to rationalise this presence.

"Moments connected by intention, desire and hope."

"And what is this moment?"

"This is your moment. Here. Now. Give yourself to it, but not with your mind. The mind analyses, compares, confuses. It will only remind you of your hunger, your conflicts. The heart thinks, clarifies, speaks the truth. It will confirm your intent, strengthen your conviction. Trust in its judgement."

In silence, Noor thought about these words.

"Why do you want to die?" asked Time finally.

"Love brought me into this world," Noor replied, "and only love should be allowed to remove me from it. My father ran away from love to our detriment. I wish to run towards Love to cleanse the fate of those I cherish. If I live, if I take up the burden of responsibility for my family and my community, I will only perpetuate the cycle of enslavement."

"And if you die, what will happen to those who love you? Treasure you?"

"When I die, hope, strength and compassion will remain in remembrance. This body will perish and no longer make demands of me. My dying wish is to know my father's love taught me, guided me, and allowed me to complete my journey. I wish to remain sincere to my intention.

"I am drunk on madness and wish to lose myself to my affliction. Dear Time, do not continue to torture me by keeping me here. I no longer care for this world, and my thirst can only be quenched by the release from all that binds me."

Without words, he sensed the warm glow of certainty wash over him as the universe conspired to race him toward *his* moment in time.

***

As Noor continued his journey towards the Light, Rukhshana noticed life in the village settled into a new rhythm. Although Shahzor was a new, less benevolent leader, the farmers still tended their crops, and the women still cooked the family meals and looked after their children.

Shahzor soon lost interest in Rukhshana. He often went on raids to nearby settlements, leaving Halima to run the day-to-day business of the village. While there were more mouths to feed than before, the village had always produced a surplus bounty, and the farmers soon became skilled at setting aside enough food for their families.

Left to her own devices, Rukhshana helped the older members of the village and acted as an intermediary between the villagers and Halima. Her thoughts regularly returned to Noor. The villagers who visited him on told her of his transformation — and she often stood at the edge of the village, staring at the folds of the distant hills, trying to picture him.

"You miss him?"

Rukhshana turned to find Halima beside her.

"He is my husband," said Rukhshana simply.

"That is as it should be. Walk with me."

The two women walked along the river; the clear water rushing over the pebbles accompanying the silence.

"I've been watching you," Halima said.

Rukhshana didn't reply.

"The people trust you, respect you."

Still Rukhshana said nothing, unsure of Halima's intentions.

Halima stopped. "We should work together."

Rukhshana frowned. "You would use me? To what end?"

"To make life easier." Halima sighed. "We came here as conquerors, and I came for revenge, but now — we need to find a way to make the peace work to the benefit of all."

"You killed my father-in-law, banished my husband, and now you want me to trust you?" said Rukhshana, hands on hips.

"Trust? No. Trust is earned, not given." Halima looked around as if the right words were on the breeze. She took a slow breath. "I cannot undo what I've done, but I don't want the rest of my life to be measured by my past."

Rukshana gave no response, preferring to retain composure by focussing on the ground.

Halima's tone wavered, testing terrain she'd never treaded before. "At least give me the benefit of the doubt. Use your knowledge of the village and the people to make life easier for all of us."

Rukhshana reflected on Noor's guidance as she studied Halima's face. "I will work with you," she said finally. "But if I see any sign you're using me, I'll do everything in my power to oppose you."

Halima nodded. "Thank you. That is as it should be."

And so, Halima and Rukhshana entered into an uneasy alliance. Halima had the trust of the soldiers, while Rukhshana had the trust of the villagers. With Shahzor often gone on raids to nearby villages, between them they ran the village and resolved the petty disputes that inevitably arose.

***

Alone in the mountains, Noor noted the passing of the seasons. As the cooler weather reached the high ground, his body still made its demands, but he chose to ignore the physical and focus his energy on

315

his chosen path. Over time, the body's demands grew weaker, its cries became fainter, until that glorious day when Noor no longer noticed them, so certain was he of his journey.

Once he was no longer tempted by his body's incessant needs, he could devote his entire being to a path from which there was now no return. Each passing day brought him closer to his destiny, brightening the light that shone in, through and around him.

The villagers made further attempts to win him over to their cause, but the Noor they had known was no longer with them. He refused their food, offers of new clothes and pleas to lead them against the bandits.

As the days blurred into each other, his clarity and foresight slowly strengthened his connection with the Divine, until it was no longer possible to tell whether the light shone on him or from within. Noor was the light; the light was Noor.

The mountain animals were drawn to him, the rabbits and weasels staying close for warmth in the wind and rain, the wolves dropping remains from their kills by his feet, which he left untouched. Despite their love for him and their attempts to feed him, he grew weaker and more ephemeral with each passing day, his only connection with his past being the messages he still sent to Rukhshana.

Yet, he was tranquil. His sole wish was to remain true to his father's teachings. Noor prayed without fail for forgiveness and understanding for leaving his wife, and to be released so he could journey in union with the Beloved.

His visitors from the village no longer tried to convince him to lead them. The initial conflict between their desire for him to become their leader and his desire to complete his spiritual journey passed, like a brief rainstorm on a hot summer day. As the weeks passed, they began to revere him. Tales of mystics who renounced the physical and turned to the spiritual were common in their religion, but to see it happening, and to someone they had known and loved, was unheard of. They came, in twos, threes, fours, to the holy man of the mountains, as he embraced the Divine, seeming to glow with an inner light.

CHAPTER 9

Meanwhile, life in the village continued much as it always had. The river still flowed, the sun still shone, the rain still fell. The crops grew and were harvested, babies were born, old people died. And then Rukhshana became sick.

Halima was the first to see it, to notice how listless she was as she went about her chores. At first, she thought it might be caused by worrying about Noor's pitiful state, but day by day Rukhshana weakened until the morning she could no longer climb from her bed. Halima felt her brow — she was hot and feverish. As the day progressed, her fever climbed, and she became lost in fever-driven nightmares that caused her to thrash around and cry out.

The village healer was called, an old woman with bent limbs and white hair, but after spending whole day with Rukhshana, she announced nothing could be done. After the healer had left, Halima stood over her bed, watching. Rukhshana was her son's wife, and they had proven an effective team. But they had also, little by little, become friends. Halima could not stand by and watch her die. The village needed her. Halima needed her.

So, she did what she had avoided for years uncounted — she opened her books. The pages drew her in as she searched for a remedy that might save Rukhshana. She no longer saw pure darkness in them, something that had poisoned her. They had the potential for good and bad, and her intent had made the difference. If she approached them looking for power and the ability to control and manipulate people, that is what she would find. But if she turned to them seeking truth, love and healing, she would discover them.

Over time, she found the vacuum left by Aasim's death created a space that could be filled with redemption. While she could not save Aasim from her anger, she now felt the need to save Noor's wife from death. Halima had once thought her salvation would be in the death of someone who wronged her, but this had not given her the peace she craved. She realised true redemption lay in the salvation of all that was beautiful in her son's eyes.

Even so, as Halima read, the tentacles of darkness crept out from the pages, offering her power untrammelled, secrets that would transform her into a mighty priestess of great power, and even greater darkness.

But Halima shut her mind to the temptations and focused on her love for Noor and her higher purpose — to heal another. In time, she found a simple herbal remedy.

Once darkness fell, she crept from her tent to the hills, searching for the necessary herbs. On her return, she whispered a dua while preparing a bitter tea.

Rukhshana was too ill to sit up and drink, so Halima stayed by her bed all night, dipping a small cloth into the brew and squeezing it into the corner of her mouth.

As the first light of dawn crept over the hills, the cup that had held the brew was empty. There was nothing more Halima could do, and she fell into a heavy, dreamless sleep on a blanket beside Rukhshana's bed.

***

"Halima?"

She slowly opened her eyes, stretched her aching back and sat up suddenly as she realised the voice was Rukhshana's.

319

Halima touched Rukhshana's forehead. "We are blessed by the Beloved." The fever was gone. Her eyes were clear. A healthy flush had returned to her pallid cheeks.

Rukhshana looked around the small room and nodded at the dried herbs in the corner, the pestle and mortar, the small pot sitting over the embers in the fireplace. "You healed me?"

Halima brushed her unkempt hair from her face then gently held Rukhshana's hand between her palms. "At first, I feared you were ill from sorrow at your husband's condition, but as your fever rose, I realised it was something more."

"I have long ago resigned myself to Noor's decision," Rukhshana whispered. "But why did you help me?"

Halima looked at the ceiling for a moment. "Family looks after family," she said, then lifted one hand to her heart and wept tears, releasing her from the binds of her past.

***

It didn't take long for word of Halima's healing powers to spread through the village. The villagers began coming to her whenever they or their children were injured or unwell. At first, she wanted to turn them away, not wishing to draw attention from Shahzor, but the numbers increased as knowledge of her powers spread to villages in the adjoining valleys.

As she became increasingly busy, Halima took Rukhshana under her wing, teaching her how to find the right herbs, how to prepare them as soups, teas, potions and poultices. To Halima's surprise, Rukhshana cherished her new role. Halima's knowledge had become a tool used to heal, not destroy. The village's burgeoning reverence aided her transformation, filling her longstanding bitter void of rejection. Her newfound acceptance, however fragile, gave her the strength to accept all she was afraid to embrace before and become more than she would otherwise have been.

Rukhshana was not just a quick learner; she possessed a wisdom far beyond her years. Soon, not only were people coming to see the two women when they were unwell, they were also seeking out Rukhshana to share their problems and listen to her kind, insightful words. The alliance that had started in the summer was bearing a full crop as winter crept from the hills.

***

Shahzor was not happy with the change in his mother and her growing relationship with Rukhshana. The emergence of her loving, nurturing side was a sign of weakness that could undermine their control of the villagers and risk losing everything they had gained.

Each day, more people waited outside his mother's house, seeking help and attention from Halima and Rukhshana.

What was wrong with her? She used to be so strong, so powerful. She had taught him to have the heart of a lion, the viciousness of a hyena, the cunning of a fox. And now she was healing people and listening to their woes. She was also spending more and more time with Noor's wife, the two women seemingly happy in each other's company, when they should be implacable enemies.

But how could he go against her? Despite his fearlessness in battle, Shahzor was afraid of his mother. He might wield a mighty sword, but she had the power of words. Whenever he tried to challenge her on something, she had a way of making her position seem the only reasonable option, while his arguments sounded weak, stupid and childish.

Shahzor started taking long walks around the village, his rage building with each stride. This conquest had not turned out as he had expected. His men were turning from soldiers into farmers and had lost their appetite to conquer new villages and move from this fertile land; his mother was becoming respected and revered; he was no longer needed. He missed the old days of raiding, plundering and killing, and the fear and respect he had commanded from his own men and those they attacked. Courage and violence were his tools, not a hoe or plough. What would happen to his reputation, his control, if he relaxed his iron grip?

On one of his evening walks, Shahzor noticed that, as the villagers passed the apple orchard at the north end of the village, they gave a little nod of respect towards the distant hills. He frowned. He knew of no shrine in that direction. As he looked at the brown slopes commanding the valley, a villager scurried past and nodded towards the hills.

Shahzor grabbed him by the shirt and pointed. "What's up there? Why do you give the mountains such respect and none to me?"

The man quaked and tried to avoid Shahzor's fierce gaze. "It is nothing, master, just a stupid superstition."

"Don't lie to me," growled Shahzor.

"Please, master, I'm just a simple farmer," the man whimpered. "Don't hurt me."

"Hurt you? Why would I hurt you?" He pushed the man to the ground. "Go!"

The people had no respect for him. They feared his cruel temper and sharp blade, but they didn't respect him. He gazed at the distant hills again, now shrouded in darkness. A faint light shone in the distance, high up on the mountain. That's where the villagers' respect lay! With his brother, Noor, living in the hills, his light a symbol of goodness and hope.

Shahzor's brow creased in anger. His mother had advised him to spare Noor, saying that to let him live would serve as a constant reminder to the villagers of Shahzor's power, but it had become the exact opposite. It was a sign of Shahzor's weakness and the first sign of his mother's weakness — the moment when Shahzor started to lose his grip on power.

End Noor's life, end the villagers' foolish adoration of him, and things would return to their rightful state. Shahzor would once more be feared and respected, and his mother could again take her place by his side, supporting him as she once had done.

CHAPTER 10

Shahzor set out at dawn to find Noor. He had told no one, not even his mother, of his plans. His aim was simple: find Noor, kill him and bring his body back to the village. That would show them once and for all who was in charge.

As he climbed, his eyes scanned the hills, looking for any signs of his half-brother. As he approached the spot where he'd seen the flickering light the previous evening, he found the flock of sheep that had followed Noor to the hills.

Shahzor marched through them, and they bleated as they scampered away. Weak, pitiful creatures like his brother.

And there was Noor.

Shahzor swallowed hard, eyes wide. Noor's body was skeletal and burned dark by the sun, his clothes filthy scraps, his beard and hair long and matted. He sat on a flat rock facing the morning sun, his eyes closed. Several birds perched on one side of him, a family of rabbits on the other.

Shahzor smiled, loosening his sword in its sheath. How could this feeble shell be a threat?

As he approached, the animals scattered, and Noor opened his eyes. He didn't seem surprised or afraid to see his brother. "You came," he said softly.

Shahzor scowled. "You're a distraction. My people need to know who is in control and to stop looking towards you."

"They do as they choose," replied Noor.

"But why do they revere you so, when they hate me?" whined Shahzor. "I can bring wealth and prosperity to the village, whereas you are nothing but a shadow of a man, hiding in the hills. You have shirked your responsibilities, while I am the leader I was born to be. They should revere me!"

"Should?" Noor gave a long sigh. "People rarely do what they should. All we can do is try to live our lives according to our beliefs and allow others to draw their conclusions."

"And what is the example you offer them? What conclusion should they draw? That they should give up when confronted with difficulties?" Shahzor snorted. "I thought it was a mistake when my mother left you alive because you might lead your people in an uprising, but instead I find not a man but a wraith."

Shahzor stepped closer and unsheathed his sword. He admired the curved blade as it gleamed in the sun's dying light. "You offer them weakness, while I offer them strength."

"There are many ways of showing strength," said Noor calmly. "I have chosen not to perpetuate the violence, the rivalry, but to be true to my beliefs."

"That's cowardice," snapped Shahzor. He stepped closer, his dark shadow looming over Noor's frail body.

Noor looked up at his brother with a calm, unconcerned gaze. "It is my experience that neither people nor animals bow easily to the will of others."

"We shall see!" Shahzor towered over Noor and raised his sword. "Do you have any last words?"

"I feel only love for you, brother," said Noor.

His answer enraged Shahzor further. "How can you say you love me when you know what I will do?"

"I know your suffering," replied Noor simply.

"Enough!" Shahzor roared, lunging forward and swinging his sword at Noor's head. But before the blow could land, there was a growl and a flash of grey as the wolf landed on Shahzor's back.

Shahzor and the wolf fell to the ground, and the wolf sank its teeth into his throat.

As Shahzor's life blood spilled into the dusty ground, the wolf looked at Noor, its jaws drenched with blood.

Noor's face remained impassive. He held out his hand to the wolf, and the fearsome beast trotted onto the rock and sat by his side.

All day long, Noor sat, unmoving, his eyes fixed on his brother's body. Around him, the birds and animals of the mountains gathered — the rabbit beside the wolf, the mouse at the feet of the crow, apparently oblivious to or unbothered by the other.

Not one of them touched Shahzor's body, seemingly content to be close to Noor.

As evening approached, Noor gave a deep sigh, extended his hand towards Shahzor's corpse, then slipped away from his body, releasing himself from the torture of his physical form and the concerns of this world.

His body crumpled to the ground. At once, the animals began to howl, moan and call, lamenting his passing.

***

Halima wandered the village, looking for Shahzor. He was not in his tent, nor by the river sharpening his sword. She asked the villagers if they had seen him, but they all shook their heads.

An old lady approached her. "You're looking for your son? I saw him this morning, leaving the village."

"Leaving?"

The old woman nodded to the hills. "He climbed up there, his sword at his side."

As the old woman shuffled off, a wave of fear gripped Halima's heart like a winter's frost. In that instant, she knew her sons were dead.

***

A group of villagers watched Halima march out of the village.

"Where is she going?" said one.

"To the hills, like her son," said the old woman.

The villagers looked at one another. "They are both gone," they murmured.

CHAPTER 11

As Halima climbed, a huge flock of birds circled high above. She used them as a guide to where her sons lay. As she approached, the animals drew back.

Halima stopped, her legs tired, her lungs raw from the cold wind. Before her lay the bodies of her two sons — Shahzor bloodied and torn, Noor no more than a wisp of flesh, bone and hair.

She fell to her knees and a primal cry ripped from her throat. Her scream echoed around the barren hillsides, but rather than flee, the animals and birds closed around her, somehow knowing she was the mother of their beloved Noor.

***

Halima lay sobbing for a long time, and when she opened her eyes, it was dark. Two luminous yellow eyes were staring at her.

The wolf with the white blaze was standing over her. Halima shrunk back as the wolf gazed at her for a moment, then turned and trotted off.

Halima sat up and looked around. As her eyes adjusted to the darkness, she saw her sons" bodies side by side, as united in death as they had been divided in life.

She forced herself to her feet, stumbled to the bodies and began to scrape at the earth with her bare hands. The harsh ground tore at her skin until her fingers were raw and her nails torn, but she kept scraping until she had dug a shallow grave. Slowly, tenderly, she rolled her sons into the ground, then spread the earth over them.

Exhausted and grief-stricken, she forced herself back to her feet and stumbled down the mountain.

***

"There she is!"

As Halima entered the village, several men rushed towards her, grabbed her and dragged her to the hall. The whole village was gathered inside, their faces lit by the flickering torches. The men hauled Halima to the centre and threw her to the ground, where she lay unmoving, too shocked by the death of her sons to react.

When she finally looked up, a group of villagers was standing over her. Halima understood. With Shahzor dead and Halima in the hills, the villagers had killed the soldiers and taken back their village.

"What should we do with her?" said one.

"Kill her," said another. "Her son killed our people and enslaved us, and she killed Aasim. It's what she deserves."

"Kill her! Kill her!" shouted others.

"Wait!" Rukhshana pushed her way through the crowd and stood over Halima. "Noor?" she asked her.

Halima looked up, her eyes full of sorrow. "Dead. Both of them," she whispered.

A chill washed over Rukhshana. Noor had sealed his commitment to his people with his life.

***

In the vacuum of a moment frozen in time, Rukhshana's chill was replaced by a surge of calm and clarity, as though Noor were holding her hand, his love and certainty strengthening her.

329

She turned to the villagers, their vengeful eyes tainting everything Noor had wished them to overcome. "We should spare her," she said. "She saved my life and helped many of you."

"Her son killed scores of our people," shouted a villager. "Someone should pay."

"Kill her! Kill her!" others chanted.

Rukhshana held up her hand, and the excited crowd fell silent. "Before you pass sentence," she said, "you should at least know her story." She explained how Aasim had abandoned her, leaving her alone and pregnant, how the darkness had crept into her soul, the desire for revenge driven by the betrayal and abandonment. Rukhshana looked round, catching the eye of person after person. "Who among you could put your hand on your heart and swear you would have not done the same if you'd been treated this way?"

The villagers silently looked from Rukhshana to Halima.

"What would you have us do with her?" one asked.

"Show her mercy," Rukhshana replied. "If she will ask our forgiveness, we should accept it. Noor would have wanted this for his mother." She looked around the room. "If we love Noor, we have to forgive her."

There were some mutterings, but no one challenged Rukhshana.

Halima slowly stood and looked around the crowd. "I have done a terrible thing and paid the ultimate price, losing both of my sons and the only man I loved," she said softly. "I knew a thousand ways to take a life, but not a single way to save one, until Rukhshana came into my life. She has taught me wisdom and forgiveness, allowed me to turn my knowledge to good use. Now, with your consent, I would like to continue my work as your healer."

One by one, the villagers nodded.

"But who will be our leader?" asked an elderly man, his straggly white beard quivering as he spoke.

"Rukhshana," said Halima.

There were gasps of surprise.

"But she's a woman!" protested the old man.

"True, she is a woman," Halima said loudly over shocked murmurs, "but she is also a wise and compassionate healer. She has loved and suffered great loss, yet still she has the strength to show forgiveness, and has proven herself over and over these past few months. Can you name anyone better?"

"I see the reflection of Noor in her heart," said one villager, amid stunned looks from some others.

"I trust her," said another.

One by one, the villagers nodded in agreement.

"I believe she will be a great and considerate leader," Halima concluded, her eyes challenging them all. "So, I ask again: Can you think of anyone better to lead the village back to health?"

***

It was decided. Rukhshana became the elder of the village, carrying on the good work of Aasim and Noor, healing the wounds that Shahzor had created, while Halima's life was spared.

Under Rukhshana's direction, the villagers climbed the mountain and extracted Noor and Shahzor from their shallow grave to give them a proper burial, side by side.

The whole village gathered around the grave. The people stood on one side, the wild animals, who had crept down from the mountains one by one, on the other.

A soft breeze whipped around Rukhshana's ankles as she stood at the head of the grave, her palms facing the heavens. She prayed for the souls of her husband and his brother. The people bowed their heads, and the wolf's plaintive howl rang from the dark hills as Noor's soul was lifted from the earth and set free one last time.

Rukhshana looked up. She thought she glimpsed Noor's soft smile looking down on them and heard him whisper, "The minute I heard my first love story, I started looking for you, not knowing how blind that was. Lovers don't finally meet somewhere. They're in each other all along …"

Returning to the Place of Souls

334

"If I adore You out of fear of Hell, burn me in Hell!

If I adore You out of desire for Paradise,

Lock me out of Paradise.

But if I adore You for Yourself alone,

Do not deny to me Your eternal beauty."

Rabia al-Adawiyya (Rabia al-Basri)

CHAPTER 1: SERGEI'S JOURNEY HOME

Sergei lifted from his corpse. The sense of calm as he took his last breath met with a long-forgotten feeling of warmth, safety and love. It was a familiar feeling, welcoming him home, as if all his years had been but a gestation, each step drawing him closer to the self he was written to become.

As Sergei drifted through a translucent tunnel towards a warm, bright light, he was bathed in a vapour of pure energy. As he was being cleansed of the exposure to Earth, he evolved from scent to taste, from mere form to existence, from pursuing objects of love to being unified with the Origin of Love. He felt the waves of the eternal ocean where he and his friends had once communed.

A familiar form approached from the distance. Sintra smiled like a loving confidante, and her embrace said what a thousand words could not.

"Welcome back, Sergei. How are you?"

He wanted so desperately to sound positive and grateful in the presence of his guide but was bone-weary from his experiences. "I'm tired, Sintra," he admitted, "so very tired. I never realised that life would take so much out of me. I'm home now and I feel safe, but I know that I failed." He sighed. "I'm so sorry to everyone I hurt, so sorry to you and the group. I let you all down."

Sintra gave him a curious look. "Did you?"

"I was so isolated, so alone. I couldn't be the role model my men needed, or the strong, dependable man my wife so desperately wanted, and as my life spiralled downward, I took the coward's route to alcohol."

"Your chosen path was one of the more difficult within the group, but you would never have been tested beyond your ability. Do you remember the life you agreed to before being born?" asked Sintra.

"I agreed to sacrifice what I loved the most on Earth to allow it to grow. I agreed to become an alcoholic hoping my daughter would develop the strength she needed to complete her life, but I fear that even in that I failed," replied Sergei.

"The love of a father is rarely recognised, and its absence quickly chastised, but it has no equal. Many a good man has been broken by a tacit expectation that they should provide, protect, and be strong at all times without being deserving of reciprocal love, support or acknowledgment," Sintra said.

"But why did I need to suffer so long?" he asked.

"All the time you were suffering, Anya was admiring you for not giving up. Your daughter developed her inner strength and resilience from you — the strength she needed to grow and progress in her journey. Had you given up, she would have too," Sintra explained. "She may not have always liked you, but she never stopped loving you, especially when you lay dying in hospital."

"I didn't fail?"

"Come and see for yourself," said Sintra, waving her hand across the familiar translucent pool. Sergei gasped as he saw Anya standing at the front of a large lecture room. "She's a teacher?"

"At the university," confirmed Sintra.

Sergei shook his head in wonder. "She looks so beautiful." He sighed. "I never told her how much I loved her..."

"What do you see in her eyes?"

"She looks so calm, so confident," said Sergei. "How can she be so peaceful after what I put her through?"

"Because every time you turned to your base self and your demons, Anya saw another example of what she wouldn't allow herself to be. It forced her to search deep within to find the best part of herself."

"And my granddaughter?" asked Sergei nervously. "What does she remember of me?"

"Her memories are based on the stories Anya told her; bedtime stories you told Anya."

"Baba Yaga and Zmey Gorynych, the three-headed dragon?" asked Sergei, wide-eyed.

Sintra nodded. "And in every story, the helpless villagers are rescued by Sergei the Strong, a mighty warrior who wields a huge two-handed sword, perfect for beheading dragons."

Sergei shook his head in amazement.

"You made Anya," Sintra told him, "and Anya made a version of you that her daughter would be proud of."

"I was always afraid my actions were no different from those who are intentionally evil," said Sergei.

Sintra shook her head. "You acted out of blind duty towards your country and your family."

"And what of all the innocent people I slaughtered?"

"Their spirits haunted you for the rest of your days as their demons became yours," replied Sintra.

Sergei looked around. Translucent bubbles filled the air. "Are they here?"

"Yes."

"I need to see them … all of them."

Sintra tilted her head, studying him. "Why?" she asked, her tone sharpened, as if testing the resolve behind his request.

A silence passed between them.

"I lived in perpetual hell on earth," Sergei said finally, his voice low. "I woke every morning already condemned, drinking to drown the screams I couldn't silence — theirs and mine. Their faces faded over time, but their eyes never left me. They stared at me in silence, night after night. I always knew what the right thing to do was, but fear and guilt crippled me."

His light flickered as he remembered his daughter. "That can't be the legacy Anya inherits."

He took a deep breath. "I need to ask each for their forgiveness and the forgiveness of their children, for ripping away their fathers and mothers."

Sintra nodded gently. "They're waiting to meet you."

As Sergei stepped forward, the orbs surrounded him. He ebbed and flowed with them, merging and separating in a graceful dance as he met every man, woman and child he had killed in the name of his country's defence.

Some received him warmly and accepted his apologies; others struggled to acknowledge him. Seeing how forgiveness reshaped their children's destinies, Sergei vowed to return as often as needed, until all were freed from their family's bitter legacy. Although time didn't exist in the Place of Souls, the burden of pain swirled turbulently inside Sergei, wave after wave, with only brief moments of respite before the next emotional onslaught.

***

"How do you feel now?" asked Sintra when Sergei finally returned. They stood in a small glade, soft grass at their feet, verdant trees around them, dappled sunlight playing across their faces as the trees swayed in the breeze.

"I wanted to be admired, to be the wise man and not the war hero," Sergei admitted.

"But had you been the wise man, how do you think your daughter would have turned out?" Sintra nodded slowly. They both knew the answer.

Sergei reciprocated. "And was she able to forgive me?" he asked.

"She was able to celebrate you!" laughed Sintra. "And to this day, that is how she chooses to remember you."

At Sintra's words, a great weight lifted from Sergei's shoulders. He could finally breathe freely, unencumbered.

"What did you value most about your life on Earth?" probed Sintra.

"That's easy," replied a rekindled Sergei. "The birth of Anya. As she emerged into the world, I became nothing and she became everything. I asked for her burdens to be given to me so she could become more than I could ever be."

"And that is what you did." Sintra smiled. "I think you're ready to meet up with the others."

CHAPTER 2: THE FRIENDS REUNITE

Sergei felt himself move into an endless space, first floating, then drifting at an increasing pace on a guided line of travel. As he gave himself to the journey, other souls joined and left the stream from various tributaries as they all blended into one unified consciousness.

Eventually, he was drawn into a narrower, quieter side stream. Utter peace and joyous anticipation radiated from within him as he watched other souls moving past, each looking like an illuminated grape on a wispy filament of light from the Divine tree. Random thoughts reached out to him as he drifted past, but this was not his place, his group.

His joy increased as he felt himself slowing down, drawn to familiar minds reaching out to him from his own group. He was home. The others rushed to greet him, an overwhelming feeling of love and acceptance from the happy greetings, hugs and kisses.

They floated amongst each other until their surroundings crystalised into the familiar field of wild flowers. The group clustered beneath the branches of the ancient Divine tree, each clad in translucent robes through which the colours of their souls shone.

They gathered around an altar-like table, joking and teasing each other about their recent lives, the silly things they did and how serious it all seemed when they were down there. Their recollections felt like distant daydreams.

On the table lay 'life books', one for each of them, showing live images from their recent experiences. In turn, each opened their book to share what they had learned during their lifetime. The images came into focus as they slowly turned the pages, and the memories, the laughter and the reassurance bathed them in the pure, soft light of growth and renewal.

CHAPTER 3: LIFE LESSONS

Budoo opened her book, whose cover was light brown and dusty, as if covered in the sands that had surrounded her for so many years.

"Look at the size of your book!" gasped Anaïse.

"That's what you get for living for centuries," said Budoo. She leafed through the thick pages. "During my thousand-year existence, I pursued false gods in the form of money, power and ego satisfaction through the manipulation of others. Even when love came in the form of the farmer who accepted me, defended me, and offered tenderness without condition, I couldn't embrace it. My jinn hubris and princess stature wouldn't allow me to love a simple man and admit everything I had been taught about humanity was wrong. It was only in my dying moments that I understood the beauty of Love, declaring myself a willing servant to it by releasing attachment to everything else. Those closing moments were the most beautiful of my life. My declaration was rewarded with worldly veils falling to reveal Love's embrace."

"It sounds like the story of the Phoenix my father told me," said Anaïse.

"It was exactly that," said Budoo. "No matter how hard I tried to push Love away, the opportunity to submit to it was omnipresent. In the end, I gave myself to its intoxication and willingly drowned in it."

Sintra smiled. "Fire can make a hot air balloon fly high above the ground or burn a forest to the ground. It can turn solid gold into liquid, liquid water into vapour. The essence of fire is constant, but its manifestations are infinite. These manifestations are the shades of the human experience." She turned to the others. "How did you deal with the adversities of life?"

"I drank, and in rare moments of clarity, I begged for salvation," admitted Sergei, the gently swaying branches dappling his stern face with splashes of soft golden light. "Salvation for my family, my soldiers, the people I killed, those they left behind."

"Not for yourself?" asked the Boy.

"No, never. I assumed that, since I was already damned, my prayers would never be answered. I was afraid I would find something better to believe in than alcohol, and I liked the release, the lack of accountability that being drunk afforded."

"Did it lead you away from your addiction to alcohol?" enquired Noor.

"Pleading in submission didn't remove me from the world," replied Sergei. "It reconnected me with the universe and allowed me to be woven into it. It cleansed the dirt I collected during the day."

He paused, recalling those fleeting moments. "There were times when I fell to the floor, so great was my pain. As I sat up, I felt pulled out of the Earth with an appreciation for the life I was given. Sometimes I would fall again, only to realise how close my face was to the ground and the gateway of death I would eventually travel through."

"During my life, time slowed down as Light and Love washed over me in those moments. Was it the same for you?" asked Noor.

"It was as though I was taking back time's dominion over me," replied Sergei. "The closer I got to the Light, the more time expanded, allowing me to remain immersed in that transient moment."

"Travelling at the speed of prayer! I like it," joked the Boy. The others laughed, nodding.

"And you? How did you find peace and clarity in testing moments?" Noor asked the Boy.

"I grew up believing the only way to succeed in life was to gather possessions," said the Boy, "but when I looked around, all I saw were people enslaved by self-built cages. Greed, paranoia and fear were the tools of their misery. I didn't want that."

"So, you died poor?" teased Anaïse.

"That's one way of looking at it," replied the Boy. "But I'd prefer to say I died complete." He paused. "We all try to do our best, right? That's the point of this whole thing."

"What did you do?" challenged Anaïse.

"I focused my life on providing people with a place where they could get away from the pressures of life, reconnect with nature, maybe have some space to think about their lives. Didn't always work, mind you, but at least I gave it a good try, right?"

"How did you keep the lure of material trappings at bay?" asked Anaïse.

"It's not easy, is it, with a world full of temptations? I replaced greed with charity and money with blessings from those I helped." He grinned. "I ran a community garden."

"And did you find peace in your garden?" queried Noor, recalling his own life under the starlit heavens over the Afghan hills.

The Boy nodded.

"We should all give like the sun and the earth, which nourishes the seed as it grows into a beautiful rose," said Anaïse quietly.

Noor smiled softly. "We were each heated by the intensity of the sun, burning away the impurities that veiled us from the omnipresence of the Beloved."

As the friends looked through Noor's book, Budoo pointed out pivotal moments, each of which had the potential to lead Noor to the darkness of the base self she had succumbed to.

"What was your single life-defining moment?" she asked.

"Acknowledging that my father was not the perfect man I had thought him to be, and accepting the path I would have to follow to prevent my parent's legacy from being perpetuated in my village."

The others nodded.

"And just as Sergei submitted to prayer to lose himself from the pain of the world," continued Noor, "I turned to removing all distractions that tried to deny me the Love I needed to fulfil my obligation."

"Did you ever feel you were running away from your responsibilities, from the destiny chosen by your people?" asked Budoo.

"To take revenge and assume the place of my father would have been the easier option," replied Noor, "and it tugged at my ego every day, telling me I was being weak and I needed to fight back. I cried every night until my body was dry, knowing the perpetual danger in which my actions placed my friends and family. Fasting allowed me to withdraw energy from my physical senses, redirecting my focus to seek guidance from the Beloved. And when Time witnessed my devotion, Mercy answered by cleansing not only me but all the people I loved. And with nothing in my stomach to dampen the sound, the music of my soul resonated with Love."

"The merit of fasting is not in the hunger, just as the merit of medicine is not in its bitterness," said Budoo.

"Al-Ghazali?" asked Anaïse.

"Al-Ghazali," acknowledged Budoo with a gentle nod. She tipped her head as she looked at Anaïse. "And you — did you ever find love again after losing Amato?"

"I did, many years later, in between reciprocating the love and care my father had given me," replied Anaïse, "… and becoming a master watchmaker," she added with a smile.

"Really?"

"What else would the daughter of a master watchmaker, obsessed with precision in everything, do? After all, I had the best teacher I could wish for, and I was used to beating the boys at their own game from a young age."

"Did your old life ever catch up with you?" asked Budoo.

"On a couple of occasions, especially as I became known for my handmade timepieces, but just as Noor couldn't be swayed from his path, I didn't wish to squander the chance to mend, love and create."

"Did you spend the rest of your life in Le Sentier?"

"No, it was a pilgrimage my heart needed to make to remedy itself of all that had held me back," replied Anaïse. "My true calling was in the arms of my deepest wounds. After Amato died, I tried so hard to tune in to his inner guidance. Everything I went through, I needed to go through so that I could return home to complete my journey. And just as with every pilgrimage, the time came to leave and resume my life, armed with the tools that always existed in me."

"Yes, yes, that's all very nice … but who did you fall in love with?" pressed Budoo.

Anaïse smiled. "A good man whose beauty I would never have recognised had Amato and my father not been the men they were."

"The root of all suffering is attachment," reflected Budoo.

"The Buddha?" enquired Anaïse.

Budoo nodded.

Before Anaïse could punch the air, all the friends mimicked her gesture in unison and laughed, echoing her joy. Sintra sensed Budoo dwelling silently on her own lost loves. "I'm so proud of how far you've all come, and especially your reflections on each other's lives," she said. "Let's put the books aside and walk a while..."

The friends followed Sintra to the wheat field where they had started their journey, the endless ocean washing the shore in the distance.

A soft luminescence began to emanate from the horizon, growing in intensity until five distinct orbs of light materialised before them. The friends became excited as they realised who they were being reunited with.

As each soul came into focus, they hugged their respective partner and floated to a location reminiscent of their time together on Earth.

Anaïse met Amato.

Sergei met Anya.

The Boy met the Alpha.

Noor met Rukhshana.

And Budoo met the farmer, her first true love.

Sintra reflected from a distance, wondering if they had achieved the closure and detachment needed to proceed on their journeys.

***

On their return, the glow of each soul had changed colour, healed from their time with the one they loved the most. They felt complete, reborn, like being gently woken from a dream to become their authentic selves.

Sintra smiled, humbled by what they had put themselves through and what they had become. "Death is not an entrance into nothingness," she told them. "Similar to how we wake up by opening our eyes, when we die, we do not disappear; we simply open our eyes to another reality."

"On Earth, each of us lived the fragile dance of balancing duality," said Noor. "We were like delicate butterflies that come out during the day, surrendering to the solace of the sun's warmth and the fragrant nectar of flowers. At other times, we were like moths coming out at night, seeking the consuming allure of darkness, only to fly towards the flame for salvation."

Sintra's form shimmered softly, energy radiating from her as she whispered,

"They have endured their trials, living proof of hope, love, transcendence. Let their truth guide your decree."

A deep, harmonious hum resonated from the Nūrāniyān. Their collective radiance intensified, a silent, profound affirmation that swept through the ethereal space. Translucent mist swirled around the five souls. The light shone brighter, merging and blending with the mist, wrapping around them until they were a part of the swirling, glowing haze as it circled Sintra.

Eyes closed, she lifted her arms and accepted the light as it flowed with increasing intensity into her chest, a torrent of light and learning.

The distant hill shimmered, visibly warmed by the Nūrāniyān's respect and admiration.

With a gasp, Sintra opened her eyes. The only soul still with her was Noor.

He looked around. "They've gone?"

"They are part of the Oneness, for now," she said, her voice filled with a calming peace.

Noor nodded, a newfound serenity on his face. "And me?"

Sintra gestured towards the stream of light that flowed past them. "It is time for you to find your group. They are waiting for you, for your knowledge and wisdom."

"I am to be a guide, part of the Nūrāniyān?"

Sintra nodded. "You are ready."

Noor looked towards the glowing current, then back at Sintra. "And what of you?"

"It is time for me to return to my group, to my guide, and share what I have learned," she replied, her gaze already fixed on the luminous path.

Noor looked at the stream, then back at Sintra, a flicker of understanding in his eyes. "Will we all meet up again?"

"Of course," Sintra affirmed, her voice filled with ancient certainty.

Sintra stepped forward and took his hand. "Are you ready?"

Noor nodded, and they walked calmly forward, hand in hand, towards the fast-moving stream.

As they reached the edge of the light, Sintra's form shimmered and dissolved. Noor paused for a moment, bathed in radiant stillness, reflecting on the journeys of his friends in a world still on the edge.

"It's true," Noor whispered. "We don't carry our deeds with us when we return — only our intentions, and the love we offered along the way."

He glanced at the Doomsday clock, its solitary hand now indicating three minutes to midnight. "There's still Time. There's still Love. One giving the other a reason to exist."

"When we are born, the adhan, or call to prayer, is recited in our ears, but no prayer is performed. When we die, no adhan is recited, but a prayer is performed. The adhan of your birth is but a few short breaths away from the prayer of your death. That's how short life is."

Anonymous

www.ingramcontent.com/pod-product-compliance
Lightning Source LLC
Chambersburg PA
CBHW020905060726
47591CB00004B/1089